TRIAT

A TRAINII

Steve Trew

The Crowood Press

First published in 2001 by
The Crowood Press Ltd
Ramsbury, Marlborough
Wiltshire SN8 2HR

© Steve Trew 2001

British Library Cataloguing-in-Publication Data
A catalogue record for this book is available from the British Library.

ISBN 1 86126 386 4

Line illustrations by Annette Findlay.
Photographs by Nigel Farrow.

Acknowledgements
I am indebted to the many writers, coaches and athletes who have kindly contributed to these pages. In particular, I would like to thank the following: Phil Pearson, for his massive, 100 per cent input into the stretching and injury sections; Kath Atkin, for her equally important contribution to the chapter on nutrition; Dave Day, for much of the swimming section, and particularly the information on body position and drills; and Carole Trower, for the development of pool to open-water swimming.

I am also grateful to Chris Ray and Alan Ingarfield for sharing their knowledge, commitment and insight on endurance training and competition; to Andy Lee, for his academic expertise on exercise physiology; to Rob Pickard, Director of Australia's World Class Performance programme; to Barrie Shepley, National Triathlon Coach, Canada; and to Bernie Shrosbree, for all the late nights, ideas and sharing of philosophies of conditioning, and development and training of athletes.

Last but not least, I must thank all the athletes who have contributed to this book, giving me permission to use their training programmes and their ideas. They have taught me much.

Typefaces used: Galliard and Franklin Gothic.

Typeset and designed by
D & N Publishing
Baydon, Wiltshire.

Printed and bound in Great Britain by JW Arrowsmith Ltd, Bristol.

CONTENTS

Forewords

I train because I want to succeed and fulfil my potential at triathlon. I also train because I love sport and the buzz you get having pushed yourself that little harder. Then there are the friendships you develop and the laughs you share. I do, however, think training for triathlon is difficult to get right as you are often juggling three different disciplines as well as your health, your family and friends and your job (all of which I did before I became a full-time athlete in training for the Olympics). It is crucial to train efficiently and not waste time and that is why a guide like this is invaluable.

Indeed, the principles in this book are key to improving and performing to the best of your ability. Training this way means that every minute is put to good use. All the basics that are in here are those that I have used throughout my triathlon career thus far, from my age-group days right up until my Olympic debut. Follow it and you will never look back.

Sîan Brice
British Olympic Triathlete

It is very important to have a structure to triathlon training and to integrate the three disciplines; my coach, Lance Watson, believes that and this book explains it perfectly. The running programme is fantastic: the ideas on 10km-pace running are simply the best. The basic guidelines made a big impression on me and the way I prepared for the World Championships and the Olympic Games.It taught me to use my running time and training properly, and to be specific. It hurts, but it works!

Simon Whitfield, Canada
Olympic Triathlon Champion
and gold medallist

Part I
Principles and Basics

Fig 1. Sue Bathgate showing the fruits of her efforts!

CHAPTER 1
Introduction

Triathlon at last came of age when it stepped up onto the world stage at the hugely successful summer Olympics of Sydney 2000. Olympic status reflects the acceptance of one sport by others, so triathlon can be said to have officially arrived. And it was appropriate that the host country was Australia, the home of one of the sport's established global leaders.

Triathlon's journey to Sydney 2000 and Olympic status has not been straightforward. The early event in San Diego, and the first-ever Hawaii Ironman – still seen as the ultimate event – with its mere handful of starters, may date back two decades, but the best-known names from those days are still around. The original 'big four' – Dave Scott, Mark Allen, Scott Tinley and Scot Molina – still attract huge crowds to races and lectures. In the short history of triathlon, they are already legends; the remarkable Dave Scott did it all, and then returned to Hawaii at the grand old age of 40, after a five-year gap, to finish runner-up.

In triathlon, women athletes are the equal of men. They train as hard, they compete as hard, and they suffer just as much. The times are different, but athletes such as Erin Baker and Paula Newby-Fraser have rewritten the record books and redefined female achievement. Times, distances and records that were once seen as beyond the capabilities of male competitors are now well within the reach of female athletes.

A mass of élite athletes have followed in the footsteps of these six: Brad Bevan, Greg Welch, Mike Pigg, Karen Smyers, Michellie Jones, Emma Carney, Isabelle Mouthon, Carole Montgomery, Miles Stewart, Rick Wells, Loretta Harrop, Joanne King, Chris McCormack, Nicki Hackett, Spencer Smith and Simon Lessing MBE – the list goes on and on.

These may be today's heroes and heroines, but the next race, next season or next decade will bring athletes who may make their exploits seem commonplace. It's the nature of sport and competition, and what makes it so fascinating. The potential for achievement in triathlon is enormous, with three different disciplines, transitions to race through, and technology to aid, abet or control, or be controlled. Triathletes race on different courses, in different countries, on different continents. The challenge might be a fifteen-minute flash sprint in England or a fourteen-hour strongman-distance race in Japan. They have to deal with a whole range of conditions, from coaches and spectators are never bored.

Everyone needs a hero to emulate, and then possibly to overtake. Standards and records are set, and then challenged and beaten. Will this book make you a world champion? It might … but it might not. To reach the top in any sport, the first thing you have to do is to choose your parents wisely. Genetic inheritance plays a large part in setting absolute limits of achievement. This book aims to help you to make the very best of yourself – to achieve that personal best, to finish a race, maybe an Ironman distance, to beat two hours for an Olympic-distance race, to qualify for your national age-group team … or even the élite team. Why not?

Knowledge of training techniques in triathlon has come a long way in the last ten years. The same method of training will not work for everybody, but there are basic principles of training that will make a significant contribution to all triathletes and maximize their potential. There are also many ways of applying those principles, so examples of the training schedules of individual athletes are included too.

This aims to be more than just a training manual, though. I hope there is something here for all triathletes, whatever their standard. There are some new ideas, and certainly many old ones. There are few secrets any more in training and coaching – everyone watches, copies, borrows and adapts the methods and ideas of their heroes, athletes or coaches.

Sections are also included on stretching, injury prevention and rehabilitation, relaxation, nutrition, mental attitude and tapering. Paying attention to such 'extras', and putting in that little bit more effort, often makes the difference between a good performance and a great one.

CHAPTER 2
The Laws of Triathlon

LAW ONE: THIS MAY NOT BE THE TRUTH

This book sets out tried and tested principles of training that have been applied to triathlon. However, everyone is an individual and not every method of training may apply to you. Some people thrive on long, slow, distance training; some cannot live without their daily fix of intervals or high-quality work; some triathletes rarely need rest while others may find that training every other day is sufficient for massive improvement. You are an individual and need to find a way of training that is best for you alone. General principles, for you, may not represent the truth.

LAW TWO: SUCK IT AND SEE

Be prepared to try out new methods of training and see if they work for you. Perhaps the method you have been using, although in principle it is correct, doesn't work for you. Be adventurous, don't get stuck in a rut. Try something new; you never know, you might just like it.

LAW THREE: APPLY THE KISS PRINCIPLE

'KEEP IT SIMPLE, STUPID!' Sometimes it is possible to get so bound up in new-fangled theories of training that you forget the basics; the fact is, the harder you train, the better you get (although that is, of course, an oversimplification). Be aware of new methods and equipment, or your hero's favourite regime, but don't lose sight of where you are going.

LAW FOUR: APPLY THE 'CASE' PRINCIPLE

There are few secrets in training any more. CASE stands for 'Compare, Adapt, Specify, Examine', or 'Copy And Steal Everything'! Look at other athletes' methods or training and try them for yourself; play around with times, distances, rest intervals and targets, and adapt others' schedules. You can be sure that they will do the same to you!

LAW FIVE: KNOW YOURSELF

Don't fool yourself into believing that you are something that you aren't. Know what you are good at, what you are bad at, what you like doing and what you dislike. Know your strengths and weaknesses. Don't look back at the end of a season or a career and think, 'If only ...'.

LAW SIX: TRAIN TO YOUR WEAKNESSES, RACE TO YOUR STRENGTHS

Everyone likes doing what they are good at and dislikes making a fool of themselves. To make a significant improvement in triathlon, it is necessary in training to work on the weak aspects, and cut back on your strongest discipline, which may have been your specialist sport before you came to triathlon. This may prove to be hard going at first.

In a race situation, the opposite applies: work on your strengths and minimize your losses. If you can swim like Kieron Perkins and take a three-minute lead into the bike section, you'd be a mug not to take advantage of it.

LAW SEVEN: MAKE HASTE SLOWLY

Progress at the beginning can be quite dramatic, and improvements in an endurance sport are usually measured in minutes or tens of minutes rather than seconds. The rate of improvement will slow down and it is a natural reaction to want to train harder and longer in order to maintain the same rate. This risks injury, so don't be tempted. An increase in training, whether in time or intensity, must be gradual. Think in terms of months and years rather than days, look for gradual increases in training and commitment, and you will improve *and* remain free of injury.

LAW EIGHT: CHOOSE YOUR PARENTS WISELY

Unfairly, genetic inheritance governs everyone's limits of attainment and improvement. The child of a 10,000m track world record-holder and an Olympic swimmer is likely to have a special set of genes. Don't waste such a great headstart. Those who have not been presented with such an advantage (the vast majority!) will have to make the very best out of what they have, and train sensibly and systematically to maximize their potential.

LAW NINE: DON'T SET LIMITS

Don't underestimate your potential to improve. It is all too easy to look at the star in the next swimming lane and think, 'I'll never be as good as that.' Why not? It is difficult to envisage massive improvements, but it is easy to aspire to an improvement of one second on a 100m swim, or ten seconds on a 10km run. Then you make another ten-second improvement, then another, and another. Before too long that ten-second improvement has become a minute. Look to the next level of

attainment and in time you will come closer to your dreams. It may take a month, it may take five years, but it will come.

LAW TEN: DON'T BELIEVE EVERYTHING YOU READ

When sports magazines print an interview with a superstar, and include a box by the side of it headed 'A typical week's training', they should print a health warning too. They should also print another box with the heading, 'And this is what I was doing 5 years ago'. You don't have to train the same as your hero in order to emulate your hero. Train for yourself, not for anybody else.

Here's something else to ponder: if somebody interviewed you for a magazine, wouldn't you think something like, 'They'll never believe that I train as little as I do. I'd better tell them about my best-ever week'?

LAW ELEVEN: TREAT EVERY MINOR INJURY AS IF IT COULD BECOME A MAJOR ONE

Triathlon tends to attract people who like to train long and hard, whose natural inclination is to swim/cycle/run through any small niggling injury. Untreated niggles can easily progress to major niggles and become major injuries. Treat minor inconveniences as if they have the potential to become a significant inhibitor, and stop them progressing too far downhill. Be cautious, and do not ruin a season's hard work by refusing to back off.

LAW TWELVE: ENJOY

If you don't enjoy triathlon, don't do it. The sport is demanding in terms of time and commitment, and some people simply do not have the time. If you stop enjoying triathlon, stop doing triathlon.

LAW THIRTEEN: DON'T PLAY THE 'IF' GAME

You know – if only I could swim faster … if only I didn't have so many work commitments … if only I could afford better equipment … if only I could get invited to classier races … if only I didn't get injured so much … if only I was lighter/taller/heavier/smaller … Playing the 'if' game leads to frustration and bitterness; it's also a good excuse for losers. If you don't like something, do something about it. And if that is not within your power, then get on and do something else.

LAW FOURTEEN: THERE IS LIFE OUTSIDE

Triathlon is a part of life, but it is not life itself. Only a minuscule number of people are full-time triathlon professionals or make a substantial income from the sport. The vast majority who take part as age-groupers have full-time jobs and families, and take part in all sorts of other life-enhancing everyday activities. Don't let triathlon become so important that you lose sight of reality. There is life outside triathlon, and after triathlon.

CHAPTER 3
Developing a Programme

'Winter miles, summer smiles'

INDIVIDUALITY

A training schedule must be tailored to the individual. Many years ago, my running coach used to say, 'Show me twenty 400m runners and I'll show you twenty different training programmes.' With multi-discipline sports, such as triathlon, decathlon and modern pentathlon, the individual differences may be multiplied by the number of disciplines.

Before thinking of establishing a comprehensive training schedule, look at three areas:

1. The individual athlete – background?
2. The individual athlete – strong and weak points? What is required from the basic principles of training?
3. The individual athlete – aims and ambitions? How hard will they work to achieve these aims? How much time do they have available to train (and to rest)? How much sacrifice and inconvenience are they prepared to accept? What help (facilities/coaching/money) is available?

BASIC PRINCIPLES OF TRAINING

Stress

The body will adapt to almost anything that is thrown at it, coping with stress and dealing with its demands. The term 'stress' has many, mostly negative implications, but those who live without any stress at all are often unable to cope when they have to.

When people speak in negative terms about stress, they are really referring to *di*stress. The positive version of this is *eu*stress.

Training should be considered as *eustress* (positive). When too much is demanded too soon, eustress becomes *distress* (negative) and the expected adaptations fail to materialize. If training is systematic, steady and sensible, the classic principle of training formula comes into action:

Training stimulus ➔ Adaptation ➔ Training response

General Principles

Overload

Training must be sufficiently demanding to encourage the body to adapt and improve its performance capacity. The frequency, duration, amount and intensity of training in swimming, cycling and running should be determined with this in mind. However, the combined stress from working out in three disciplines, and the accumulated fatigue, may be excessive; err on the side of caution while learning and developing the training programme.

Progression

The amount of training must gradually increase as the individual becomes fitter and more proficient and adapts to training loads. For example, the amount of distance aerobic training should steadily increase during the off-season period and the quality of both aerobic and anaerobic work should improve during the period leading up to the competitive season.

Don't try to make too many increasing demands on your body too quickly. Always consolidate your gains before moving on to the next phase. A short period of easier training can be beneficial before progressing to harder work.

Overtraining

Following a hard training session, a hard week, a hard month or a hard season, the body will require a minimum time to recover. If training starts again before recovery is complete, levels of endurance, strength, speed and energy will all be below par. Training at this time will lead to poor performance and extreme fatigue. The overload principle will only work if your body is allowed enough recovery time to make the best of each training session.

Specificity

The effects of training are specific to the individual triathlete, the type of training being undertaken, and the particular discipline. To gain maximum benefit, training must be geared to individual triathletes, and their current state of fitness. Within a group, club or squad of triathletes, individual ability in each discipline will vary. Athletes and coaches should be aware of these differences and make appropriate adjustments to the schedule.

Training in swimming means that you will become a better swimmer, not a better cyclist or runner. Cross-training and crossover benefits will only occur on a limited aerobic level, and if the skills are either very similar to those required in another discipline or are entirely non-specific.

Rest and Recovery

Recovery after the completion of training is a most important part of the programme. It is during the recovery phase that adaptation takes place. Many triathletes ignore this and do not allow sufficient rest and recovery in their schedule. As a result of this, they fail to progress, and may suffer from overtraining symptoms.

One of the greatest advantages that full-time triathletes have over rivals who also have a job is not so much the time they have to train, but the time they have to rest and recover between sessions. Being able to go back to bed after a two-hour early-morning swim before a mid-morning bike ride is a luxury that should not be underestimated.

As a general rule, running training is more stressful than cycling, which in turn is more stressful than swimming (although intensities and background fitness also play their part). Anaerobic training is more stressful than aerobic training and requires longer recovery between sessions. Sessions, such as hard-intensity interval running, should be approached with caution and steps taken to ensure adequate rest time in between. There will be periods of the year when such interval running will be entirely inappropriate.

The ability of each individual to withstand various workloads differs greatly. Many beginners have little concept of how hard it is possible to train, and how much it is possible to hurt, until a good standard of fitness has been achieved.

An individual's ability to rest and recover has an important bearing on reading basic aerobic fitness levels. Even if their training and racing performances are similar, different athletes' resting and maximum heart rates will not be the same, so they are not a true measure of fitness. The speed at which the heart rate drops after exertion gives a much better indication of fitness. As the athlete gets fitter, the heart rate recovery quickens; often, the rate can drop to one-third of maximum (say, 180bpm to 120bpm), or more, within a minute. With aerobic conditioning, it is also likely that the athlete's resting pulse will drop. However, this should only be measured in relation to the athlete's previous resting heart rate, not to the heart rate of another athlete.

Reversibility

As soon as training stops, any improvements in performance that have been gained also stop. The improvements are then lost at anywhere between 50 per cent slower to 50 per cent faster than the rate at which they were gained. Once again, the principle of the individual athlete with his or her own actions and reactions is paramount. Triathletes who have years of aerobic conditioning from endurance exercise will lose fitness far more slowly than those who have only recently begun to train in the sport.

Technique

Athletes in single-discipline sports need to be technically proficient only in that discipline. A triathlete needs to have excellent technique in three quite different activities. The importance of ensuring good technique cannot be over-emphasized; time spent on practising technique will be repaid in every race.

Maintenance (the 'Simmering' Effect)

Once an enhanced level of fitness has been achieved, it can generally be maintained for a time (normally during the racing season) even with less training, as long as you train 'smart'.

The Plateau of Despondency

Periods of no improvement or even decrease in performance are common – and frustrating. However, this 'settling in' or 'complementary' period is necessary if the athlete's body is to adapt before moving upwards to a higher level of racing.

Mind/Motivation/Mental Toughness

This is the single most important factor in determining how much use athletes make of their potential. There may be a guy at your club who always comes second in training, but always wins on race day. Without being mentally strong, no one is likely to approach their physical limits.

Physical Limitations

However good or bad you think you are going to be, however high you aim, certain physical limits have been genetically determined for you. Every athlete should aspire to a personal best, but the closer you approach your ultimate capability, the harder you have to work for smaller improvements.

TYPES OF TRAINING

A number of different types of training are applicable to triathlon. How do these fit in with the individual triathlete's own strengths and weaknesses?

Background

Many athletes come into triathlon from one of the three individual disciplines. Many are disillusioned, bored and injury-prone, have had no success or fun, or are just looking for a new challenge. Unsurprisingly, the triathlete will be strongest, at least in the early days of training, in the background discipline. It is essential to ensure that the two other disciplines do not remain weak and the time that is allocated in training should reflect this consideration.

This necessitates a sometimes difficult adjustment. A would-be triathlete might have, for example, spent the last eight years swimming six days a week, twice a day; this training load might have to be reduced by one-third, and the time allocated to improving the disciplines of cycling and running. Everybody likes doing what they are good at, but triathletes must remember the maxim: 'Train to your weaknesses, race to your strengths.'

Goal Setting and Programme Planning

How often have you heard, or said, 'That's it. I'll have a short rest, then I am really going to get the kilometres and hours in for next season.'
'Kilometres and hours' of what?

The Mixture

Within each of the three disciplines there are a whole range of training methods, each of which will have a specific effect on the individual. Each method of training can be used in each discipline, but some will obviously apply more than others; in no particular order of importance, these are:

- overdistance;
- distance and endurance;
- race pace and time trials;
- intervals and repetitions;
- fartlek;
- resistance training;
- technique;
- strength;
- speed; and
- power.

Within each of the types of training there are many variations and, of course, there are three disciplines to consider too.

For an individual coming into triathlon with no sporting background, and no fitness, each type of training would be required to a lesser or greater degree on each discipline – but not all at once. Building up enough endurance to get through a race would be the first priority. On the other hand, somebody who has been involved at a high level in one of the disciplines will probably have enough knowledge and awareness to start bringing the other two disciplines up to standard straight away.

What do each of the training methods contribute to the overall fitness of the triathlete?

Overdistance

Overdistance is the laying down of the basic aerobic foundation. It involves running, swimming and cycling for long periods of time, at an intensity that is very easy to cope with. Many experienced triathletes consider that overdistance training is preparation for coping with 'proper' training; indeed, as your standard improves, you will need to do more intense workouts. Overdistance should not cause any damage. Its intensity is low, it builds up conditioning and mental strength, as you become confident about being able to continue for a long time. Because the intensity of the session is very low – you should aim for between 55 per cent and 65 per cent of VO_2max (see Chapter 5, on Exercise Physiology) – the muscle glycogen is not depleted very quickly.

Overdistance teaches the body to use fat more easily as a fuel rather than carbohydrate.

It is an essential part of the programme for Ironman-distance training, particularly for those attempting the distance for the first time. It will greatly improve the body's ability to flush waste products out of muscle tissue and bring in fresh blood, oxygen and essential fuel. Many novice triathletes find it hard to accept that even top international triathletes will do a significant part of their training at this pace, particularly in the off season and on recovery days in season.

Goal Setting and Programme Planning
What is your goal or aim?
What time is available?
What is your current state of fitness?
How will you evaluate your progress?
When is your first event?
How many events are you planning to do?

You need to answer all of the above before you can plan your future programme.

Distance and Endurance

In simple terms, endurance training gives the athlete the ability to withstand physical stress over a prolonged period of time. Distance training develops and maintains aerobic endurance.

In triathlon, a sport with three disciplines, endurance training must be considered on two levels. An élite male will finish an Olympic-distance race in 1 hour 50 minutes, or less; an élite female in around 2 hours, or less. Triathletes who are not yet as fast may look to achieving something between 2 and 4 hours, or more. Endurance training must be seen from the point of view of the total triathlon event, but also in respect of each individual discipline.

Generally, endurance training means doubling up the distance of the race, so this involves the following:

- 3000m of swimming;
- 80km (50 miles) of cycling; and
- 20km (12 miles) of running.

Swimming

The required distance of 3000m may well be achieved in a one-hour club swimming session (including a proportion of interval-type training). Once basic competence in stroke technique is mastered, it is essential not to waste time, and to employ this technique in all sessions. Without good stroke technique, you will always be at a disadvantage and playing catch-up in a race situation. Stroke technique is not an 'extra'; it should always be present.

Most triathletes will do the majority of their swimming sessions in an indoor pool. As well as doing long, endurance-type swims of 1000m and 2000m throughout the off season, and occasionally at all times of the year, athletes will often cover the distance by breaking it up into sections (with a very short recovery time). This is not usually the case for cycling and running endurance sessions.

Cycling

Most triathletes have a problem finding enough time to train, particularly in cycling. Depending on the time taken for the cycle section in a race, you should be looking for a 150–200 per cent increase in that time – but not at the same intensity. A cycle split of 80 minutes will look for endurance workouts of two hours plus. The intensity of the endurance sessions will be higher – between 70 and 80 per cent of maximum heart rate – than that of the overdistance. This is probably the type of training that most club triathletes will do on a day-to-day basis.

Running

Endurance running sessions typically take 60 to 90 minutes, but the real problem is the possibility of injury, and the likelihood of local muscle fatigue and muscle soreness. In triathlon, running is the final discipline. Covering up to twice the race distance in training gives you an important psychological advantage. When you get to the run discipline in the race, at least 75 minutes of flat-out effort are behind you and that six-mile slog on aching legs is before you, so you need to be mentally strong.

It is easy to skimp on running training, but you must not let it happen. Running can become a real bind for athletes who are continually fighting injuries and sore legs, so be sensible. Work on a progressive programme, gradually increasing distance and intensity, and make time for warming up and down, stretching and flexibility.

Race Pace and Time Trials

Racing a triathlon is the end product of all the effort you have put into training. However hard you work during training sessions, there is nothing quite like that extra buzz brought out by a race. For the athlete who has not raced in any discipline, or who has missed out completely on race-pace workouts outside the main competitive season, the first race of the year can come as a nasty shock. Avoid this by doing some sustained pace work, or some local time trials or 5- and 10-km running races in your build-up period.

Outline Types of Training Phases

1. Preconditioning/conditioning.
2. Base endurance.
3. Quality.
4. Event preparation/racing.

Pace: Swimming

The opportunity to swim a straight 1500m in a competitive situation comes about very infrequently. Even if you are a top-class swimmer, or involved in a good, comprehensive master's programme, you are unlikely to race a straight 1500m more than twice a year. There are two ways to incorporate a race-pace effort into your normal swimming sessions:

1. a longer than normal warm-up of a straight 1500m, with your swimming coach timing you. Going into a timed swim 'cold' can be a good way of simulating that first outdoor race situation (but without the flailing arms and knocked-off goggles); or

2. the timed, or 'T' swim, commonly used in swimming and triathlon clubs once every four or six weeks throughout the year. The athletes swim for a period of time (normally either 20 or 30 minutes), and count the total distance covered. All distances are logged and used as a benchmark for future swims. Results for a T30 (30-minute) swim might be recorded as follows:

December 1430m;
January 1510m;
February 1550m;
March 1625m.

Having a distance to aim at ensures a challenge (or an opportunity) and pushes the triathlete to work hard. Concentration on smooth stroke and stroke counting per length will also help to alleviate any possible boredom, and control the stroke energy output. Mind games are important in training; focusing on good technique for a long period of time means that the battle for improvement is 90 per cent won.

Pace: Cycling

The method is simple: time trials. Join your local cycling club, or at least make sure you are welcome at time trials. It's useful to put yourself on the line for a 10- or 25-mile time trial and to discover that you can push yourself further and faster than you thought possible. Despite recent rule changes and 'legal drafting' – staying just over 10m back – practised by a number of élite triathletes, the cycle section in a triathlon is essentially a time trial for most. Racing a straight time trial will make you aware of your potential for improvement.

Pace: Running

A time trial run over the amount of time that it takes to cycle 25 miles would be long and hard, with a high chance of injury, boredom or lack of focus. Try running time trials over 15 minutes and just over thirty minutes. Briefly, the 15-minute run is the test point to see how much distance is covered with maximum effort (basically an equivalent of a VO_2max test). Assuming that 3200m (7.5-minute miling pace) is run, this is the starting point from which to establish interval and repetition training times. The second timed run aims to double the distance covered – 6400m (4 miles) – in double the time plus 10 per cent, in other words, 30 minutes + 3 minutes, or 33 minutes.

In a comprehensive training programme, the triathlete attempts to bring the time down to 30 minutes over a period of 6–12 weeks and then undertakes another 15-minute test.

> 'The successful athlete is often the one who can train most consistently without breaking down with injury or illness.'
>
> *Mark Allen*

This may sound easy enough, but is your programme graduated and structured individually for *you* so that you don't break down?

Intervals and Repetitions

This is the real hard work of training, where significant improvements are made.

Interval and repetition training are often confused. Although there is no rigid dividing line between them, interval training usually has a fairly short rest between the efforts. Repetition training allows a much longer rest but will require the efforts to be carried out at a much faster speed and intensity.

An interval training session (running) might involve 6 × 800m with a 200m jog recovery in 60 seconds.

A repetition training session (running) might involve 3 × 800m with 10 minutes recovery.

The repetition runs are carried out both faster and with greater effort than those done during the interval training session. Training properly with run/swim/cycle interval and repetition sessions is physically and mentally the most demanding of all training; it also shows the greatest improvements. Interval-type training is essential.

The DIRTY Principle

Interval training depends on four factors:

- *Distance*: the distance of each run/swim/cycle.
- *Interval*: the rest interval between each run/swim/cycle.
- *Repetition*: he number of repeats of the runs/swims/cycles.
- *Time*: the time in which each run/swim/cycle is done.

Finally, there is the 'Y' factor: *you*. As with any work, interval training must be specific to the individual's strengths, weaknesses, age, physiological make-up and sporting background. All the DIRTY factors can – and will – be changed as the triathlete progresses.

A Little History

The contributions to knowledge in training methods have been worldwide, notably from Australia, New Zealand, South Africa and mainland Europe. From the world of running Franz Stampfl, Mihlov Igloi and Woldemar Gerschler all had remarkable success with their own particular brand of interval/repetition training, including Olympic gold medals and world records. In swimming, Forbes Carlisle, Don Talbot and Cecil Colwyn used remarkably similar methods of interval training, and reaped their own rewards with world and Olympic records and medals.

On the other hand, runners Arthur Lydiard, Percy Cerutty and Ernst Van Aaken also achieved tremendous results with very different work, concentrating more on what can roughly be described as periodization, resistance running, and long slow distance.

The lesson is that you should not stick with just one method of training; use a judicious mixture of what is appropriate for you as an individual. Long-distance, slow, steady work, fast repetitions, weights, circuit training, pyrometrics and low-quality intervals all have their advocates and detractors. Assess what you need and adjust the mix accordingly. The content of the mixture is important, but must be applicable to you.

Essential Needs

Conditioning
Strength.
Flexibility and mobility.
Technique. Body composition.
Cross-training. Low intensity.

Base Endurance
This is the foundation of your training.
It should be regarded as the most important phase of your training, but is often the most neglected.

Fartlek

Essentially, this is a non-structured interval session, with the triathlete choosing when to go faster or fastest, with an easier period between efforts. Without the discipline imposed by a structured session, this type of training can degenerate into a low-key workout, with little effort made during the training time. Training in a group can overcome this, by exerting peer pressure to conform to the hard work.

There are two main methods, as follows:

1. giving each triathlete a certain amount of time to lead the session. If not forced to do otherwise, individuals will prefer to train to their strengths and will make the others in their group do the same. Subsequent 'leaders' will be determined to make the rest of the group suffer at least as much as with their predecessor, and will go immediately to their own strengths. This method ensures a good mix of hard, varied work; and
2. pre-setting the criteria – for example, every hill to be attacked flat out, sprinting and jogging between alternate lamp posts, lengthening each effort by one telegraph pole, reducing the rest by 10 seconds each time, and so on. The permutations and combinations are wide, but establishing some idea of structure prior to training will help greatly.

Resistance Training
Broadly speaking, adding some form of resistance makes training harder. The obvious

Factors that Encourage Conditioning and Endurance Work

- improvement in the ability of the heart to pump blood;
- increase in blood vessels in the muscles;
- increase in muscle strength;
- development of tendons and ligaments;
- pace endurance;
- weight monitoring.

These create a stronger base upon which to put quality.

Quality
Quality can be divided into two categories:

- speed endurance (steady state, at or below);
- high intensity (race pace, at level and above).

Race Preparation
Have I done enough? Should I do some more just to see how I am going?
Keep sharp and hold form by reducing volume.
Monitoring form at this stage is crucial.
Using heart rates is essential.
For a great number of athletes, recovery is more important than training.
Mental attitude is paramount.

resistance in running and cycling is hill training; for swimming, resistance can be added by wearing baggy swimshorts, t-shirts, using hand paddles, or immobilizing the legs with a rubber strap around the ankles. Adding a braking or weight resistance on the wheel(s) can also work in cycle training (particularly for turbo training), but safety aspects must be considered carefully.

Technique

Time spent on perfecting technique is rarely wasted, whether it is done in isolation or as an integral part of a training session.

Good technique in swimming is essential. Technique in cycling has to be examined in relation to bike position, gearing, cadence and pedalling. Some triathletes would argue that a good running technique is barely relevant, but 'economy of running' is surely important. How else is it possible to explain the vastly differing marathon times of runners who have similar VO_2max readings, similar training programmes, similar best times for distances up to 10km and similar percentages of VO_2max utilization? The total event premise is viable again too. After a tiring swim and cycle, good running technique will pay dividends in the last third of the race.

Strength

Triathlons are endurance events and a large part of the training time must be geared towards fulfilling the demands of such events on an athlete's strength. The triathlete must be strong enough to carry out the training; if this is not the case, remedial work may be necessary. For example, those with a running or cycling background may need to work on their upper-body strength for the swimming discipline. It is essential to feel strong in the swimming, particularly in rough, choppy open water, in the middle of a pack of others.

Speed

'If the name of the game is speed, don't get too far away from it.' (Peter Coe, coach to double Olympic gold medallist and multiple world record-holder, Sebastian Coe.)

Speed is relative and geared to a specific event. Speed over 100m is not the same as over a mile or 25 miles, but the majority of recent research indicates that the greater the sprinting speed the more likelihood there is of carrying it over to the longer events, with the appropriate training. As sprinting is an anaerobic activity (without oxygen) and endurance relies on the capacity for using oxygen for creating energy, there is an obvious and immediate paradox. Despite this, there is much subjective and objective evidence to illustrate the tremendous range that world-class swimmers, cyclists and runners possess:

- Kieron Perkins (Australia), swimmer: world record-holder 1500m freestyle, and 52 seconds for 100m freestyle;
- Greg Lemond (USA), cyclist: Tour de France winner and short-distance (sub 30 minutes) time triallist;
- Peter Snell (NZ), runner: world record-holder 800, 1000, 1500m, and 2 hour 24 minute marathon runner.

Many other great athletes have given wide-ranging performances. The above examples do seem to indicate that it is never advisable to get too far away from some kind of speed training. The whole idea of racing is to go as fast as you can over the prescribed distance. That means speed, however relative. Train for it.

Power

Power could be defined here as the ability to explode into speed; sprinting flat out is one example. In a triathlon lasting two hours or more, the opportunities for using power are limited. However, there are instances – such as breaking away from another competitor by sprinting around a turning buoy, accelerating into and around a corner or making a fast break on a hill climb – when it will have a place in your racing repertoire.

MORE ABOUT INTERVAL TRAINING

Cutting through all the theory, the basic principles behind interval training are as follows:

1. You swim, cycle or run fast for a period of time to gain speed.
2. You repeat the effort a number of times to gain endurance.
3. The shorter the effort and the longer the resting interval, the more the speed will increase.
4. The longer the effort and the shorter the resting interval, the more the endurance will increase.

5. Interval training hurts.
6. Interval training results in improvement.
7. The critical factor in training for a triathlon, which is primarily endurance, is the resting interval.

There is little doubt that the phenomenal improvements seen in swimming and running times, from national to world level over the last 40 years, and more recently in cycling, have been because of the extensive use of interval training. The late, great runner Emil Zatopek had a 'favourite' training session of 20×200 metres, 20×400 metres and 20×200 metres, all with a short jog recovery of half the running distance. The total of the 'hard' running is 16km (10 miles), plus the jog recovery, warm up and warm down. No wonder the man was unbeatable at his peak.

It is reported that past world 10,000m champion Liz McColgan has a session of ten by 1-mile repeats, each run in 5 minutes, with just 30 seconds recovery. (The session totals 10 miles in 54 minutes 30 seconds, including the recovery period.) Her results speak for themselves. A male triathlete, who competes regularly at the Ironman distance and also takes part in ultra-distance events, attempted this session and was unable to walk the next day.

Start within your capabilities and gradually extend your limits. Do not attempt to copy slavishly a top sportsperson's training schedule without taking into account your own standard at the time. Otherwise you risk disappointment and disillusionment. You might be influenced by the training schedule of someone like Spencer Smith, for example, but Smith had ten years of competitive swimming training behind him before he burst on to the triathlon scene. Remember: your training requirements are specific to you. Analyse what others are doing and try it to see if it works for you, but don't assume that just because a 'name' is doing it, it must be right. Some sportspeople have got to the top *in spite of* how they are training rather than because of it. Remember, what is right for other athletes, may, or may not, be appropriate for you.

DEVISING A PROGRAMME

The Starting Point

The dream for the novice triathlete is to finish a triathlon. Many aim to finish a 'real' one, over the Olympic distances of 1500m, 40km and 10km. First, you need to analyse exactly where you are in terms of the following:

1. standard of performance in each discipline;
2. level of motivation;
3. self-discipline; and
4. what you are prepared to give up.

If there is an inherent weakness in one of the disciplines, your starting point must be to bring that discipline up to a reasonable level. It would be ridiculous to enter a 1500m lake swim when you struggle to complete a 25m length of the local pool. Before devising a training programme, you must be sufficiently competent to complete the distance in each discipline without putting yourself in danger. Once you are happy that you can cover the distance, you can start to make constructive improvements. By ensuring that you train to cover the distance, you are developing the habit of consistent, year-round training, and laying the foundation for your future in triathlon.

Working out a Schedule

How many hours are you able to train each day/week/month/year? What other commitments do you have? Is your partner supportive? How good do you want to be? How much are you prepared to sacrifice to achieve your aims?

Be realistic about your own availability for training.

How easy is it to get access to a swimming pool? Are there structured sessions or is it just a free-for-all? What about a running track? Is your area 'good' for cycling or do you have a hundred sets of traffic lights and articulated lorries to get past? Do you own a turbo trainer?

All these factors, and hundreds of others, have to be taken into account before you can even start to plan out your programme. Take some time for self-analysis, in order to establish realistic aims. Examine the truth and then you can set out the starting points of your training.

TYPES OF TRAINING

The list of training methods should focus you on what you will need to include in your outline training plan. Remember that triathlon is an *endurance* event. It is individual, but the philosophy of *training phases* will help you select what type of training is suitable and appropriate for you at any particular time of year.

- stretching/flexibility;
- weights/circuits;
- technique;
- resistance (hills);
- cross-training;
- fartlek;
- intervals/tempo;
- evaluation;
- mental attitude;
- experience;
- racing.

CHAPTER 4
The Athlete

'If not you, who?
If not now, when?'

TRIATHLETE PROFILE: SELF-ANALYSIS

Before embarking on a training plan, it is important to make a detailed assessment of the raw materials – the athlete. Filling in the following form for analysis will give the athlete and coach a realistic starting point.

The medical data at the beginning of the form is basic, but it may be necessary at some time. The record of training times gives an initial idea of and introduction to time management; the tests indicate basic fitness; the final section makes the athlete think hard about the future and his or her aims.

All triathletes start from different levels, largely dependent on genetic inheritance, but success in triathlon results from consistent training over a period of time. It is the product of careful short- and long-term planning.

THE SELF-ANALYSIS FORM

Outline and General Health
Name: _____
Age: _____
Date of birth: _____
Address: _____

Telephone numbers: _____
Weight: _____
Height: _____
Blood pressure: _____
Resting pulse: _____
Body fat percentage (mm):
   1. _____*mm (bicep)*
   2. _____*mm (tricep)*
   3. _____*mm (iliac crest)*
   4. _____*mm (subscap)*

Total mm measured, indicating percentage of body fat: _____

Medical Background
1. Do you have any medical conditions?
2. Do you take drugs or medication?
3. Do you get chest pains at rest/after exercise?
4. Do you get headaches/dizzy spells/fainting fits?
5. Do you have any allergies (for example, to penicillin, aspirin, paracetamol)?
6. Do you ever get bouts of coughing?
7. Do you suffer from back pain (particularly lower back)?
8. What previous injuries have you had? What previous illnesses have you had?
9. Do you have easy access to medical support? Doctor? Physio? Masseur?

Basic Fitness Indicators
What are your best times for the following?

Swimming
100m _____
400m _____
800/1000m _____
1500m _____
2000m _____

Cycling
400m _____
1000m _____
1 mile _____
5 miles _____
10 miles _____
25 miles _____
30/50 miles _____

Running
40m _____

100m _____

400m _____

800m _____

1500m/1 mile _____

5000m/3 miles _____

10,000m/6 miles _____

What club(s) are you a member of?

_____

_____

_____

Have you had a coach before? _____

Fitness Tests and Mobility Tests

Flexibility

1. Shoulder girdle and upper body

How far can you bring your arms together behind your back? _____

Do your hands touch? _____

Do your arms cross over?

(By how many centimetres?) _____

Draw a diagram below to show where they cross/how far they come together.

2. Legs, adductors and hamstrings

Can you touch your toes with your legs held reasonably straight (but not forced back)?

_____

With your fingertips? _____

With your wrists? _____

With your elbows? _____

If you can't touch your toes, how far away are you? _____

Lie face down and pull up your feet behind your back so that your chest is off the floor. How high is your chest (taken from the hollow in your neck) from the floor?

_____

Stand upright. Hold the knee of one leg into your chest, come on to the toes of the other leg and fall forward in a giant stride.

What is the distance between your feet:

With the right leg forward? _____

With the left leg forward? _____

Speed Endurance/VO$_2$ Indicator

(Running Test)

THIS TEST IS VITALLY IMPORTANT. *Try to do it as accurately as possible, preferably on a running track, or in a place where the distance can be measured accurately.*

Run for 15 minutes. What distance (to the nearest 25m) did you cover?

_____

How many of the following exercises can you do in *one* minute?

1. Press-ups? _____
2. Bent-knee abdominal sit-ups? _____
3. Squat thrusts? _____
4. Chin-ups on a bar? (either over or under grip) _____

Hop 25m on each leg. How many hops did it take you to cover the distance?

Right leg? _____ Left leg? _____

Do a standing long jump (both legs together) into a sand pit or on to a padded mat. What was the distance covered? _____

Do a sergeant jump: stand sideways next to a wall with arm and fingertips extended and make a mark where the fingertips are; bend down and leap as high as possible banging your hand against the wall and making a mark. What distance is the second mark above the first? _____

How much weight can you lift above your head? _____

How much weight can you curl? _____

How much weight can you half-squat with?

_____

Warning! if you're not used to handling free weights, get expert help.

(These tests give an indication of your flexibility, aerobic, anaerobic, muscular endurance, leg strength and power/weight ratio. There is absolutely no point in influencing the result of any of the tests. They reveal a great deal about your potential, and can also indicate your susceptibility to injury.)

Training Possibilities

What training facilities do you have available?
Running track? _____
Grass area for running? _____
Swimming pool? _____
Turbo trainer? _____
Gymnasium? _____
Weight-training/fitness room? _____

Do you have others to train with?
Swimmers? _____
Runners? _____
Cyclists? _____
Triathletes? _____

Time Commitments/Time Available for Training
How much training time do you have each week?

_____

What is already blocked in (group sessions in the swimming pool, on the running track, etc.)?

_____

What race commitments do you have to fulfill (school/university/college swimming leagues, cross-country leagues, etc.)?

Commitments				
	Morning	*Lunchtime*	*Afternoon*	*Evening*
Monday				
Tuesday				
Wednesday				
Thursday				
Friday				
Saturday				
Sunday				

Are there any days which are unavailable on a monthly, termly, yearly basis? Does the situation change dramatically at different times of the year? For example, between school term time and vacation time?

_____

Goals and Aims

What are your goals and aims for next year? Worlds? Europeans? National championships? To finish an Olympic-distance race? Other races? Other aims?

List your aims in order of priority.
1. _____
2. _____
3. _____
4. _____
5. _____

Key Questions

How serious are you about triathlon?
What do you expect from your coach?

CHAPTER 5

Exercise Physiology for Triathletes

'Know your body.'

An understanding of the basics of exercise physiology is invaluable. The principles provide the base for training programmes and devising a suitable training schedule for each individual triathlete.

There are a number of misconceptions in sport about some of the terms used in exercise physiology. They may be defined as follows:

Aerobic: with oxygen, in other words, the presence of oxygen is essential.
Anaerobic: without oxygen, in other words, anaerobic processes do not require the presence of oxygen; however, an anaerobic process can take place even if there is plenty of oxygen present.

Oxygen debt: the increased oxygen taken in after the triathlete has stopped exercising (*see* Fig 2.)

EXERCISE PHYSIOLOGY

A number of areas of exercise physiology are relevant to triathlon.

Energy Systems

For a muscle to be able to contract, there must be a source of energy available. The body's energy carrier is a molecule called ATP (adenosine triphosphate) and a constant supply of

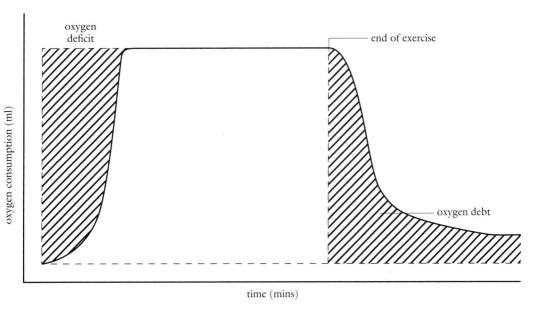

Fig 2. Graphical representation of oxygen debt.

ATP is required by the body. There are five systems in the body by which ATP can be generated:

1. from ATP stores in the muscles;
2. from creatine phosphate stores in the muscles;
3. ADP + ADP = ATP + AMP;
4. glycogen = ATP + lactic acid; and
5. carbohydrates, fats + O_2 > ATP + water + carbon dioxide.

(The first four processes are all anaerobic; the fifth represents the aerobic energy system.)

These energy-producing reactions do not work independently of each other; one will predominate, depending on the intensity and duration of the exercise. The anaerobic systems can produce ATP very quickly, but at a cost (the athlete is soon fatigued); the aerobic reaction takes longer to generate ATP but can produce very large amounts over long periods of time.

When racing, triathletes will get most of their energy from the aerobic reaction (even in sprint distance triathlons).

The Aerobic System

The two main fuel sources for the aerobic system are carbohydrates and fats. Carbohydrates are stored in the body as glycogen in the liver, and in the muscles; glucose also circulates in the bloodstream. Fats are stored as triglycerides in various sites in the body, including the muscles. Triglycerides consist of a glycerol molecule, to which three fatty acid molecules are attached. When fats are needed as a fuel, the triglyceride molecules split up into glycerol and FFA (free fatty acids).

The glycogen stored in the liver is broken down into glucose by a process called glycogenolysis; the glucose enters the bloodstream and is taken to the working muscles. Here, the glucose from the blood and from the muscle's own supplies of glycogen (which also undergo glycogenolysis) is changed to glucose-6-phosphate and enters the process of glycolysis.

The end product of glycolysis is pyruvic acid. This substance then enters the mitochondria (the 'engine room' of the muscle cells) and is eventually converted to water and carbon dioxide. This process leads to the formation of ATP.

While some ATP is produced by glycolysis, the reactions in the mitochondria (collectively known as the Krebs Cycle, the Citric Acid cycle, or the TCA cycle) create much greater quantities of ATP. Oxygen is not essential for glycolysis to take place, but the reactions in the mitochondria do require the presence of oxygen, otherwise they soon stop. As the production of ATP from FFA occurs in the mitochondria (via the same processes as pyruvic acid), oxygen must be available if FFA is to be used as a fuel.

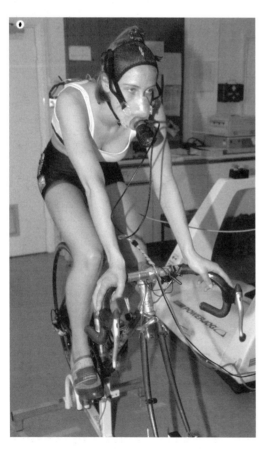

Fig 3. British International triathlete Joanna Hinde is tested at the British Olympic Medical Centre (BOMC).

Using fats in addition to carbohydrates as a fuel source has advantages over the use solely of carbohydrates. Fats yield more energy, weight for weight, than carbohydrates (fats produce 39kJ/g, while glucose produces 16.7kJ/g). The body is also able to store far greater quantities of fat than glycogen. It is estimated that, if each fuel was used by itself, glycogen stores would last about 90 minutes while fats could keep the body going for more than 50 hours.

The drawback in using fats is that, in order to release the same amount of energy, they need more oxygen than carbohydrates. A triathlete exercising at a particular workload and using fats *and* carbohydrates will have to take in and transport more oxygen. Using fats, the triathlete will need to use less glycogen to go at the same speed, so the role of the oxygen transport system becomes important.

The Oxygen Transport System

The oxygen transport system consists of the lungs, heart, blood vessels and blood, known collectively as the cardio-respiratory system. The purpose of the cardio-respiratory system is to transport oxygen to the parts of the body that need it and to remove the carbon dioxide produced.

The lungs provide the mechanism by which the oxygen in the air we breathe is transferred into the blood. The air enters the trachea (windpipe) through the nose and mouth; the trachea divides into two bronchi, one entering the left lung and the other the right lung. In the lungs, the bronchi carry on dividing until the alveoli (air sacs) are reached. The exchange of gases (O_2 and CO_2) between the lungs and the blood vessels takes place in the alveoli.

Generally, breathing is more efficient when deeper, less frequent breaths are taken, rather than shallow, quick ones.

While the lungs are obviously important for taking in air, their capacity is not greatly increased by training (by 10 per cent at the most). The amount of oxygen available for exchange in the alveoli is only very slightly increased, if at all. However, the system for transporting the oxygen does show great improvements with training.

The cardiac output (the amount of blood pumped by the heart) is governed by heart rate and stroke volume (the volume of blood pumped by each beat of the heart).

Cardiac output = heart rate × stroke volume

Training does not raise the maximum heart rate of a triathlete – indeed, it can actually fall – but the stroke volume will be greatly increased. With this improvement, the same cardiac output can be achieved at a lower heart rate. With an increased stroke volume, more blood is pumped by each beat of the heart.

Additionally, aerobic training causes more blood vessels to form in the muscles so that the amount of blood in the body rises. The greater volume of blood means there is more haemoglobin – the molecule that carries oxygen around the body.

Maximal Oxygen Uptake

While training leads to increases in the amount of oxygen transported by the cardio-respiratory system, there is still a limit to how much oxygen that can be carried to and utilized by the muscles.

A swimming, cycling or running triathlete will use more oxygen than when at rest; their oxygen uptake rises. At a particular work intensity, the oxygen uptake of each individual will reach a plateau – the maximal oxygen uptake or VO_2max per minute. If the triathlete exercises at a greater intensity, the oxygen uptake will not increase, because the body is now taking in and using all the oxygen it can.

Maximal oxygen uptake (also known as maximal aerobic power) can be calculated as follows (note that this is not the same as maximal aerobic capacity, which is equivalent to the anaerobic threshold; *see* page 28):

VO_2max = maximum cardiac output × a–v O_2 difference
(maximum cardiac output = maximum heart rate × maximum stroke volume)
(a–v O_2 difference = oxygen content of arterial blood – oxygen content of venous blood)

Maximal oxygen uptake is most accurately assessed in a physiology laboratory using a gas analyser that measures the levels of oxygen in the air breathed in and out by the athlete. Other, less accurate methods of measurement give information that may be used by coaches and athletes, with a degree of caution.

If the figure produced by testing is divided by the individual's body weight, the VO_2max value can be expressed in terms of millilitres of oxygen used per minute per kilogram of bodyweight (ml/min/kg). This allows comparisons to be made between athletes. Maximal oxygen uptake values will vary depending on the triathlete's age, sex and level of fitness.

While VO_2max is often used to assess aerobic fitness, it must be remembered that athletes with a similar performance level can have very different VO_2max scores, while athletes with similar VO_2max values can have very different performance levels.

Training can lead to increases in an athlete's maximal oxygen uptake (15 to 20 per cent) but improvements seem to be limited by genetic factors. Although, after a regular training programme, a triathlete may only show a small rise in the VO_2 result, their endurance capacity may have vastly improved. The triathlete is now able to exercise at a greater percentage of their VO_2max without becoming fatigued. This level of intensity has been called the anaerobic threshold.

EXERCISE THRESHOLDS

Aerobic Threshold

Two important exercise thresholds are relevant to triathletes. The lower (easier) of the two is the *aerobic threshold*. The adaptations in the body that result from training – increased numbers of mitochondria, better blood supply to the muscles – take place above this threshold.

Below the aerobic threshold, very few significant changes occur in the body. The training load must be at an intensity that is greater than the triathlete's aerobic threshold before training effects become apparent.

Anaerobic Threshold

A number of energy systems produce ATP, combining together, with one system dominating, depending on the duration and intensity of the exercise. As the triathlete increases velocity, more and more of the ATP needed will be produced by anaerobic metabolism. It is *not* correct to think that, at a certain velocity, the triathlete switches from using solely aerobic mechanisms to using only anaerobic energy supply.

The intensity at which anaerobic metabolism starts to make a significant contribution to ATP production has been called the *anaerobic threshold* (AT). (The AT will be lower than the maximal oxygen uptake in all athletes.)

The concept of the anaerobic threshold has been the subject of much discussion. However, it can be defined as a certain level of exercise intensity above which a triathlete will fatigue quickly and have to slow down. As work intensifies above the AT, lactic acid starts to accumulate and breathing becomes more strained. The intensity at which the breathing rate dramatically changes is called the *ventilatory threshold* (VT or T vent). While many researchers have found that the AT and VT coincide, other studies have shown that the two thresholds do not always occur at the same point.

The anaerobic threshold is sometimes referred to by the names *lactate threshold* (T lac) or *OBLA* (onset of blood lactate accumulation). OBLA is not always the same as the anaerobic threshold. OBLA is taken to be the same specific concentration of lactate (4mm/litre) for everyone and does not change with training, although the work intensity at which OBLA occurs can change.

It is ideal for the triathlete to race just below the anaerobic threshold, with short periods when the threshold is crossed (as when cycling or running up a hill).

Both the aerobic and anaerobic threshold can be expressed as a percentage of a triathlete's VO_2max value – in other words, as an oxygen uptake figure such as 3 litres/min, or in terms of work intensity (for example, 300 watts). Both have their drawbacks, and triathletes commonly use heart rate as an indication of training thresholds. Heart rate linearly increases with the rise in intensity of exercise, although this relationship breaks down as the triathlete approaches maximal oxygen uptake.

The Karvonen formula can be used to calculate the heart rates that correspond to a triathlete's aerobic and anaerobic thresholds:

Heart Rate = [loading factor × (Max HR – Resting HR)] + Resting HR
(loading factor = percentage of maximum heart rate that coincides with the threshold to be determined)
(Normal loading factors are 0.7 for the aerobic threshold, in other words, 70 per cent of maximum heart rate, and 0.85 for the anaerobic threshold, in other words, 85 per cent of the maximum heart rate.)

For a triathlete with a resting heart rate of 55 beats per minute and a maximum heart rate of 185 beats per minute, the Karvonen formula gives the following answers:

$$
\begin{aligned}
\text{Aerobic threshold} &= [0.7 \times (185 - 55)] + 55 \\
&= [0.7 \times 130] + 55 \\
&= 91 + 55 \\
&= 146\text{bpm}
\end{aligned}
$$

$$
\begin{aligned}
\text{Anaerobic threshold} &= [0.85 \times (185 - 55)] \\
&\quad + 55 \\
&= [0.85 \times 130] + 55 \\
&= 110.5 + 55 \\
&= 165.5\text{bpm (round} \\
&\quad \text{down to 165bpm)}
\end{aligned}
$$

The idea of using heart rates to gauge training and racing intensities may be appealing *but* they should not be used in isolation. The following factors should be remembered:

1. Accuracy: in order to find out whether the triathlete is near to the anaerobic threshold, the heart rate must be measured during activity, not afterwards. It is impossible for a triathlete accurately and safely to measure their own heart rate while cycling hard on a public road, for example. An accurate and reliable heart rate monitor (not a fingertip or ear-lobe model) will need to be used.
2. Personal differences: in exercise physiology, mean (or generalized) results are calculated and this can be problematic. For example, it is possible to estimate maximum heart rate by subtracting the individual's age from 220, but the result is likely to be inaccurate. It is better for the triathlete to undertake a maximal exercise test. The loading factor in the Karvonen formula, given as 0.7 and 0.85, will vary from athlete to athlete. For the less fit individual, the anaerobic threshold may be reached at 50 per cent of maximum heart rate (a loading factor of 0.5). The only way to determine accurately an individual's anaerobic threshold is to measure blood lactate concentrations at various work intensities. This is usually impractical, so the loading factor has to be estimated each time. Overtraining can increase the resting heart rate, as can a rise in perceived stress levels. Certain medication can also influence heart rates.
3. Environmental factors: environmental factors include temperature, humidity and altitude. In a hot and humid climate, until the triathlete is acclimatized, heart rates will be higher than normal. More of the blood is diverted to the skin surface, in order to promote cooling, so the heart has to work harder to provide the muscles with the required volume of blood.
4. Fluid intake/cooling: all triathletes should ensure that they take in enough liquids before, during and after exercise. In hot weather, the body may also be cooled by splashing water on it. By being hydrated in training and racing, the triathlete will be able to exercise at a higher pulse rate before fatiguing.
5. Reassessment: it is important to assess a triathlete's progress regularly, particularly when heart rates are used for making decisions on training or racing intensity. As the triathlete improves, heart rates corresponding to the aerobic and anaerobic thresholds will change. A triathlete who fails to make regular assessments may train at the wrong intensity.

Heart rates should only be used as a guideline. With good coaching, all athletes can learn to recognize when they are training at the appropriate intensity, and racing at their optimum pace.

MUSCLE FIBRE TYPES

There are three types of muscle fibre: slow-twitch and two types of fast-twitch (and recent research suggests there may be more). Slow-twitch fibres take longer to contract than fast-twitch ones. The differences are as follows:

1. Slow-twitch fibres (also called slow-oxidative, red or Type 1 fibres) have a plentiful supply of blood carried by a dense network of capillaries (the tiny blood vessels in the muscle), hence the name 'red'. They can receive great quantities of oxygen and fuel, and waste products can be quickly flushed away. Additionally, these fibres have great numbers of mitochondria and high concentrations of the enzymes required in aerobic metabolism. Slow-twitch fibres are ideal for aerobic energy production as they can repeatedly contract, without fatiguing, for many hours.
2. Fast-twitch fibres are also called white or Type 2 fibres, divided into Type 2A (fast oxidative glycolytic) and Type 2B (fast glycolytic). While both types have fewer capillaries than slow-twitch fibres, Type 2A fibres can work aerobically or anaerobically; Type 2B fibres mainly work anaerobically. Fast-twitch fibres are adapted to producing ATP swiftly but they fatigue far more quickly than slow-twitch fibres.

Each muscle consists of a combination of all three fibre types, but the percentage of each type in the muscle will differ from person to person. People with a higher percentage of slow-twitch fibres in their muscles will be more suited to endurance sports, such as triathlons. However, no one should be excluded from any sport just because their muscle fibre mix is 'wrong'. Enjoyment and satisfaction are the important factors.

It is useful to understand the order in which the fibres are recruited when a muscle is working. Generally the slow-twitch fibres are used first, at low loads; then the Type 2A fibres are brought in as the work gets harder. Finally, with a further increase in intensity, the Type 2B fibres come into play. The recruitment pattern depends, therefore, on the load on the muscle and on the required speed of movement.

LACTIC ACID

There are a number of misconceptions about *lactic acid* (also called *lactate*):

1. Lactic acid is not a 'poison'. Even at rest, there is a small quantity circulating in the bloodstream – normally about 1 millimole of lactate per litre of blood (1mmol/L). Slow-twitch type muscles and other organs in the body, such as the heart, are also capable of converting lactic acid into pyruvic acid, which can then enter the Krebs cycle.
2. Lactic acid is not only produced when there is a lack of oxygen in the muscles. Lactate production also occurs when fast-twitch muscles are used and when more pyruvate is produced that can enter the Krebs cycle.
3. Increased production of lactate does not automatically mean there will be a higher concentration of it. The concentration depends not only on the rate of production but also on the rate of removal and conversion.
4. Lactic acid is not the cause of pain in muscles the day after exercising. The acid is cleared away and converted relatively quickly, especially if the triathlete warms down properly. The reason for the discomfort (called delayed muscle soreness or DMS) is not definitely known, but leakage of fluids and other substances are believed to be the main causes.

There have been suggestions that optimal endurance training effects take place at a lactate concentration of 4mmol/L, but this single value cannot be valid for everyone. Even with a lactate analyser, lactate measures should not be used as the only indicator of training intensity.

FATIGUE AND RECOVERY

The main reason a triathlete slows down near the end of a race is *not* a build-up of lactic acid. There are a number of causes of fatigue in endurance activities, but the main one is the depletion of the triathlete's glycogen stores, which leads the body to rely more on fats for its fuel. Pacing is a crucial factor in successful triathlon racing.

Fig 4. South African international cyclist and triathlete Annelle
Rabie goes through her paces on the wind trainer.

A triathlete might expect always to feel fatigued during everyday training, but this should be avoided, especially with novice triathletes. Many triathletes overtrain and this may affect their enjoyment, and their race results. High-intensity training sessions lead to significant glycogen depletion and it can take up to 48 hours for levels to return to normal. This is one of the reasons for having a recovery day, particularly after a hard training run or cycle session.

ADAPTATIONS TO TRAINING

The following adaptations occur with endurance training:

1. Greatly improved neuromuscular function, with more fibres contracting together and with greater efficiency.
2. Increased heart stroke volume, resulting in a higher cardiac output for the same heart rate.
3. Increase in the number of red blood cells (and, therefore, more haemoglobin).
4. Increase in the volume of blood in the body.
5. Increase in the number of capillaries in the muscles.
6. Increased amount of myoglobin (the molecule that transports and stores oxygen in muscle cells) in the muscle fibres.
7. Increase in the number of mitochondria in the muscle fibres.
8. Great improvement in the capacity of the fast-twitch muscle fibres (principally the Type 2A fibres) to produce ATP aerobically.
9. Sweating starts sooner when exercising. Sweat is more dilute, with about a 50 per cent reduction in the concentration of sodium, potassium, magnesium and chloride in it.

(Numbers 3 and 4 may lead to the triathlete being diagnosed as anaemic, or having a lower than normal concentration of haemoglobin. Although the *total amount* of haemoglobin increases, the increase does not match the rise in blood volume and, consequently, the *concentration* of haemoglobin is reduced.)

Because of these adaptations, the triathlete is able to use fats at an earlier stage when exercising; the muscles are able to use more oxygen; more ATP is produced aerobically; and the point at which lactic acid starts to accumulate is delayed.

The maximum oxygen uptake value will probably be higher and the anaerobic threshold raised, so that the athlete will be able to perform at a greater percentage of VO_2max for a longer period of time.

The aim of triathlon training is to cause changes in the cardiovascular system and improvements in aerobic muscle endurance (local muscular endurance). Any form of aerobic training will lead to the cardiovascular adaptations, but the physiological changes in aerobic muscle endurance will be confined to the muscles used in that training session. By mixing different types of training session and training in all their disciplines, the triathlete aims to improve both the cardiovascular system and local muscular endurance.

IMPLICATIONS FOR RACING

Some knowledge of exercise physiology can help triathletes when it comes to racing.

The key word in racing is *pacing*. You must swim, cycle and run at a speed that is appropriate to your level of fitness on that day and to the distance of the race. If the intensity is too high, your anaerobic threshold will be overtaken, fatigue will result and you will have to slow down. (Remember, too, that speed is not a direct measure of intensity; weather, terrain and local conditions can all affect it.)

At the start of the swim and after each transition, be careful not to sprint away. While some lactic acid will be produced at these times, a sensible pace will mean that large amounts will not be accumulated and glycogen stores will be spared. Similarly, on hills and when trying to break away from a competitor, you are likely to be working at an intensity above your anaerobic threshold. Gauge the amount of time you can afford at that increased intensity, based on the distance left to race, the severity of the rest of the course, and your state.

Finally, sports science is not an exact science – find out what works best for *you*.

CHAPTER 6
A Practical Application of Exercise Physiology

'The difference between good and great is a little more effort.'

Athletes and coaches who refuse to acknowledge the benefits of exercise physiology, or turn a blind eye to them, and prepare for competition by relying on 'gut feelings', are not making the best use of coaching and athletic expertise. Exercise physiology is closely related to everyday training and racing – an extra tool to be used for the good of the athlete.

PLANNING YOUR YEAR'S PROGRAMME

Most of the factors that constitute a year-round training programme can be divided into three main phases:

1. base/foundation/conditioning/endurance training;
2. transition (speed endurance) training; and
3. speed (incorporating taper) work.

Base/Foundation/Conditioning/Endurance Training

This is undertaken during the athlete's off season. The establishment of a strong aerobic base on which to place subsequent and more intense training is the main aim. Physiological benefits will include the following:

- enhancement of myocardial function and oxygen transport;
- an increase in blood volume;
- enhancement of mitochondrial and oxidative capacity of skeletal muscle; and
- improved fat mobilization and utilization.

During this base period, the overall training is maintained below the threshold at which the athlete would be overworked. This conditioning phase typically works the athlete at fairly low intensities, perhaps at 65–70 per cent of VO_2max or 70–80 per cent of max heart rate (MHR), for long time periods. Training is for at least half an hour up to several hours each day, with 7–12 (or more) sessions each week,

APEX

SPEED (incorporating taper) WORK — RACE SEASON

TRANSITION (speed endurance) TRAINING — PRE-SEASON

BASE/FOUNDATION/CONDITIONING/ENDURANCE TRAINING — OFF SEASON

BASE

Fig 5. Planning your year's programme: speed, built upon speed endurance, built upon base work.

and for as long as possible (3–6 months), depending upon the time constraints of the previous and next season's competitive phases.

Can this sort of base training – up to six hours a day at speeds that are very much slower than competition pace – prepare athletes for individual phases that, at élite male level, will last for less than 20, 55 and 33 minutes? Despite much research, it is still not certain whether such training (which is undertaken by the majority of endurance athletes), compared with the higher-intensity work that is more specific to race pace, does result in better race performances.

Transition (Speed Endurance) Training

This is the hard work phase. The objective is to expose the physiological systems to sustained effort at an intensity equalling the athlete's best steady-state pace. Physiological benefits will include the following:

- enhancement of lactate kinetics; and
- stimulation of muscle fibre recruitment required during a race.

Training during this phase will include both intervals and sustained efforts (time trials) at the less than race distance. Intensity will be at the anaerobic threshold (perhaps 85 per cent of VO_2max/90–95 per cent of MHR), or equivalent to best race pace for each of the three disciplines. There is still little scientific evidence to back up intensities of work based on blood lactate concentrations, despite the recent popularity of measuring training by this method.

A typical interval session might include 6–8 repetitions of 5 minutes at best race pace with a maximum of 60 seconds active recovery between; or, in training terminology shorthand, 6–8 × 5 mins (rec 60 secs). A 31-minute 10km runner would aim to cover 1600m (1 mile) in each 5-minute effort.

As the athlete's fitness improves, the distance covered is increased or the time is reduced.

Speed (Incorporating Taper) Work

This is undertaken at faster than race pace. The objective is to expose the physiological system to max or sub-max efforts. This phase uses high-intensity efforts with long recovery intervals.

A typical session might include 6–8 repetitions of 1.5 minutes with a 5-minute active recovery between; or 6–8 × 1.5 mins (rec 5 mins). The intensity of this type of training cannot be monitored effectively by heart rate measurement. The heart rate will frequently still be rising as the intense exercise period ends.

In the final approach to the race, the volume and frequency of training are reduced but the intensity is maintained, or even increased. This type of taper (HIT) is far more effective than either a reduction of training intensity (LIT) or total rest (ROT).

PHYSIOLOGICAL OBJECTIVES

Each phase of training emphasizes one or more specific physiological objectives, which can be loosely divided into seven areas:

- maximum oxygen uptake (VO_2max);
- fractional utilization of oxygen uptake;
- peak sustained power output;
- fatigue resistance;
- anaerobic/lactate threshold;
- economy of movement; and
- fuel utilization.

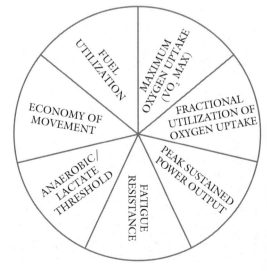

Fig 6. Planning your year's programme: the seven considerations.

Maximum Oxygen Uptake (VO$_2$max)

Maximum oxygen uptake (VO$_2$max) is the greatest rate at which oxygen can be consumed by an athlete during exercise. Under controlled conditions, it is a reflection of the individual's maximum rate of aerobic energy utilization.

As early as the 1920s, it was understood that VO$_2$ increased with running and swimming speed, and that the fastest athletes had the highest oxygen uptakes. Over the next fifty years, credibility was given to the belief that VO$_2$max was a good predictor of athletic potential in endurance sports.

Today, the vast majority of swimmers, cyclists, runners and triathletes still believe that VO$_2$max is the single best predictor of athletic potential. However, high values of VO$_2$max, such as those seen in middle- and long-distance runners with values of over 75ml/kg/min, are

Fig 7. Olympian and World duathlon champion Steph Forrester is tested on the turbo trainer.

almost certainly not as critical for athletes taking part in prolonged endurance events of over one hour. This obviously includes triathlon and therefore is highly significant in training for the standard distance of 1500m/40km/10km.

Fractional Utilization of Oxygen Uptake

Fractional utilization refers to the percentage of an athlete's VO$_2$max that can be utilized at a specified speed or work rate, such as race pace. Male marathon runners who run under 2 hours 20 minutes can sustain up to 85 per cent of VO$_2$max for the duration of the race; the slower runners would sustain approximately 75 per cent for the same distance. Similar differences are also noted in cyclists doing 40km (25-mile) time trials. It would seem therefore that the percentage of VO$_2$max that an athlete can sustain or tolerate for prolonged periods of time is related to the accumulation of lactic acid in the active muscles. In well-trained endurance athletes there is no increase in blood lactate concentration until there is an exercise intensity of over 70 per cent and up to 85 per cent of VO$_2$max.

Peak Sustained Power Output

Peak sustained power output is an excellent predictor of endurance performance. In runners, the peak velocity achieved during a maximal test is as good a predictor of endurance performance as any physiological variable currently measured. It has been proposed that times over short-duration, high-intensity events (such as 800m and 1500m in running) might also determine performance in more endurance-orientated events. Similar evidence exists in cycling.

Fatigue Resistance

Fatigue resistance is, simply, the ability of the athlete to resist fatigue during prolonged exercises, or, 'How much can I hurt?' This capacity is the major adaptation to endurance training.

Anaerobic/Lactate Threshold

The anaerobic/lactate threshold is the speed of movement at which a specific blood lactate

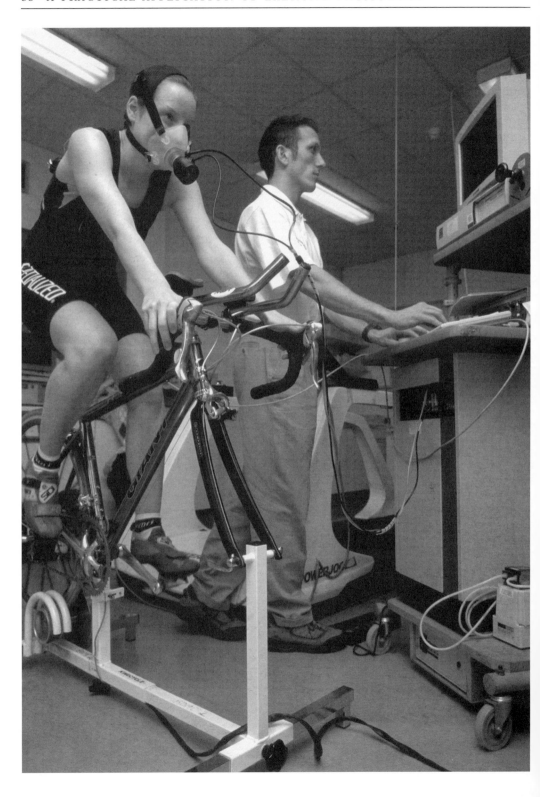

concentration (usually 4mmol/L) is observed. This simply reflects the highest intensity of exercise that the athlete can sustain without accumulating the amounts of lactate that limit performance. In running, endurance training increases the speed at the lactate turning point and this change correlates closely with improvements in running performance.

It seems unlikely that Conconi's proposal of lactate threshold coinciding with heart rate deflection is valid.

Economy of Movement

Economy of movement could be summed up as 'the awesome moment of looking good'. The best endurance athletes – swimmers, cyclists and runners – are usually the most efficient.

High weekly running mileage increases running efficiency, leading to a decrease in stride length and increase in stride frequency.

Similarly, cyclists use high cadence/low gear to develop a smooth action. In swimming, the distance covered with each armstroke is an excellent predictor of performance in all events from 50m upwards. The greater stroke distance at any speed is the most efficient. Again, this is achieved by the enormous distances covered by swimmers during training.

Fuel Utilization

At higher intensities of training, there is a greater reliance on carbohydrate for fuel. Well-trained endurance athletes can make greater use of fat as a fuel during high-intensity submaximal exercise than less well-trained athletes, thereby conserving muscle and liver glycogen stores.

Interestingly, though, the concept of training longer and further to increase the ability of the muscles to utilize fat remains contentious.

Needs for Excellence in Performance

1. A high, but not phenomenal VO_2max.
2. The ability to utilize a high percentage of VO_2max for sustained periods.
3. The ability to sustain high power outputs and resist muscle fatigue during prolonged exercise.
4. A high power output at the lactate threshold.
5. An efficient technique.
6. The ability to utilize fat as a fuel during sustained exercise at high work rates.

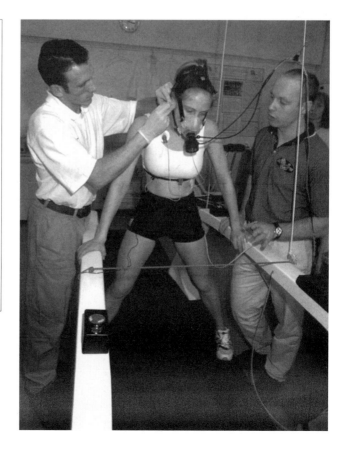

(Left) Fig 8. Ceris Gilfillan, an Olympian and an international cyclist, duathlete and triathlete, is tested at the BOMC.

Fig 9. Joanna Hinde undergoes an increasing demand test on the running machine.

CHAPTER 7

Training with a Heart Rate Monitor

'Train smart.'

WHAT IS A HEART RATE MONITOR?

A heart rate monitor accurately measures your cardiovascular and physiological response to exercise. It is much more reliable than checking your heart rate by putting fingers to wrist or throat, and provides immediate feedback. It is the key to regulating the intensity and quality of your workout. Guessing and going by your 'perceived effort' is inefficient. Precisely monitoring your training allows you to maximize every workout, making it unique to your physiological make-up.

A heart rate monitor uses two electrodes mounted on a sealed electronic transmitter that is attached to the chest with an adjustable elastic belt. These units pick up the electrical impulses from the heart and relay the information to a wrist monitor. On newer models, the chest belt and transmitter are combined into one component, and there may be extra features that will help you train with greater precision.

Fig 10. Heart rate monitor strapped to the body.

The chest belt is hooked around the athlete's waist, then pulled up to just below the nipples. The two electrodes are moistened with water or saliva and the transmitter is worn under the clothing. The wrist monitor is set to display the heart rate and the starting heart rate is noted.

USEFUL TERMS

Resting heart rate (RHR): the number of beats in one minute when at complete, uninterrupted rest. It is usually taken when you first wake up in the morning, before doing anything.

Maximum heart rate (MHR or Max HR): the highest number of times your heart can contract in one minute. It can be measured by taking a specific test while using a heart rate monitor.

Safe heart rate: the rate that is prescribed for beginning exercisers, whatever the aerobic activity chosen. This range is usually 60 per cent (or less) of the MHR and represents the least amount of stress you can place on your heart and still receive a beneficial exercise effect. There is a misconception that low-intensity training and exercise is an absolute must for burning fat rather than carbohydrate. The truth is that high-intensity exercise burns *more* fat than low-intensity exercise; however, low-intensity workouts burn a higher *percentage* of fat, while high-intensity work burns a higher *percentage* of carbohydrate than fat.

Karvonen training heart rate: the rate used in the formula (*see* page 29) to determine training levels – it is particularly important to get a realistic range of heart rates at which to work. Some examples are given here without using the RHR but, if you want maximum

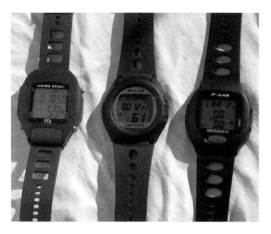

Fig 11. Different heart rate monitors.

benefit from your training regime, you should use the RHR.

Heart rate reserve (HRR): the total number of beats (the specific heart rate range) that you have between your resting heart rate and your maximum heart rate. MHRR is the maximum heart rate reserve, and is sometimes called the 'working heart rate'.

Recovery time or recovery heart rate (Recovery HR): the time after your exercise that is used to measure the reduction in your heart rate.

Total recovery heart rate: the time between when you stop exercising and the time it takes for your heart rate to return to normal. Different recovery HR intervals will be appropriate for different types and intensities of training.

MVO₂ heart rate (MVO₂ HR): the heart rate at which you hit your maximal oxygen uptake effort. On the average, you hit your MVO₂ HR at 95 per cent of your MHR; this will differ with individuals.

Anaerobic threshold heart rate (AT HR): the heart rate at which you enter the physiological point where you are producing more lactate than you are able to synthesize. (The point at which things start to hurt.)

VARIATIONS IN HEART RATE

Heart rates vary tremendously among individuals. Resting heart rates can vary by as much as 50–60 beats in two people of the same height,

weight and age. They can vary greatly between males and females as well, with women averaging about 5–7bpm more than men; women's hearts are proportionately smaller.

Fit people also have a lower heart rate, with some as low as 40bpm (known as *bradiacardia*). Sedentary, unfit people have a high resting heart rate, sometimes over 100bpm.

Your heart rate can be viewed as an efficiency rating for your entire body. It can indicate the amount of blood your heart is pumping. The higher the heart rate, the more energy is required for you to pump it. A heart with a lower rate requires less energy to pump the same amount of blood.

The heart is a 'work now, pay now' muscle. (Skeletal muscles are 'work now, pay later' muscles.) The heart requires continuous fuel or 'metabolic replenishment' while, for limited durations at least, skeletal muscles are able to contract without meeting their immediate metabolic fuel needs.

The heart's cardiac output is based on how often the heart beats per minute (HR or bpm) and how much blood is being pumped (stroke volume or SV). The total cardiac output formula is pretty simple:

$$\text{Cardiac output} = \text{HR} \times \text{SV}$$

If the heart is weak, causing the stroke volume to decrease, it will maintain the same blood volume by beating faster. If either the HR or SV changes, the other factor will work to adjust itself accordingly, in order to keep the cardiac output consistent. While the cardiac output increases with exercise, the HR and SV keep in close relationship with each other, each changing as the other changes.

A key indicator of your heart's efficiency is the body's heart rate reserve (HRR), the difference between the heart working at its maximum and minimum rates. Expanding the heart rate reserve will reduce the chances of the body's demand for oxygen exceeding the supply.

The lower resting HR that results from physical conditioning also allows a longer rest interval between heart beats. This means that the heart chambers have more time to fill with blood. The more blood that fills the ventricles the more they are stretched, which means a stronger contraction and a greater ejection of blood.

Aerobic conditioning of any kind causes the cardiovascular system to strengthen and become more efficient, and results in a lower resting HR. The benefits are reversible – when conditioning is lost, there will be an increase in the resting HR.

Heart rates are affected by a variety of factors, such as the person's emotional state. An athlete's heart rate may rise before a race; this is called 'anticipatory heart rate increase' and is the result of the endocrine and nervous systems signalling for help. Other factors resulting in a response might include stress, caffeine, moods, images, feelings, thoughts, attitudes, and differences in the amount of food and liquid consumed.

The heart rate response to intense exercise is almost immediate. The higher the intensity of the exercise, the higher the heart rate. Even in non-sprint events, a trained athlete's heart rate may rise to 180bpm within 30 seconds of the start of a 1- or 2-mile run. After this quick increase in heart rate, further increases are more gradual, usually with several plateaux being reached during the run. This intense response is common, except in swimming. A swimmers' maximum heart rate tends to be 10–13bpm lower than that of other athletes. One of the reasons for this is the fact that they exercise in the prone position and use upper-body muscle groups, which are relatively smaller than the large leg muscles in the lower-body muscle groups used in most sports.

Sports psychologists have long been aware that the mind both consciously controls *and* unconsciously affects the body. Resting and submaximal exercising heart rates can be controlled voluntarily, but this requires practice. Control anticipatory heart rate increase and exercising heart rate by watching your wrist monitor and focusing on relaxing, and breathing deeply and fully.

MAKING ACCURATE ASSESSMENTS

Triathlon training is designed to improve performance in each discipline so that the athlete does better in competition. The body is stressed by training hard over and over again (using the overload principle), and made to adapt to such repeated demands so that it is able to handle the same amount of training with less stress. The training is then increased until the body adapts again, and the spiral continues upwards. But how do you know that you are doing the right thing? Starting at the right point? Making the correct increments in training?

Athletes constantly monitor improvements in speed and recovery times, the number of repetitions the body can handle, and overall how much training the body can take. Such records do not always give a sufficiently accurate assessment – particularly to the coach – of precisely how the athlete is feeling, and the amount of physiological stress being endured at any specific point during training. A heart rate monitor allows an exact assessment of the stress put on the body by training and exercise.

Establishing Maximum Heart Rate

Maximum heart rate can be established using a variety of tests. Usually these are of the 'increasing demand' variety and last for 12–15 minutes.

To work out the maximum heart rate for cycling, the athlete starts in a gear at which 90/100 pedal revolutions per minute (RPM) can be maintained; every one to two minutes, a harder gear is selected while maintaining the same RPM (this is 'increased demand'). The process should be continued until exhaustion point is reached.

The procedure for testing running maximum heart rate is similar, particularly if a treadmill is available. A speed is selected at which the athlete feels comfortable and the pulse rate is steady, then the speed is increased every 2 to 4 minutes until exhaustion is reached.

It is interesting and important to note that, with an increased speed or load, the heart rate of some individuals will jump up and then drop off a few beats; others will gradually rise and then hold steady.

When athlete and coach have established the athlete's maximum heart rate – bearing in mind that it is worth going through the test procedure at least a couple of times, ten or fourteen days apart, to check the accuracy of the readings – the relative intensities of training and the appropriate percentage of maximum heart rate can be set as follows:

1. For long, slow distance (fat-burning) (recovery zone) 60–70 per cent of MHR;
2. For aerobic threshold 70 per cent of MHR;
3. For aerobic range 70–80/85 per cent of MHR;
4. For anaerobic threshold: 80/85 per cent of MHR;
5. For anaerobic – VO$_2$max: 80/85–100 per cent of MHR.

The appropriate percentages are worked out from the Karvonen formula, which uses both testing and maximum heart rates.

The Karvonen formula is the most accurate method of working out true heart-rate zones. The Karvonen method uses the range of heart rates between resting and maximum. For example, a female triathlete whose resting pulse is 45bpm and whose maximum is 195 has a heartbeat range of 150 (195 – 45). For her, 60 per cent would equal 60 per cent of the range plus the resting heart rate, or:

Resting heart rate (RHR) 45bpm (beats per minute)
Maximum heart rate (MHR) 195bpm
Heart rate zone 45–195bpm
Range 150bpm

Max (195) – Min (45) = 150
$\qquad$ 150 × (60 per cent effort) = 90
Add the resting pulse back on:
$\qquad$ 90 + 45 = 135bpm

Other percentages of effort are indicated below:

60 per cent = (0.6 × 150) + 45 = 135
70 per cent = (0.7 × 150) + 45 = 150
80 per cent = (0.8 × 150) + 45 = 165
85 per cent = (0.85 × 150) + 45 = 173
100 per cent = (1 × 150) + 45 = 195

This example shows the risks of relying simply on maximum heart rates. Assuming the same Max HR of 195bpm, the percentages without the input of RHR are as follows:

60 per cent of 195 = 117bpm (a difference of 18bpm)
70 per cent of 195 = 137bpm (a difference of 13bpm)
80 per cent of 195 = 156bpm (a difference of 9bpm)
85 per cent of 195 = 166bpm (a difference of 7bpm)
100 per cent of 195 = 195bpm (same).

For a truly accurate personal training intensity, use your RHR.

There is a further complication: individuals' percentages of Max HR will not always fit nicely into the percentages at the various threshold levels.

Spotting Early Warning Signs

Knowing your heart rates – resting, maximum and at various levels of effort – can be valuable in spotting excessive tiredness or identifying overtraining. (Note that triathletes who are always tired may need to look carefully at their lifestyle, including rest, diet and social activities.)

If the resting heart rate in the morning is 5 beats or so higher than normal, this is a warning sign; training should be restricted, with either an easy day or a rest day. A tired athlete will often have a considerably higher heart rate than normal at any particular work rate or, perhaps, difficulty in reaching the required heart rate due to too much hard training on previous days. The athlete should *not* try to push though this. Failure to heed early warning signs will lead to failing adaptation, disillusion with training and triathlon and, sometimes, even chronic fatigue syndrome. The sensible athlete and coach will make the difficult decision to back off.

LACTIC ACID

Analactic, alactic and *lactic acids* are usually grouped together under the single heading of *lactic acid*. Lactic acid is a waste product created during exercise. Blood lactate begins to rise when the muscles are working hard, and continues to rise as the intensity of training increases. Eventually, the level rises so much that it is intolerable. Clearly, the more the athlete's body can tolerate lactic acid, the faster the athlete can train without having to stop. Such an athlete saves a lot of 'wasted' training time.

Many triathletes now have access to testing facilities, but using them may not be absolutely necessary. Results from both cycling and running indicate that lactate levels tend to rise in line with rising heart rates, critically at around 80–85 per cent of the maximum heart rate. (However, this is not *always* true.)

The female triathlete in the example (*see* page 41) has a maximum heart rate of 195 and a minimum of 45. Her training minimum level of 80 per cent would be 165 beats per minute or, at 85 per cent, 173 beats per minute. This is the anaerobic threshold level.

CALCULATING MAXIMUM AND RESTING HEART RATES

Training causes physiological adaptations to higher levels of athletic performance. To improve performance, athletes must co-ordinate and focus on all of the factors involved: frequency and length of workouts, type of training, speed, intensity, duration and repetition. In the past, coaches would have all their athletes do the same workout at the same intensity level, ignoring the adaptation rates and genetic abilities of each individual athlete.

Today, it is recognized that training intensities need to be set for each individual's fitness level. One person's high level of intensity might be below the training threshold intensity for another, who is in better shape or who is genetically gifted.

Maximum Heart Rate (Max HR) vs Maximum VO$_2$ (Max VO$_2$)

- Maximum Heart Rate (Max HR): the heart rate at which increased intensity of exercise does not cause an increase in heart rate.
- Maximum VO$_2$ (Max VO$_2$): the maximum volume (V) of oxygen (O$_2$) that the body

can utilize, regardless of training intensity increases. It is synonymous with maximal oxygen consumption, maximal oxygen uptake, or maximal aerobic power.

These two measurements are accurately related to one another within plus or minus 8 per cent above the 50 per cent range. When training at a given percentage of Max HR, they are at a predictable percentage of their Max VO$_2$:

Relationship of Max HR to Max VO$_2$	
Percentage of Max HR	*Percentage of Max VO$_2$*
50	28
60	42
70	56
80	70
90	83
100	100

The Age-Adjusted Formula

It *is* possible to use the old formula – for men, 220 minus athlete's age, and for women 226 minus age – for calculating maximum heart rate, but this is not the most accurate assessment. There are many 40-year-olds with a Max HR of 180bpm, but you will always come across examples of those who have 160bpm, while others may be as high as 200bpm.

The formula should never be used with children.

Maximum Heart Rate Tests

Max HRs seem to be determined by genetic background, and do not change with training of any kind, but athletes will see an increase in their maximum heart rate as they learn just how much hurt they can tolerate! Age is the only factor that changes Max HR, by lowering it.

Max HR is dependent on the specific activity. Max HR in cycling will be slightly different from that in swimming or running, in both fit and unfit individuals.

The following tests are basically different versions of increasing demand tests. Max HR is usually the highest heart rate registered toward the end of the testing period.

Running

The 12-Minute Test Also known as the VO$_2$max test, this can be repeated as needed to determine improvement in conditioning. It was developed by Cooper in his original book *Aerobics*. After warming up, run at an even pace for at least 10 minutes and then at an all-out pace for the last 2 minutes. Measure the total distance covered during the 12 minutes. As fitness improves, you should be able to cover a longer distance in the same amount of time.

The One-Mile Test Run as fast as you can for one mile, or four laps around a 400m track. Keep track of the total elapsed time during the one-mile run, as you should be able to improve your time as you become more fit.

Hill Repeat Test Find a relatively steep hill that you can run up in about 90 seconds. After a warm-up, run four times up as hard as you can, after each ascent running or jogging down the hill to recover.

Graduated Test Take your best one-mile time. Start at a pace that is one minute per mile slower than your fastest predicted one-mile time. Then, gradually increase the pace, so that by the fourth lap you are at your top one-mile speed, and then give it all you've got for that last 200m.

800-Metre Format Run 400m, building to about the 95 per cent level, then, on the second 400m, simulate a real race situation by trying to run as fast as you can.

Swimming

(Be aware that the swimming test has shown several inaccuracies and variables in testing.)

Swim 50m fast, then rest for two minutes. Using the time from your first 50m, add ten seconds to get your starting pace. Now, swim six lengths, starting at this calculated pace. Each length, try to decrease the length time by five seconds until you can no longer increase your speed. Stop every 50m and look at your heart rate monitor. Your highest value during the test is equal to your Max HR.

Cycling

Flat Begin a 'ladder' of 30-second intervals. At each 30-second 'step', increase the speed of the bike by half a mile per hour (or 1 km/h). There should be about 4–8 steps in the ladder, so your beginning speed needs to be about 2mph slower than the rate of your fastest mid-distance, racing speed.

Hills Find a long uphill or a series of hills. After warming up, hit the bottom of the hill relatively fast. Work the hill extremely hard until you approach exhaustion.

Calculating Resting Heart Rate

Resting HR is best tested in the morning, immediately after waking up and before getting out of bed.

FIVE TARGET HEART RATE ZONES

There are five heart rate training zones. Training in one or all of these zones can play a part in your overall fitness or programme, depending on your individual goals. Think of training in the range within your target heart rate zone, say, from 135 to 145bpm.

The five different heart rate training zones of five different levels of exercise are as follows:

1. long slow distance (fat burning/recovery) zone: 60–70 per cent Max HR;
2. the aerobic zone: 70 per cent Max HR;
3. the aerobic range: 70–80/85 per cent of Max HR;
4. the anaerobic threshold zone: 80/85 per cent Max HR;
5. the maximum, anaerobic, VO$_2$max zone: 80/85–100 per cent Max HR.

Recovery Zone/Long Slow Distance

Training at this level will strengthen the heart. The long slow distance (LSD) is the training zone that works the heart hard enough for it to get stronger and ready for a steady, pain-free, moderate pace.

To work out your LSD zone, multiply your Max HR by 60 per cent for the low value and 70 per cent for the high value (*see* table below).

LSD Heart Rates: Max HR × .60 =   bpm;
                 Max HR × .70 =   bpm

Remember, using your RHR (Karvonen formula) will give a more accurate figure.

Aerobic Threshold and Aerobic Range

Training your respiratory system increases your endurance. When training within this range, you enhance your aerobic power (the ability to transport oxygen to and carbon dioxide away from the sport-specific muscles). At 70–80 per cent of your Max HR, your times and effort levels will both begin to drop after several weeks. Multiply your Max HR by 70 per cent for the low value and 80 per cent for the high value (*see* middle table below).

Aerobic heart rates:
                 Max HR 190 × .70 = 133bpm;
                 Max HR 190 × .80 = 152bpm

	Max HR										
Training intensity zone (per cent Max HR)	150	155	160	165	170	175	180	185	190	195	200
Long slow distance (60–70 per cent)	90–105	93–109	96–112	99–116	102–119	105–123	108–126	111–130	114–133	117–137	120–140

	Max HR										
Training intensity zone (per cent Max HR)	150	155	160	165	170	175	180	185	190	195	200
Healthy heart (70–80 per cent)	105–120	109–124	112–128	116–132	119–136	123–140	126–144	130–148	133–152	137–156	140–160

	Max HR										
Training intensity zone (per cent Max HR)	150	155	160	165	170	175	180	185	190	195	200
Anaerobic (80–90 per cent)	120–135	124–140	128–144	132–149	136–153	140–158	144–162	148–167	152–171	156–176	160–180

	Max HR										
Training intensity zone (per cent Max HR)	150	155	160	165	170	175	180	185	190	195	200
Maximum (90–100 per cent)	135–150	140–155	144–160	149–165	153–170	158–175	162–180	167–185	171–190	176–195	180–200

Again, using your RHR (Karvonen formula) will give a more accurate figure.

Exercising in the aerobic heart rate zone burns a higher percentage of carbohydrates than fats as fuel, and also strengthens both the heart and the lungs.

Anaerobic Threshold Zone

At some point within this zone, from 80 to 90 per cent of Max HR, you will be training at or near your anaerobic threshold. The primary benefit is to increase your body's ability to metabolize lactic acid, allowing you to train harder before crossing over into the pain of lactate accumulation and oxygen debt. For the anaerobic training zone, multiply Max HR by 80 per cent for the low value and 90 per cent for the high value (*see* bottom table left).

Anaerobic threshold heart rates:
Max HR $185 \times .80 = 148$bpm;
Max HR $185 \times .90 = 167$bpm

Anaerobic/VO$_2$max Zone

This is the highest-intensity training. You should only train at this level if you are extremely fit. You will be operating in oxygen debt, under the 'work now, pay later' principle; going as fast as possible for short periods, training the fast-twitch muscle fibres. For triathletes, particularly, this intensity of training may well be appropriate only for a limited time pre-season, and then in some aspects of the tapering phase (*see* table above).

Maximum heart rates:
Max HR $175 \times .90 = 158$bpm;
Max HR $175 \times 1.00 = 175$bpm

DIAGNOSING PROBLEMS USING A HEART RATE MONITOR

Illness/Overtraining

A heart rate monitor can be used to provide a warning that an athlete is training at intensities, frequencies, or durations that are too demanding. Overtraining is common with athletes who fail to take a systematic approach. One of the best indications of overtraining is your morning Resting HR. If this is 10 beats per minute higher than normal, there is cause for concern. A high Resting HR could indicate that you may be overtraining, suffering from fatigue, slightly injured, or fighting off a virus or a stress-related problem. There is a simple solution: rest.

A number of problems can arise during training or racing. These can sometimes be more easily diagnosed by using an HR monitor (*see* table overleaf).

RACING WITH A HEART RATE MONITOR

A heart rate monitor worn during racing can provide valuable information on fitness levels, signs of overtraining and whether race pacing has been good.

Knowing their anaerobic thresholds, athletes can use a monitor to pace themselves. In a short race of less than one hour (such as a 10-mile cycle time trial or a 10km running race) it is possible to maintain a heart rate 3–5 beats above the AT. For a longer race (marathon, standard-distance triathlon, 10km/40km/5km duathlon), the athlete is likely to be 3–5 beats below AT.

A good race graph should be roughly even throughout. If the graph tails off in the latter stages of the race, the athlete has started too fast or is insufficiently rested for the race. If the graph starts to go up in the latter stages, it may indicate dehydration or hyperthermia (overheating). Often, an athlete's cycling heart rate (and AT) will be 5–10 beats lower than the running heart rate; similarly, swimming rates will be lower than cycling rates. A smaller muscle mass is used when cycling, and swimming is done in a prone, water-supported position. With good swimming and cycle training, the rates can be brought closer together.

Heart Rate Monitored Diagnosis

Problem	Possible causes	Solutions
Heart rate high on an easy ride or run	Tired, overtrained	Rest
	Not recovered from previous day's workout	Go easy or rest
	Cold, flu, viral infection	Stop training until recovered
	(If very early in the season)	Lack of fitness
Inability to reach normal AT heart rates when doing intervals	Overtrained, tired	Abandon intervals and have a recovery session, or rest
Heart rate starts normally on long run/ride but elevates in latter stage	Dehydration	Take more fluids
Heart rate drops in latter stages of long race/long training session; athlete feels terrible	'The Bonk' – not enough energy eaten/drunk or not enough long slow distance training to enhance fat metabolism	
Heart rate elevates by more than 5–10 beats when going from a lying to a standing position	Overtrained, tired	Reduce training volume; no intervals, no intensity
Heart rate responds sluggishly; when climbing a hill, heart rate is slow to elevate and, when the hill is crested, slow to come down again or, after an easy run, heart rate is very slow to come down again	Overtrained, tired	Reduce volume; no intervals until problem disappears

CHAPTER 8
Cross-Training and Back-to-Back Training

'If you can steel your heart and nerves and sinews to serve their time long after they are gone,
  And still hold on when there is nothing in you, except the will that says to you, "hold on!" ...'

WHAT IS CROSS-TRAINING?

When one muscle group is exercised, a corresponding muscle group will also show increased strength, even if it is kept stationary, so long as the motor nerves to the inactive part are uninjured.

As long as fifty years ago, physiologists were discovering that training one muscle group results in significant improvements in the (symmetrical) partner group on the other side of the body, even if that group is unexercised. For example, a footballer with a broken leg in a plaster cast could maintain some strength in the injured leg, if the uninjured leg continued to be exercised. The term used was *cross education*, and it was applied to both skill training and strength improvement. Importantly, the training in the active limb needed to be done at an intense level, in order to provide the equivalent effect of an easy training session on the unexercised limb.

It is still unclear why this occurs. The theory is that the nerves that cross over from the muscles in the active limb to the inactive muscle on the other side of the body are stimulated sufficiently during overload (high-intensity) training to create an effect.

The body's system is interdependent – a complex, interconnected mechanism rather than a series of independent parts. In a sport such as basketball, in which players are expected to be able to shoot with either hand, training regimes will concentrate largely on one side, and the carry-over to the other is anticipated.

BENEFITS OF CROSS-TRAINING

In current sporting terms, the theory of cross education is summarized as the benefits and improvements to one sport that carry over from training in another. The benefits from training in more than one discipline include the following:

1. building and maintaining a good, strong aerobic capacity;
2. increased flexibility from training and using muscles that are not used in the dominant sport;
3. avoiding injury from the 'overuse' syndrome (most distance runners, for example, have to take time away from training because of sore muscles or locked knees);
4. avoiding boredom; and
5. maintaining strong antagonistic muscles.

All the above points are inter-related.

Aerobic Effect

The respiratory system will be the first to benefit from the crossover effects in an endurance activity such as triathlon, duathlon, distance running, cross-country skiing or cycling. There will also be a carry-over in the circulatory system and, to a limited extent, in the area of muscle use.

Any aerobic training – swimming, cycling, running, or whatever – will increase the amount of oxygen getting from the lungs to the muscles in action via the bloodstream.

However, only the muscles being exercised at any particular time will be affected. Muscular transfer between disciplines is very restricted, and only muscles that are used in more than one activity will receive any benefit.

There *is* some transfer of muscle use. For example, hill running and cycling on the flat, and hill cycle climbing and flat running use some of the same muscles, so there will be a crossover effect. Similarly, many cyclists use a static rowing machine in the off season, because this will exercise many of the same muscles.

Working out aerobically carries over the type of training effect between the same type of muscle fibres. Distance training works the slow-twitch fibres and the efficiency of these will improve whatever the aerobic training method used.

Mobility and Flexibility

Distance runners and professional cyclists have been notorious in the past for their lack of mobility and flexibility. Even international swimmers with tremendous upper-body suppleness may lack leg mobility.

The cross-training athlete would expect to get the benefits of extra flexibility by exercising muscle groups that a single-sport exponent would not use, particularly if attention is paid to stretching and warming up. However, it is not always easy to become flexible, especially when coming from a single-sport background of cycling or running, where patterns of movement may have been firmly established.

Other factors may also affect the amount of mobility in an individual. These include genetic make-up, muscular development, amount of muscle-fibre elasticity, previous sporting background (which may add or detract from flexibility), age and, of course, how hard the athlete works at it.

A word of caution: if gaining flexibility becomes so important that you are in stress or pain trying to achieve it, it is highly likely that you will be working against yourself and will break down with muscle aches or even injury. As with any training, a gradual increase in the workload is best.

Injury

High-quality athletes in most sports tread a fine line between super-fitness and breaking down when they start to increase their training, either in time or in intensity. In running, for example, the stress put on joints and muscles by the downward force of every foot plant makes fitness/injury a delicate balance.

Cross-training – in which one discipline does not dominate – can benefit this balance. Increased aerobic capacity results from any of triathlon's three component activities, and each set of muscles does not have to be overused. Great care must still be taken when adding speed training to the schedule without adequate preparation.

If the cross-training athlete does become injured and unable to take part or train in any particular activity, aerobic fitness can still be maintained by working out in a different endurance sport. This is already established practice in many sports. When runners are injured, they take a leaf out of the triathlete's book and go for a swim or a cycle ride. Injured runners in the US have made use of swimming pools and the cushioning effects of water for more than thirty years. Some wear buoyancy vests and go through the motions of running in the water, without their feet ever having to touch any hard surface.

Boredom

You certainly won't get bored with cross-training. Professional cyclists can spend the greater part of every day in the saddle; thousands upon thousands of serious distance runners cover more than a hundred miles a week; competitive swimmers can be in the pool twice a day covering 5–10,000m each time. The cross-trainer has the best of all worlds. A different environment, different training companions, or a solitary workout if that is what is needed, can all be accommodated in a comprehensive training schedule. If one discipline becomes intolerable, for whatever reason, there is always an alternative. A missed day's training in one activity can always be caught up, as long as other training continues.

Fig 12. Switzerland's Olympic bronze medallist Magalli Messmer speeds through transition.

Antagonistic Muscles

Movements in the body are governed by the *agonist* muscles, which initiate the movement by shortening. The *antagonist* muscles are those that lengthen and oppose the movement. One of the main reasons why injuries occur in single sports is because the antagonist muscles are not strong enough to work efficiently against the agonists. In cross-training, the opposing muscles are more likely to be strong, having been worked in a different discipline.

SPORTS SPECIFICITY

Cross-training is not the panacea to all sports improvement. Performers in a single sport need to spend as much time as possible concentrating on their speciality. *Sports specificity* means training specifically for the individual sport, in order to develop and improve that sport. Improvements come about with added cross-training because the cross-training is just that – extra – and not a substitute.

The extra hours of training result in improved general fitness, which helps the athlete's specific fitness; those extra hours might not be possible in a single discipline without risking injury. However, there is only a limited amount of time in the day, and it must be remembered that training for a different sport will prevent athletes from developing the skills and strengths that are required for their own sport.

BACK-TO-BACK TRAINING

Some athletes have unlimited time at their disposal and can add to their training by taking part in other activities. Sometimes, this means going directly on to working out in a different sport after training in the major one.

For example, running is an immensely taxing activity. Before the body breaks down, the athlete can improve endurance by continuing to work out aerobically on a static cycling machine. This continuous training in one sport followed by another is known as *back-to-back training*. In the above example, the stiffness that can follow a long training run will be dispersed to a considerable extent. The waste by-products of exercise that are accumulated in the legs by running will be washed away by the less traumatic action of cycling.

Even if the immediate effects of back-to-back training are not felt, it is an extremely taxing and fatiguing method of training. Particularly in the early stages of experimentation, athletes should be prepared to feel very fatigued, if not immediately, then at some time later in the day. Rest can make all the difference.

One of the fascinations of triathlon, both for the competitor and the spectator, is seeing how each participant copes with the demands of the three different disciplines. When an athlete is experienced and has raced many times, it becomes less important to train back-to-back, as the frequency of racing causes the body to adapt. However, in the early days, when the transitions are quite literally a shock to the system, it makes good sense both mentally and physically to follow training in one discipline directly by training in another. The intensity of these back-to-back sessions should be monitored carefully in order to avoid injury and mental staleness.

The normal order of a triathlon is swim, cycle, run. Some back-to-back training sessions will need to be done in this order – swim/bike or bike/run – to acclimatize the body to the race's demands. However, this is not always essential and many productive general fitness sessions can be undertaken by run/bike, swim/run or, indeed, any combination of two or three activities.

In many cases it makes good sense in terms of time management – and time is always at a premium for triathletes – for certain sessions to follow directly on from each other. If you live within running distance of your local pool, try jogging there carrying your swimming costume and towel in a backpack. It may feel uncomfortable to pull on damp running clothes for the return journey, but you will save a lot of time and will have exercised aerobically for a much longer time than if you had split the training sessions up. If the pool is too far for running, jump on your bike; the same extra aerobic effect is gained and cycling home will also give you some idea of what to expect during a race.

After a certain point, there will be limited triathlon (as opposed to general fitness) benefit in such combined sessions. Then, you need to have a look at the specific back-to-back sessions and their individual effects.

Swim/Cycle

This session prepares you for the effects of blood pooling in the arms and for the sensations you might experience during a race as you exit the swim/cycle transition area. As most of the muscular output of swimming is in the arms and upper body, this is where the blood is directed during exercise. When the triathlete gets on to the cycle section, the blood has to be rapidly redirected to the legs.

Swim/Run

This session will give similar benefits to that of the swim/cycle. The arm blood pooling will have to be redirected to the legs.

Cycle/Run

This transition from cycling to running is considered to be the hardest. The legs are already fatigued from being worked hard during the cycle stage, and then they are immediately called upon to work even harder for the run section. The blood is already centred in the legs, but mainly in the quadriceps, on the front of the thighs.

Racing out of transition and into the run results in a truly remarkable sensation for the first-timer. Nothing adequately prepares you for the feeling of having 'lost control of your legs'. Blood is urgently required in running's prime movers, the hamstrings, and the first few minutes while the blood transfers are not pleasant. It does get better and easier with experience, and practice does help to ease the discomfort.

The ability to run well during a triathlon race is not always directly related to how well the individual can run in a single event. The triathlete's performance depends far more on an ability to cope with the accumulated fatigue and on management of the ensuing discomfort and pain.

Run/Swim

Blood pooling transfer will be experienced in a run/swim session, as it is redirected from the legs to the upper body. If you run to the pool in order to save valuable training time, you will probably need a longer warm-up than usual before your arms will behave as if they belong to you.

Cycle/Swim

This can be a similar situation to the run/swim workout, although the effects are not normally as marked. There is more than one time trial-type triathlon, where the athlete first cycles to the pool.

Run/Cycle

This session can be particularly effective, for three reasons. The risk of injury to a long-distance runner attempting a big mileage can be lessened by shortening the run and transferring immediately to the bike. When the run needs to be for longer than two hours, when preparing for a marathon, for example, the chances of an overuse injury are dramatically increased.

Many athletes have experimented with dropping the run time to 90 minutes and then getting straight on to a wind-trainer mounted cycle for three-quarters of an hour. This has the added benefit of increasing total training time. The aerobic effect of training will be maintained by the immediate transfer to the bike. As with run/swim and cycle/swim, this session can now be specific.

BRICK SESSIONS

Brick sessions represent a very demanding method of training, and are one of the few training methods that are special to triathlon and duathlon. As with the single disciplines of swimming, cycling and running there are distinct phases of the year when particular emphasis is put on endurance, strength, speed endurance and speed.

Brick sessions *must* be tailored to the individual. For some athletes, they are an excellent way of training; for others, there may be little benefit. The Dutch and the French have long used brick, or back-to-back type sessions.

Dutch Method

In the Netherlands, long-distance triathlon attracts much more attention than standard-distance. The following is a classic session used by Dutch distance triathletes as a staple in training:

Long-distance cycle (up to 5 hours); rest for 30 to 60 minutes; long-distance run (up to 2 hours). Obviously distances can be adapted here as appropriate.

During the rest between the cycle and the run, no stretching is done.

The theory is that this method simulates the fatigue felt during a race, when the athlete will be tired and have 'sore' legs going into the run. This distance training is also used by standard-distance triathletes in the endurance phase of training. All athletes will use the early-season standard-distance or sprint-distance races as their 'speed' work, without tapering or specifically preparing for them.

French Method

Some French triathletes have experimented with doing a great majority of their training as brick work. This follows the standard year pattern of endurance, leading into endurance and strength, leading into specific preparation before the competition period.

Each training session breaks down the total distance into manageable amounts of each cycling/running discipline. For example, immediately pre-season, when the total distances covered might be racing distances, the session might be made up as follows:

Cycle 20km, then run 5km, then cycle 12km, then run 3km, then cycle 8km, then run 2km. (Total distance covered during training session: 40km of cycling and 10km of running.)

For many, both of the above examples might be seen as too restrictive. Most triathletes will choose to carry out their training as a mixture of single-discipline sessions and brick sessions.

Yearly Programme of Brick Training

There is usually little place for brick training in the rest and recovery phase of the year as it is generally too demanding.

Phase 1: The Start of Endurance (General Preparation) Training

At this stage, the athlete is beginning to build up the quantity of training, without putting too much stress on to the body. There is probably little call for brick sessions here.

Phase 2: Endurance and Strength

After the first six weeks of preparation, brick sessions can be introduced. As these are for endurance and strength, they will be distance-orientated, with little pressure in terms of speed or effort. The main aim is to condition the body to be able to run after cycling, or to cycle after swimming. A typical session might be as follows:

Cycle for 90 minutes, followed immediately by a run for 45 minutes, *or*, cycle for 60 minutes, followed immediately by a run for 45 minutes, followed immediately by a cycle for 45 minutes, *or* (for experienced athletes), a 3-hour cycle ride followed by a 6–8 mile run, gradually increasing pace.

The emphasis in this phase is on endurance and strength.

Phase 3: Endurance, Strength and Preparation for the Specific Phase

The primary aim is still to build strength and endurance, but there is now also a need to look at preparation for the next phase and one element of each brick session (occasionally more) will become a little bit more specific. Sessions might be as follows:

Run 30 mins; cycle (turbo) 50/60 mins; run 30 mins.
The first run is steady; the second run includes 5 × 3 minutes (1 min rec) at 10km pace only or up to 5km pace if feeling strong. Cycle is at a steady HR of Max HR less 40bpm.
or
1-hour ride plus 1-hour run.
(If turbo, HR at 35 beats below max; if on road, 1-hour hard ride or TT. Run to have

4 × 1 mile or 5 minutes (2 mins jog rec), done at 3km/5km race pace so HR is almost at anaerobic threshold.)

These sessions provide endurance and start to focus on running speed specific.

Specific Pre-Season Phase

1-hour ride plus 1-hour run.
(If turbo, start at 23mph and increase by 0.5mph every 7 or 8 minutes; if on the road, try to do the same, or 1-hour hard ride or TT. Run to have 30 × 30 secs done at 1500m/3km pace with 30 secs recovery, so HR almost at anaerobic threshold.)

Such training aims to begin to simulate the conditions and pain felt during a race, but still maintains an endurance element (the 1-hour run). After this phase, you start to focus much more specifically on speed. Two very similar sessions have proved to be efficient in building speed and strength:

1. Fast brick. 5km cycle/1km run × 5 sets. 5km on turbo at 42–43kph (26–27mph), going hard on all runs. No recovery between run and next cycle.
2. As above, fast brick. 5km/1km × 5 sets. 5km on turbo at 42–43kph or faster. 3–4 minutes recovery between each set.

(Each of the five runs are slightly faster – for example, 3.40 for the first, 3.30 for the second, 3.15 for the third, and so on.)

It is important to emphasize that brick training can be physically and mentally very demanding. Be cautious and take advice from your coach and from more experienced athletes when embarking upon this type of training.

Part II

The Practicals

Fig 13. A group squad training session in Lanzarote.

CHAPTER 9
Swimming

*'The three most important things in swimming are:
technique, technique, and technique.'*

THE IMPORTANCE OF TECHNIQUE

Of the three disciplines in triathlon, swimming is by far the most technical. It is sometimes difficult for newcomers from running or cycling to understand that improvements in swimming do not result from more hours of physical work in the pool. Runners and cyclists are used to making great physical efforts to improve, but this does not necessarily apply in the pool.

The essence of being a good swimmer – particularly in triathlon, where the distance is 1500m – is a good stroke. It is vital to work on technique and stroke drills designed to ensure that your swimming is efficient. Far from bringing times down, a technically poor swimmer may even swim *more slowly* in a race after continuing to train extremely hard. A poor stroke ensures that swimmers are working *against* themselves, by grooving in an inefficient stroke. Every good swimmer allocates some time in a training schedule to refine and redefine good technique. This is even more important for a triathlete, who has a great deal more improvement to make.

Some say that swimming in open water bears very little resemblance to swimming in a pool, but this is untrue. There are many differences, but there are also many great swimmers turned triathletes, such as Robin Brew, Benjamin Sanson, Rick Wells and Loretta Harrop. They are evidence that good pool swimmers do make good triathlon swimmers, with the appropriate adjustments in training, and an understanding of the conditions to be found in open water. Some pool swimmers, of course, do not make a good crossover.

FRONT CRAWL TECHNIQUES

Front crawl is the fastest of the swimming strokes. In the early days of triathlon, a variety of strokes were seen. Times have changed, however, and no good competitor would now do anything other than front crawl. With this stroke, the force is directed backwards and there is continuous propulsion (with the minimum of retardation). Being better streamlined than any other, the stroke is efficient particularly for long-distance, when it can be physically advantageous to be prone and working anteriorly.

Body Position

The body should be in a flat, horizontal position, stretched and streamlined just below the surface. The pull should be kept within the body width and the kick within the body depth. The kick must be deep enough to work effectively, but the wetsuit gives so much buoyancy that anything other than a very light kick with the purpose of balancing the stroke will result in wasted energy. The face should be in the water, hips close to the surface, back straight and legs kept in the water.

The head position and the leg action are the key to the body position. The head should be in line with the body in a natural position, not lifted or buried, with the eyes looking down (at about 45 degrees) and with the water breaking somewhere between the hairline and the middle of the head. The head is kept steady and central, except when breathing. Buoyant swimmers will ride higher in the water (the wetsuits make every triathlete more buoyant than they would otherwise be), but all swimmers should assume a natural position and avoid attempting to ride higher by lifting the head or arching the back.

The answer to faster swimming is both to streamline and apply propulsive forces more effectively. Variations in poise (and therefore of streamlining) may be caused by the following:

- lateral deviation, caused by the lifting and lowering of the head to breathe, pulling outside the body line and/or a wide arm recovery;
- vertical deviation, caused by the lifting and lowering of the head to breathe, pushing down at the beginning of the pull and pulling up at the end of the pull;
- rolling, caused either by stiff shoulders (the need to roll to recover the arms) or by attempting to make the pull more efficient by bringing in the large muscle groups of the body – the pectorals, deltoids and latissimus dorsi. (Note: as long as the body is moving in a straight line, rolling can be an advantage.)

Body Roll

Proper body roll can make your front crawl much more streamlined and efficient. Most top swimmers and top triathletes allow their shoulders, hips and legs to roll from side to side as one arm begins its pull and the other recovers. This rolling motion not only makes the stroke look almost effortless, it actually does make it easier to perform. (Note that breathing bilaterally may be disadvantageous to body roll since it can make the swimmer swim flat in the water with insufficient body roll in either direction.)

How to Do It

As the right arm enters the water, the swimmer rolls on to the right shoulder. When the right arm extends, the swimmer should 'ride' on that arm to give the palm and forearm a good 'feel' for the water. At the same time, the swimmer lifts the left shoulder higher out of the water as the left arm finishes its stroke and begins to recover.

The left shoulder continues to go higher as the left arm reaches its highest point in the recovery. At the same time, the right arm is coming under the body and the right shoulder is at its deepest point. At this point of maximum rotation the line between the two shoulders will be almost directly perpendicular to the surface of the pool, straight up and down. As the stroke continues, the shoulders will reverse positions. The right shoulder will come up as the right arm finishes the underwater stroke and the left shoulder will come down as the left arm enters the water and starts to pull.

Shoulder roll has the following advantages:

- It allows your pulling arm and hand to go deeper and get a better 'grip' on the water.
- It allows you to have a longer underwater pull by making your reach in front and finish at the back longer.
- It makes your recovery easier because your recovering shoulder is up (this is especially helpful for those who do not have very flexible shoulders).
- It cuts in half the resistance of your upper body in the water.

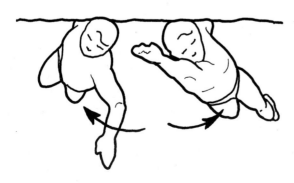

Fig 14. Body roll in front crawl can be as much as almost 90°.

Fig 15. British International Richard Stannard transfers his excellent technique from the pool to open water.

Body Roll Drills

A number of drills can be used to assist and accentuate body roll:

1. Breathing to a wall: during a session, pick one side of the pool to breathe to all the time. Emphasize the lift of the shoulder on the breathing side to help the roll. This can be good for dominant-sided breathers.
2. Turning the chin towards the non-breathing side when the breathing arm is extended helps lift the non-breathing shoulder higher.
3. Catch-up – where one arm is extended in front as the other pulls through – is good for working on body roll to the non-breathing side, as is single arm but be sure to roll completely in both directions.
4. Kicking on the side with the lower arm extended and the other by the side simulates the body movement. Progress by changing from side to side, using a front-crawl stroke, every twelve, ten, eight, six and four kicks.

This is a particularly demanding drill for those triathletes who do not have swimming as their background discipline, but it is worth persevering with it. The improvements gained will give you the confidence to deal with what feels like an uncomfortable position and environment in a demanding open-water swim.

Leg Action

Triathletes have to wear a wetsuit for many open-water swims, and the leg kick is less important in these conditions, but it should still be worked on during training. It is vital to develop an efficient leg kick right from the start. Neglecting the legs will lead to decreased efficiency, and there will be occasions when the triathlete has to swim in open water without a wetsuit.

The legs help to achieve and stabilize a horizontal body position, and balance the arm action. Indeed, the leg kick is primarily concerned with balancing. The legs move close together in an alternating vertical movement. The whole of the leg is used, with the knees alternately bending and straightening with the feet extended and the toes pointed (plantar flexed). The ankles need to be loose and flexible throughout.

Downbeat

The kick is initiated at the hip and the thigh is swept downward as the foot passes the hips during the previous upbeat. The knee and ankle joints are relaxed, allowing the pressure of the water beneath the leg to flex the knee and push the toes upwards and inwards. As the downbeat nears completion the legs are snapped straight and the feet outwards. The whip-like action brings the largest area of the feet in contact with the water pressure in a backwards and downwards direction.

Fig 16. Even wearing a wetsuit, good technique is of paramount importance.

Upbeat

The leg should rebound upwards as the previous downbeat is completed. It will be relaxed at the knee and ankle so that the water pressure above the leg maintains it in an extended position as it travels upwards. During this time the soles of the feet and backs of the legs press upwards and backwards against the water. Only the heels break the surface and the feet should not come out of the water.

The kick will be about 30–45cm (12–18in) deep – not so deep as to cause resistance, but deep enough to be functional, and maintained within the body depth. Intoeing is a natural reaction and both the size and flexibility of the feet will be important considerations. The flexibility of the ankles will determine the amount of propulsion gained by the legs whatever variation of kicking pattern is being used; inflexible ankles will cause drag.

The knee is kept straight on the upbeat and is bent on the downbeat. On the downbeat the pressure of the water forces the ankles to hyperextend. The more flexible the ankles, the more effective the kick.

Timing

There are three rhythms predominant today:

1. The six-beat kick: the normal kick for sprinters, although more and more variations have been introduced as the arms have become more dominant. Nearly all other kick patterns are a variation on this rhythm. Three leg kicks accompany each armstroke, in the following sequence: during the downsweep of the armstroke, the leg on the same side kicks down (right arm, left leg); the leg on the same side kicks down during the upsweep (right arm, right leg). The sequence is repeated on the other side, creating six beats per stroke cycle.
2. The two-beat kick: exists in cross-over and straight forms. Cross-over kicking is often caused by a wide arm recovery and it is a mistake to force some swimmers to kick with a straight vertical movement. One leg kick accompanies each armstroke, with the downbeat of each leg occurring as the arm on the same side is completing the insweep and starting the upsweep. Very buoyant swimmers with high elbow recovery sometimes use the two-beat without a cross-over. Either way, the action is almost solely a balancing one and often looks like a drift of the legs. It is a technique that is particularly advantageous to middle- or long-distance swimmers and triathletes.
3. The four-beat kick: a combination of the previous two rhythms. The swimmer kicks three times during one armstroke and only once during the other.

Most triathletes prefer the two-beat kick, or a variation of it. For many – swimmers and others – it is not a technique that comes naturally. However, it is economical and energy-saving and is worth practising during early-season outdoor swims when getting used to a wetsuit again after a winter spent in the pool.

Often, swimmers have different strokes for different races. In distance swimming, the leg kick can be reduced, since the swimmer is not pulling so powerfully and does not need to balance so hard. In addition, the large muscles of the leg require considerable amounts of oxygen so their workload needs to be reduced as much as possible.

Kicking Drills

1. On float.
2. On float, with head held high for resistance (conditioning).
3. On board, arms outstretched with face in water, breathing every six kicks. (Improves streamlining and VO_2 capacity.) Add additional boards for resistance.
4. Arms extended, hands overlapped, face down between arms, breathe to the front on sixth kick. Repeat, but with head up to improve power of kick.
5. Arms at side, face in water, breathe to alternate sides every sixth kick. Repeat, but with head up.
6. Arms extended – underwater – feeling use of leg in kick. Repeat, but with arms at side.
7. Pearl-diver: breaststroke arms, front-crawl kick.
8. Extended doggy paddle.
9. Kicking on the side, one arm spearing out in front, other arm lying along the side. Change to other side using a full stroke every twelve, ten, eight, six and four kicks. Repeat, ensuring head remains in middle.
10. Kicking with flippers (develops flexibility).
11. Kicking on front, head up and hands back.
12. Vertical kick in deep water with hands both up and down.
13. Kicking silent front crawl.
14. Kicking exaggerated front crawl.
15. Kicking with board held at right-angles to the water.

Emphasize the following techniques:

- kick continuously;
- kick with legs long and with flexible knees and ankles;
- kick within the body depth; and
- kick from the hips.

Arm Action

The main propulsive force is derived from the arms and the action is an alternating one with continuous movement. Imagine climbing a rope, with one arm pulling while the other recovers.

Entry, Catch and Underwater Stroke

Entry is in advance of the head, between the outside line of the body (the shoulder) and

Fig 17. If anyone was in doubt that top-class swimmers have excellent body roll, Craig Watson proves otherwise.

the mid-line, ensuring that the hand does not cross over the mid-point. The arm is slightly flexed, with a downward slant from elbow to fingertips. Just prior to entry the hand and wrist are elevated to facilitate a fingertip entry, with the hand 'slicing' into the water. The hand goes down into the entry hole, quickly followed by the forearm.

Catch is where the purchase on the water takes place; a quick catch is important. The hand reaches forwards in a straight line about 5cm (a few inches) under the surface while the other arm completes its underwater phase. Care should be taken to prevent the elbow dropping below the hand as it reaches forward. The 'dropped elbow' is one of the main reasons for an inefficient stroke.

As a generalization, sprinters usually enter directly to catch while distance swimmers and triathletes lengthen out their stroke. At this point, think about starting to rotate the upper arm to achieve a high elbow position. This elbow bend is a vital leverage factor, which increases power. Elevation of the shoulder should be avoided since this places the arm in a weak position; use the shoulder and chest muscles as much as possible.

The underwater armstroke consists of three distinct sweeping motions:

1. Downsweep: as the opposite arm releases the water the hand is cupped and swept down and out, with the palm pitched slightly outwards (Fig 18).
2. Insweep: as the downsweep nears completion, the insweep begins. The elbow is gradually flexed and the hand is swept backwards, inwards and upwards, until the elbow is flexed, between 80 and 90 degrees, under the shoulders and near the mid-line of the body. The palm of the hand is gradually rotated in and up during the insweep (Fig 19).
3. Upsweep: as the upsweep nears completion, the pitch of the palm is changed to backwards and outwards and the hand is pushed backwards, outwards and upwards towards the thigh. Ensure that the palm is kept flat, with fingertips pointing at the bottom, until the hand reaches the front of the thigh. During this phase the triceps are in operation and the length of the phase varies a

great deal between different swimmers; those who stroke faster tend to lift out early. Generally, triathletes should try to keep their stroke long and keep their hand in the water as long as possible without going so far that efficiency is lost (Fig 20).

During the start of the underwater stroke the arm rotator muscles are used with the arm depressors to achieve the high elbow, which is essential if the stroke is to be efficient. The wrist must be held firm and flexed throughout. Overall, the pattern of the stroke is much like a shallow, inverted 'S'.

Release and Recovery

On the *release*, as the hand passes the thigh, the pressure is released and the palm collapsed inwards. The momentum of the upsweep is allowed to carry the hand upwards and outwards over the water with minimal resistance. Exit is with little finger first.

On *recovery*, the elbow should remain flexed slightly as the upsweep is completed and should then lead the hand out of the water (Fig 21). The hand should exit where it went in, giving the feeling of pulling the body over the 'entry hole'. Ideally, the elbow leads the recovery, utilizing the momentum of the upsweep, but in a relaxed state and with the least amount of interference with the stroke. The muscles used are the deltoids, supra-spinatus and trapezius, while the chest adductor muscles relax during this recovery phase. The minimum of energy should be expended in recovery.

One feature of a good front crawl is a high elbow position, which encourages good balance in the recovery and good rotation along the axis of the body, aiding streamlining. Tightness in the shoulder will obviously affect the stroke and there are three main types of recovery:

1. high elbow, wrist pick-up, placing forward of the hand;
2. high elbow, swinging round of the lower arm; or
3. straight swinging action of the whole arm.

A wetsuit with full arms may lead to slightly restricted mobility on the recovery phase.

Fig 18. After the entry and catch, the hand is cupped and pitched outwards on the downsweep.

Fig 19. With the elbow held high, the hand sweeps back, in, and up.

Fig 20. The pitch of the hand continues to change to pushing back, then out, and finally up.

Fig 21. A high elbow and relaxed movement are essential on recovery phase.

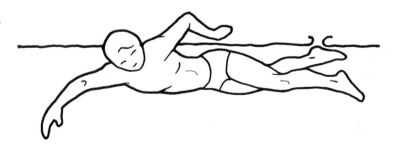

However, the increasing use of more flexible materials in their manufacture means that they are less restricting than before.

In terms of *timing*, one arm should enter the water as the other is completing its insweep (Fig 22). After the hand enters the water it begins an outward and downward sweep. During this, there is a slight increase in propulsive hand force. This increases as the hand continues a downward and outward press. At the lowest point of the downsweep the hand and arm begin to move inwards and upwards (insweep). This results in a further increase in hand force and a large increase in forward velocity. The

(a)

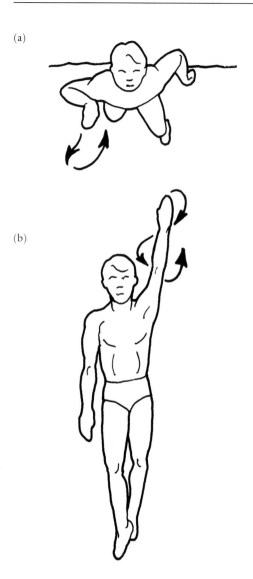

(b)

Fig 22. The timing of the arm stroke is not, as many people think, a mirror image of each other, but rather one entering the water as the other finishes its insweep.

final phase of the stroke involves an outward and upward movement of the hand (upsweep). The largest propulsive forces occur during this phase of the stroke, when a swimmer's forward body velocity reaches its peak. As the hand releases or exits the water the opposite hand has begun the downsweep portion of the stroke.

Armstroke and Co-Ordination Drills

Drill numbers one to seven are basic drills, recommended for novice swimmers and triathletes. All drills are based in appropriate groups.

1. Hand, wrist, elbow drill. Stand in waist-deep water and stroke, arms entering with hand first, then wrist, then elbow.
2. Hand, wrist, elbow drill, in front of mirror.
3. Hand, wrist, elbow drill, walking with head up.
4. Hand, wrist, elbow drill, swimming.
5. Bobbing – breathing drill.
6. Side-breathing drill, shallow end. Roll the shoulders.
7. As for 6, but walking.
8. As for 7, but swimming.
9. Stretched body swims, streamlined, and no breathing.
10. One-arm swims with one arm extended, no breathing.
11. As for 10, with breathing.
12. Stretch-up or catch-up front crawl.
13. Heads-up crawl, water polo.
14. The scooter drill on the board – single-arm swimming.
15. Bilateral breathing drills.
16. Rolling doggy paddle.
17. Single-arm swimming with free arm at side. Breathe to non-stroking side.
18. Front crawl with one leg bent and out of the water.
19. As for 18, but with head up.
20. Swim the rope drill.
21. 'Chicken wing': swimmers put thumbs in armpits, and kick front crawl, breathing every three and stroking with their 'chicken wings'. (Do not spend too much time on this; it simply serves to emphasize the importance of the high elbow action and to show how the rotation on the shoulders aids recovery.)
22. A few strokes on 'chicken wing', then start to push the forearm and hands forward to entry position (high elbow and hand drag).
23. Begin as 22 but push water forward with back of hands, recovering with high elbows and dragging hands through the water.

24. As for 23 but touch fingernails on the surface from leaving water to entering (aids relaxed, low recovery of arms).
25. Swim 100: 25 chicken wings, 25 with hands pausing at armpits before entry, 25 with hands pushing forward and 25 clearing fingernails. This helps swimmers to develop a compact crawl with high elbow recovery, hands low and close to the body width.
26. Using fists, emphasizing pulling with arms.
27. Fists on downsweep and insweep, hands open on upsweep.
28. Reverse 27.

Things Fist Swimming Helps

- develop the execution of the power phase in a straight line;
- correct any glideaway of hands after entry;
- ensure the stroke is not performed too far from the body;
- stop the hand trailing the elbow;
- prevent an arm recovery that may be too wide and flat.

---

29. Kicking, single-arm swimming, with the arm pulling from in line with the shoulder down the centre-line. Push back and out by the swimming costume with the elbows leading the hand until in line with the extended position. Concentrate on the complete arm movement.
30. As for 29 but swimming close to the wall for high recovery.
31. Catch-up with a definite pause.
32. Catch-up on to a board or pencil.
33. Full stroke with thumbs touching armpit on recovery.
34. Arms only, legs apart and drifting.
35. Arms only with pull-buoys and bands around ankles.
36. Arms only with band or tube.
37. Swim using paddles, pull-buoys and bands.
38. Swim using paddles and pull-buoys.
39. Swim using paddles, legs trailing.
40. Single-arm with paddles.
41. Catch-up with paddles.
42. Kicking on side, changing to other side with full stroke.
43. Swim touching thumb to thighs before release.
44. Swim brushing ears with shoulders.
45. Keeping head still, swim exaggerating roll of body.
46. Swim one arm extended out of the water, while opposite arm strokes continuously.
47. Stroke counting.

Stroke Counting

Stroke counting is a useful exercise for improving the armstroke. Many swimmers, especially young ones, tend to pull hard and then recover the arms too early. The upsweep is essential for efficient technique. Count the number of strokes needed to do 25 or 50m, checking the time taken. If you swim, for example, 10×50 on strokes, and average 37 seconds, try to reduce strokes while maintaining or improving the time. Stroke counting is an important indicator of tiredness.

For more on the importance of counting, amount and speed of stroke, *see* Chapter 15.

Emphasize the following armstroke techniques:

- Elbows up on the recovery and stroke.
- Initiate recovery in the shoulder and elbow.
- Hand under and just outside the elbow on recovery.
- Hand, wrist, elbow enter water in that order.
- Arm falls downwards as it passes the shoulder in recovery.
- Sweep out, sweep in, bend arm to accelerate, sweep back and out.
- Turn the chin to follow the shoulder roll to breathe.
- Inhale through the mouth, exhale through the mouth or mouth and nose.
- Look at the water surface just in front of the mouth when breathing.
- Begin to turn the head to breathe when the stroking arm on the non-breathing side enters the water.

Breathing

Breathing in swimming has to be taught, because it must come at a time when it interferes least with the stroke. It contributes nothing to propulsion, but a swimmer can only go so far without it.

The breath is normally held during the propulsive phase and taken at the end of the upsweep, when one arm is in a catch position and the other is just leaving the water. *Early breathing* means the breath is taken as the hand finishes the pull; *late breathing* is done under the armpit, as the hand and arm are in the recovery position. Although the method used will depend on the experience of the swimmer, most competitors prefer the latter.

The face and entire body, including shoulders and hips, should be rolled towards the breathing side without moving the head away from the mid-line. The amount of roll should be about 45 degrees on the breathing side and only slightly less on the other. The head begins to turn for a breath when the hand opposite the breathing side enters the water. This is the natural place to breathe in the stroke cycle, since the roll of the body at this point allows the face to be exposed to the air with the least amount of head movement. The head should be turned and not lifted and it is important that the head returns to the body line before the entering arm has passed the face.

In *explosive breathing* – normally used in sprints – the air is expelled quickly and a quick inhalation is taken when the head is turned into the 'trough' created by the bow wave. *Trickle breathing* is more rhythmical and much more suited to distance swims and triathlons. Breath is exhaled through the nose and mouth while the face is submerged and the breath is then taken with a gulping action as the mouth clears the water. (Remember, swimming is just one of the disciplines in triathlon and the triathlete should not emerge from the water in an exhausted state.)

Bilateral breathing uses both sides, usually alternately every third arm pull. This causes minimum interference to the stroke and is useful for correcting faults, such as a swimmer who pulls harder with one arm, has a weak leg kick or is having difficulty balancing the stroke. It is essential for competitive swimmers to be able to see both sides without breaking stroke.

Alternate breathing involves breathing every stroke cycle and *breath-holding* can be a good conditioner, as well as working on the start and finish of a race. It provides a fixed base for the levers to work, ensures little head movement and is also good for beginners in establishing an even stroke. However, bilateral breathing is not to be recommended during a triathlon. The emphasis must be on economy of energy and breathing should normally be on every arm cycle.

Fig 23. Olympic coach Steve Trew demonstrates high elbow and breathing below the level of the water in the trough formed.

Breathing Drills

Emphasize different breathing techniques and patterns, and experiment. (Note that holding the breath until the head turns to breathe 'out and in' causes hesitation in the stroke.)

- Breathing to the left side.
- Breathing to the right side.
- Bilateral breathing.
- Breath-holding across widths or down lengths. (Hypoxic work can be good but is of limited value for triathletes.)

Summary

Normally, timing and co-ordination in front crawl will be developed from practice and drills that improve the timing of legs-arms-breathing and the number of leg kicks per stroke cycle. The best practice is *thoughtful* swimming.

PROBLEMS AND CORRECTIONS

Variations

Mechanically, front crawl is the most efficient and the fastest-known stroke. It is also very natural and normally the first stroke taught. Each individual should adopt the technique particularly suited to their own strengths or weaknesses, which may be any of the following:

- buoyancy;
- predominantly strong arms, causing pronounced rolling and balancing action of the legs, generally a cross-over;
- stiff shoulders, with a low sideways arm recovery producing lateral movement of the legs;
- stiff ankles can be a particular problem for cyclists-turned-triathletes and can lead to retardation and wasted energy. Leg action is only to maintain body position but even this may not be accomplished effectively;
- weak arms and an emphasis on leg action. Again, non-swimmers from leg-dominated cycling or very lean distance runners are likely to over-emphasize the legs. There

Fig 24. Olympic coach Archie Brew takes a swimmer through correct technique.

may be a gliding action of the arms at the catch point.

Correcting Faults

Generally:

- If hands enter thumbs down, overcorrect and get the little finger entering the water first.
- If the head lifts before the hand is in the water (wide entry), try to see the fingers in the water before breathing or change the breathing side.
- Overkicking causes catch-up.
- Over-reaching of the arms causes excessive body roll.

In general, extra clothing – tights, T-shirts, extra costumes – can be a useful training aid. The majority of triathletes will benefit from

Some Faults and Their Correction

Problems	Correction Tip	Problems	Correction Tip
RECOVERY		ARMSTROKE *continued*	
'Windmill'	Drag hand/'chicken wing'	Short finish	Thumb to thigh – flip hand
Flat	Drag hand/'chicken wing', and thumb upside	Long finish	Elbow up – thumb to costume
Close to body	Touch wall		
Flip at finish	Take hand out of pocket	BODY POSITION	
		Head high	Look at line
ENTRY		Head low	Water at eyebrows
Flat, splash	Hold head up	Shoulders flat	Alternate breathing/ shoulder-up – windmill
Wide	Cross-over, reach in front		
Dropped elbow	Move fingers, don't reach	Zigzag body	Stop arm/leg cross-over, change breathing side
Gliding on arm	Quick pull, breathe late		
CATCH		KICK	
Dropped elbow	Over-barrel – push	Too big	Sole in water
Deep catch	Hands near surface in front	Too small	Use flippers – soleout
ARMSTROKE		BREATHING	
Cross-over	Hands outside body	Forward look	Breathe later – to side
Straight arm	Bend to 90°	Back look	Look forward – watch early
Hand near chest	Deeper – more angle	Poor timing	Breathe opposite side or when opposite arm
Pull wide	Slight cross-over		

working on drills. However, while drills are progressive steps in preparation for a total stroke their overuse can be a disadvantage, causing some more experienced swimmers to think too much about their stroke.

FRONT CRAWL CHECKLIST

Whole Stroke

- Body streamlined in near-horizontal position throughout.
- Avoid lifting of head and shoulders.
- Avoid radical body movements (up and down or 'snaking' motion).
- Feet deep enough for effective kicking action.
- Proper stroke mechanics with both arms.
- Balanced, maximum power with both arms.
- Roll of body, including shoulders and hips, about its longitudinal axis approximately

symmetrical, only slightly greater to the breathing side.
- Avoid wasted efforts that do not aid propulsion or breathing.
- One arm always applying effective force to water. Avoid 'stop and go'.

Arms

- Arms enter water at shoulder width. Hand first, little finger up and elbow slightly bent.
- Momentum from the recovery causes the elbow to straighten (but without elevation of the shoulder) and the arm to sink towards an early catch as the wrist rotates so that the palm is flat down.
- Relatively low catch.
- Wrist action permits early catch.
- Elbow up early in pull and remains up for as long as possible. Avoid dropping it.
- Aim for the sensation of pushing the elbow up and forwards.

- Palm and inside of forearm in vertical plane that is roughly parallel to pool and wall early in the pull and for as long as possible.
- Water held behind hand and arm for as long as possible, with minimum of slippage.
- Angle between forearm and bicep (vertex at elbow) approximately 100 degrees as elbow bends during 'bottom-heavy S' course of hand.
- Wrist action permits palm of hand to be held flat against the water for as long as possible during upsweep.
- Have the feeling of moving water towards the feet throughout the stroke, with a feeling of pressure on the hand and forearm.
- Acceleration of 'pull-push' from relatively slow catch to 'whip-like' finish.
- Elbow leads recovery, with the hand following.
- In recovery, elbow is always higher than hand.
- Arm relaxes for as long as possible during most of the recovery – a 'ballistic-like' movement utilizing momentum generated during the short period at the beginning of the recovery.
- Momentum of recovery is absorbed by the water upon entry.
- Avoid placing the arm in the water by muscle control of momentum developed during recovery.
- Depth of armstroke due to amount of elbow bend should be appropriate for the race and for the physical characteristics of the swimmer.

Legs

- Toes generally pointed throughout the kick.
- Knee straight during the upbeat.
- Toes churn the surface of the water without coming out of the water.
- Flexibility of the knee permits the thigh to start a downkick while the foot continues upwards and the knee bends.
- Accelerating downwards thrust of the foot should result in complete knee extension.
- Noticeable whip action. Ankle hyperextended during downbeat.
- Ankle flexibility noticeable.

- Flexibility of the knee permits the thigh to start the upbeat while the foot continues downwards and the knee straightens.
- Angle between upper and lower leg (vertex at the knee) is approximately 145 degrees when knee bend is at maximum.
- Maximum vertical spread of the feet should be 20–40cm (8–16in), depending on the age and size of the swimmer.
- Kick helps maintain body alignment.
- Kick helps maintain feet relatively high.

If you must use a wide recovery because of poor shoulder flexibility, use a cross-over kick to counterbalance the lateral movement of the hips. With a high elbow recovery the arm should leave the water for recovery as the leg on the same side kicks downwards.

Breathing

- Turn head to side by rotating neck on longitudinal body axis.
- Avoid lifting or lateral displacement.
- Breathing coincides with body roll.
- Gradually exhale through nose and mouth the entire time nose and mouth are underwater.
- Explode remaining air out of the mouth just prior to gulping a deep breath.
- Inhale while mouth is below calm-water level, in trough of wave created by the head.
- Body roll and head turn towards non-breathing side should be sufficient to balance the stroke.
- Avoid lopsided appearance.

Summary of Front Crawl Techniques

Get the body position right.
Keep the legs kicking.
Bent-arm stroke.
High elbows on recovery.
Ensure head is only turned slightly to take breath.

CHAPTER 10

Swimming: Adapting Training to Open Water

'Don't swim more, swim smarter.'

For most triathletes – experienced and novice – the season usually runs from around May to September. The remaining months of the year are used to prepare and improve both technique and endurance. Triathlons take place in all types of water – rivers, lakes, the sea and pools – and in all conditions. However, most triathletes in the northern hemisphere will be doing their training for the swim section in the pool.

The transition to open-water swimming for such athletes should start as early as possible. Strokes should be adapted and modified to allow for all types of swims. Drills and exercises must be incorporated into swim sessions to improve technique in preparation for the upcoming season. Technique is all-important in triathlon. All triathletes, whether they are strong or weak swimmers, should aim to complete the swim distance in a comfortable condition, in a good time, with as little energy expended as possible.

The transition from pool to open water can be a traumatic experience for even the most confident of swimmers and every eventuality should be covered. The following drills and exercises will help the athlete and coach to adapt swim sessions to include open-water techniques.

TECHNIQUE TRAINING

Technique is essential and the only foundation for improved performance. It is the key to faster, more relaxed swimming and can give a tremendous boost to confidence, which will improve performance.

Stroke Drills: BLABT

The importance of stroke work that breaks the stroke down into its main components – *B*ody, *L*egs, *A*rms, *B*reathing and *T*iming – cannot be stressed too much.

The correct *body* position is all-important. Adaptation may be slow, but it will come. The desired flat body position, just under the water surface, is often difficult to achieve, particularly for men, who tend to have strong trunk and leg muscles. This can cause the lower half of the body to sink. In addition, well-developed shoulder muscles produce a lack of flexibility and mobility in the upper body.

Listed below are some of the most popular stroke drills; there are many more, and many variations on these.

Arms Only

- Strengthens arms.
- Enables the swimmer to concentrate on specific aspects of the arm action whilst using a pull-buoy produces improved body position, as would be achieved with a wetsuit.

Legs Only

- Strengthens legs.
- Enables the swimmer to concentrate on kicking from the hips with a straight relaxed action emphasizing relaxed and flipper-like action.
- Improves ankle and hip flexibility.

Doggy Paddle

- Emphasizes the pull/push phase of the arm action, and highlights any weakness in the stroke. Every effort should be made to keep the action within the body line.
- Emphasizes control of leg kick to keep the body in a 'high' swimming position.

'Chicken Wing'

- Emphasizes the high shoulder and elbow action of the arm recovery. The fingertips/thumb are recovered up the side of the body to the armpit before the arm is recovered over the water into the entry position.

Extended Stroke

- Encourages the swimmer to slow down the arm action and emphasizes the long extension of the stroke.
- By using a shoulder roll, maximum propulsion can be achieved from the pull phase of the stroke.

Catch Up

As above, except fingertips catch up before the pull phase begins.

Single Arm

(One-arm extended swim using one arm only.)
- Very beneficial in showing the strength/weakness of each arm.
- Good practice for breathing to both sides.

T-shirt Training

The wearing of a T-shirt should be incorporated into specific parts of training sessions. The T-shirt causes drag and resistance, and the resultant altered body position, breathing patterns and physical effects will help a lot. A full-length, long-sleeved T-shirt can simulate the restrictive effect and drag caused by a wetsuit.

Not all training should be attempted with the T-shirt. It is a good idea to do a time trial wearing a T-shirt, maybe 400 or 1000m, and use this as a benchmark for future comparisons.

Swim Drafting

Drafting (following closely behind another swimmer) is allowed during triathlons and should be practised regularly in preparation for the mass-start open-water swims. The person in front does the hard work, allowing the follower to conserve energy and get a faster time.

To practise drafting in the pool, pair up with a swimmer of about the same standard. The following swimmer should 'sit on the feet' of the lead swimmer, trying to swim 10–15cm (4–6in) off the front swimmer's toes, but slightly to the side. This method should achieve the desired slipstreaming effect.

Incorporating drafting into a training session allows everyone to experience the effect of this technique, by sharing the roles. It also teaches swimmers the best way to use this type of swimming to their advantage and how not to upset leaders by tickling or tapping their toes. (If you do annoy a leader, you might receive a painful kick in the face!)

In training, the lead swimmer can also wear paddles and use a pull-buoy. Ninety-nine per cent of swimmers are considerably faster using such aids and should be able to pull away rapidly. However, if the following (or drafting) swimmer gets immediately on to the feet of the leader, this does not happen. This is a good demonstration of the drafting effect working efficiently.

Hip Drafting

It is also possible to draft off the hip of a front swimmer as well as off the feet or legs. In an open-water race situation, swimmers are fighting for space and it will often be impossible to get directly on to the feet of the swimmer in front.

Moving up to the hip of the swimmer in front gives an excellent draft. Visibility is also better than with drafting off the feet, when the legs and feet churn up the water in the follower's face.

With both forms of draft training, it is worth taking out the lane ropes and working in small groups so that a variety of drafting methods are being used. This also gives the idea of

Fig 25. The swim start in an open-water event is completely different from that of a swimming gala.

jockeying for position and the sensation of being in a tight group, as in a race situation. It is very rare to see a single line of swimmers all drafting nice and smoothly off the leader.

OPEN-WATER STARTS AND TURNS

Mass Starts

Open-water mass-start races are very different from anything experienced in the pool, with a large number of bodies fighting for a restricted amount of space in turbulent water. Other swimmers' bodies will be over the top, underneath and on both sides of you: pushing, kicking, pulling and splashing. Even experienced pool-based triathletes or swimmers need to be prepared for this.

There are three ways of getting away from the rush:

get immediately ahead;
get to the back; or

move to the side and swim a wider line around the crowd.

The last two are options for the weaker or less confident swimmers who can afford to hold back a little on the swim, and can make up time on the other disciplines.

The stronger or more confident swimmer should adopt the first option of getting out and away. The oxygen debt created will need to be dealt with, as will the immediate feeling of exhaustion after the fast start. Preparation in the pool should include fast repetition swims with little rest; sprint swims over short distances using breath-holding; or 800m time trials, with the first 200m flat out, and then holding on. This type of training can be emphasized particularly just before and into the race season.

To simulate the feelings of panic that may be experienced in that first open-water start, remove the lane ropes, and get a crowd of swimmers crammed together in as small a space as possible. Set up a big float, or get a competent swimmer to act as a turning buoy, and then bring the swimmers together in a straight line before simulating an open-water start. The start should be done from the deep end. A 'frog' kick, with the legs working *non*-simultaneously, will keep the swimmers afloat for such starts. It also gives the swimmer a little more space as others avoid getting kicked.

Open-Water Turns

Getting around the first buoy can also be traumatic; working on it in the pool before the race can help immensely.

When all the swimmers converge on the buoy, weaker swimmers may get pushed under. To avoid this, either go wide, or get ahead, or wait a little and then move up.

Some swimmers use the technique of turning on to their back for a couple of strokes as they go round the buoy. This is best taught in the pool or learned from video footage.

BREATH-HOLDING AND BILATERAL BREATHING

Bilateral breathing (breathing to both sides) is an essential skill in triathlon. It encourages a more balanced technique, and improved body and head position; more importantly, it also allows triathletes to see what and who is around them. This is a distinct advantage in all types of swims, including the pool.

Breath-holding drills and continuous swims should be gradual but maintained. For example, those who usually breathe every two arm cycles can develop bilateral breathing by using a set of 400m repetitions, breathing one length using the normal pattern and one length every 3 to 4 strokes, and gradually increasing on this.

Bilateral breathing can be a saviour in a mass start in open water. It is difficult to predict the conditions – the direction of the wind, the tide and the current, and the location of sighting objects. Swimmers breathing to one side only

Fig 26. The anticipation of a massed start can be worse than the actual event.

may be bombarded by a 1m (3ft) wave every time they turn to take in air. (Even for strong swimmers, this can be enough to destroy confidence and any chance of a good race.)

The extra control required for bilateral breathing also enhances the development of an improved oxygen uptake level. This means that triathletes will be able to dip into energy reserves for a short period of time (long enough for them to get away from the crowd), and still be able to recover composure and rhythm and clear the lactic acid build-up from the muscles.

A bilateral breathing pattern *may* also help to correct a bad swimming technique, because the head is returned to the central position after each breath. Some swimmers who suffer from lateral deviation (snaking), arms crossing the centre line and excessive rolling *have* had such problems reduced or even eliminated by a bilateral breathing pattern, but the process of improvement is not easy. The right timing and co-ordination do not come quickly.

Bilateral breathing should be introduced to the novice swimmer or triathlete very gradually. There will be lots of coughing and spluttering, but this is good preparation for outdoor swims, in which everyone swallows the occasional gulp of water.

OTHER TRAINING METHODS

Tumble Turns

A good tumble turn can save a triathlete as much as two or three seconds on every turn in the pool. Its execution develops controlled breathing, increases the efficiency of the heart and lungs and improves the ability to swim longer distances with no rest.

Grab turns give the swimmer the chance to take a rest at the end of the pool. The longer the swim the more fatigued the triathlete becomes and consequently the longer the rest at each end.

The ability to execute a good turn also gives triathletes a sense of achievement, making them feel like 'proper' swimmers and filling them with confidence. Taking time out to

learn tumble turns also breaks the routine and is a diversion from hard training sessions. It can be fun and that is, after all, what triathlon should be.

Eyes-Closed Swimming

Training doesn't always have to be serious. 'Eyes-closed swimming' may have limitations – it can be done only over short distances and only by a few at any one time – but it is fun.

The exercise can be done either in a clear pool or in lanes. Swim one length of the pool, eyes open, following the black line along the bottom, counting the number of strokes required to reach the end. The emphasis should be on a steady swim concentrating on the control of the arm action and the pull/push phase along the centre line of the body.

The exercise is repeated, with the eyes closed, imagining the black line. Depending on the skill of the swimmer and whether there are ropes in the pool or not, swimmers may swim diagonally across the pool, or zig-zag along. Some have even been known to swim in the direction from which they started. If there are lane ropes in the pool, the swimmer usually bounces from one side of the lane to the other. It provides a useful lesson: in open water, there is no black line, and no nice clear water to help swimmers see where they are going.

This exercise is useful for the following reasons:

- it shows the importance of the pull phase of the arm action along the centre line if the body is to keep moving forward in a straight line;
- it demonstrates how easily the swimmer's sense of direction is lost; and
- it is the type of activity that provokes thought.

To make the exercise even more 'interesting', wear swimming goggles filled with cotton wool.

Fins

Fins are an excellent training aid, provided they are used sensibly.

Some say that triathletes need to 'save their legs for the bike and run', but the legs should always be used properly during the swim. The leg kick within the stroke stabilizes the body. Those swimmers who are not lucky enough to be natural two-beat leg-kickers (which is not the norm) will need to know how to use their legs to keep a high body position in the water, enabling a faster and less tiring swim. If the legs are not used properly, the heavy trunk and thigh muscles will cause the legs to sink in the water. The arms will then have to work harder to drag the body through the water and fatigue will set in earlier.

Fins encourage the triathlete to use the whole leg to kick, emphasizing a flipper-like action of the foot, focusing on the 'whip' down and forward propulsive phase of the kick. Above all, they allow faster swimming.

Pull-Buoys and Leg Floats

These swim aids not only strengthen the arms but can also be used to give the triathlete the feeling of how the body position will be altered when wearing a wetsuit. It also allows those who do not have a naturally high body position in the water the feeling of what is 'ideal'.

The leg floats should be held high up between the thighs. The legs should be relaxed so that the swimmer is able to kick if this is necessary.

The triathlete must not become dependent on these aids. It is tempting to work most of the time with a pull-buoy because it helps you go faster with less effort.

All aids, including fins, pull-buoys and leg floats are excellent additions to training, but they must be used sparingly and in the correct situation.

SIGHTING

Sighting is a vital feature of open-water swimming and must be practised until it becomes second nature. Practice can easily be adapted to the pool environment and incorporated into sessions in numerous ways.

On a long pool swim, perhaps over an Olympic distance, deliberately lift the head every 'X' number of strokes to sight on a pre-arranged object in the pool area.

On shorter, faster sessions, swim, for example, one length with the head up (water-polo style), then one length with the head down. The high head position allows the triathlete to get used to the hyperextension of the neck and the resulting discomfort. (It is useful to know how the body will react to this activity before the first open-water race of the season.)

It is not easy to learn how to sight on objects, but it can save minutes in a race, enabling the swimmer to pursue a much straighter line. This in turn leads to greater confidence, and less stress and anguish.

When practising the head-up or lifting-head-to-sight drills, it is best to keep the head up for at least five strokes rather than to lift just for two strokes and then drop down. Lifting the head is disorientating, and it is easy for the swimmer to put the head back into the water without really having achieved anything.

REAL OPEN WATER

As soon as is practical and the weather is warm enough, triathletes should be encouraged to participate in open-water sessions. Such sessions should *not* be undertaken alone. There should always be someone else present, who can get help in case of difficulty.

CHAPTER 11

Swimming: Periodization and Practical Sessions

'Place, press, pull, push, makes my stroke go whoosh, whoosh, whoosh!'

The swimming needs of triathletes are not exactly the same as those of pure swimmers. Coaches in swimming clubs may not be entirely sympathetic to triathletes' needs and may lack knowledge about the demands of triathlon, and the particular problems of the swimming triathlete.

Triathletes must look at their specific needs and at their strengths and weaknesses. What percentage of training time should be allocated to swimming? What time in club or individual sessions is available for swimming? Aiming to cover 1500m in open water, 40km on a bike and 10km on foot, does a triathlete need the same emphasis on speed as a competitive pool swimmer? Who is best qualified to decide what is good or desirable for the triathlete's swimming training: the triathlete, a swimming coach, or a triathlon coach?

A triathlete is not a pure swimmer, and should remember the following maxim:

'Don't fail to plan; don't plan to fail; plan to win.'

THE SWIMMING TRAINING YEAR

One way of planning swimming training is to divide the training year into four phases, and then divide each phase into a period of ten to fourteen weeks. Improvement checks are regularly carried out. Repetition times for training are set by making use of the 30-minute timed swim (T30) to measure current endurance levels. By dividing the total time by the number of 100m swum, it is possible to find the base time for each 100m.

Target times would be as follows:

- For 100m repetitions, multiply base 100 time by 96.5 per cent.
- For 200m repetitions, multiply base 100 time by 98.5 per cent.
- For 400m repetitions and above, use a straight division.

This T30 timed swim can be used to re-test in order to establish new targets. The swimming year is outlined as follows:

October: rest or light swimming
November: increase regular number of sessions; emphasize stroke and aerobic fitness
December: continue as above
January: increase volume and frequency of sessions; emphasis still on stroke technique; introduce endurance
February: continue endurance; introduce timed swims
March: hardest phase; emphasize endurance, going into specific sets; compare timed swims in sets; introduce anaerobic work, specific work: race starts (particularly open-water and mass starts)
April: continue as above
May: continue as above, then move into race preparation, reducing volume

In the competitive season the options are as follows:

- repeat the process as above but on a mini- or micro-cycle; or
- maintain speed and endurance through the four or five months of the competitive season; the main bulk of the training then becomes recovery and maintenance.

Training Emphasis				
	Type	*Effort*	*Rest*	*Heart Rate*
Mixed aerobic	Mixed strokes	Comfortable	Short	140–160
Endurance (main area for triathletes)	Specific sets 6 × 400m or 10 × 200m	Hard, but able to maintain for 20–60 mins	Short	160–180
Anaerobic	4 × 100m or 8 × 50m	HURTS	Full recovery	Max HR
Speed	16 × 10–20m			

November/December/January

The following sessions are examples of those in the Nov/Dec/Jan phase (all front crawl unless specified). The sessions are mostly untimed, emphasizing stroke work, pulling and kicking. Distances are in metres unless otherwise stated.

Work on *stroke*, *drills*, and *feel for the water/flow*.

Build up/aim for 3000/3500 in a 1-hour session; occasionally 4000.

Build up/aim for 4000/4500 in a 1.5-hour session; occasionally 5500.

SESSION 1
Warm-up
400m full – 200m pull – 400m full front crawl.
Main set
20 × 50. Recovery 15 secs between. Alternate full stroke and finger drag drill.

Stroke, warm down.
400 pull – 2 × 100 kick – 200 pull – 200 emphasizing long stroke.
TOTAL DISTANCE 3000

SESSION 2
Warm-up
200 full – 200 pull – 200 full – 200 kick – 200 pull front crawl.
Main set
4 × 400. 1st and 3rd continuous swims; 2nd and 4th split 10 secs at each 100.
1st and 3rd full stroke, emphasizing long stroke and counting stroke; 2nd and 4th with clenched fists.
Recovery 20 secs between each.
Warm down: 50 kick – 50 pull – 50 full, repeat four times.
TOTAL DISTANCE 3200

Fig 27. A group squad training session in Lanzarote.

SESSION 3
Warm-up
400 full – 100 back – 300 full – 100 back – 200 full – 100 back – 100 full – 100 back – 100 full.
Main set
20 × 50. Recovery 20, 15, 10, 5 secs between and repeat 5 times.
1–4, 9–12, 17–20 full stroke. 5–8, 13–16 catch-up drill.
Stroke, warm down 200 crawl with three-point touch, 100 backstroke with full stretch and repeat.
TOTAL DISTANCE 3100

SESSION 4
Main set
400 full. Recovery 30 secs.
2 × 200 pull (10 secs between 200s), recovery 30 secs after both.
4 × 100 catch up (10 secs between 100s), 30 secs after the 100s.
8 × 50 kick (10 secs between 50s), 60 secs after all 50s.
Repeat three times, without kicking on the last set.
TOTAL DISTANCE 4400

SESSION 5
Warm-up
200 individual medley, repeat five times, 10 secs between each.
Main set
1500 straight swim. Alternate each 250 with full stroke and clenched fists.
Stroke, warm down.
10 × 50 easy pace. Recover 10 secs between each 50. Odd numbers down on left arm back on full stroke, even numbers down on right arm.
TOTAL DISTANCE 3000

SESSION 6
Main set
2000 swim: 400 full – 100 pull – 300 full – 200 pull – 200 full – 300 pull – 100 full – 400 pull.
Stroke 20 × 50. Four each of 'chicken wing', finger drag, three-point touch, clenched fists. 10 secs recovery between swims.
TOTAL DISTANCE 3000

SESSION 7
Warm-up
200 front crawl (50 full – 50 fists – 50 catch up – 50 pull), repeat ten times, 10 secs between each.
Main set
20 × 50. Recovery 20, 15, 10 and 5 secs between swims and repeat five times.
Out on long stroke counting, and returning with stroke turnover faster.
Try to hold same time on all despite different rest periods.
Stroke, warm down with easy 600. 100 front crawl, 100 backstroke. Stretch out and repeat three times.
TOTAL DISTANCE 3600

SESSION 8
Warm-up
1000 straight swim. Over-emphasize body roll and length of stroke.
Main set
100, 200, 300, 400, 500, 400, 300, 200, 100. Rest 10 secs only between swims.
100s, 300s and 500 on full stroke, 200s and 400s on pulling.
Stroke, warm down 200 easy backstroke.
TOTAL DISTANCE 3700

SESSION 9
Warm-up
8 × 100 easy swim, 10 secs between each. Attempt to lengthen stroke and roll body more on each successive 100.
Main set
Three sets of 5 × 200 rest 50, 40, 30, 20 10 secs between each swim and repeat three times.
1st and 3rd 200 in each set done with index finger and thumb touching to make an 'O' shape. Concentrate on feeling the flow of the water particularly on these swims.
Stroke, warm down 200 easy swim on any other stroke.
TOTAL DISTANCE 4000

SESSION 10
Warm-up
Continuous 800. Breathe on wrong side each alternate length.
Main set
8 × 50 recovery 10 secs clenched fists.

4 × 100 recovery 10 secs full stroke.
2 × 200 recovery 15 secs pulling.
1 × 400 recovery 30 secs full stroke, emphasizing long stroke.
2 × 200 recovery 15 secs pulling.
4 × 100 recovery 10 secs full stroke.
8 × 50. recovery 10 secs clenched fists.
Stroke, warm down 400 easy pace. Alternate crawl and any other stroke each length.
TOTAL DISTANCE 4000

Session 11
Warm-up
8 × 25 rest 5 secs, 4 × 50 rest 10 secs, 2 × 100 rest 10 secs.
Main set
3 × 800 rest 1 min between swims.
1st 800 full stroke concentrating on long stroke and counting.
2nd 800 split at each 100 by 5 seconds, alternate full stroke and fists.
3rd 800 split at each 200 by 10 seconds, alternate pulling and full stroke.
Stroke, warm down 4 × 200 easy pace. Recover 10 secs between each 200, 50 each of kick, catch-up, pull and full stroke (emphasizing body roll).
TOTAL DISTANCE 3800

Session 12
Warm-up
800 swim. 15 secs rest at 400.
Main set
20 × 100 in four sets of five. 10 secs recovery after each 100, 2 mins between each set of five.
1st set on fists, 2nd set full stroke, 3rd set on index finger and thumb, 4th set full stroke.
Stroke, warm down 4 × 100 kick, rest 15 secs between each 100, 400 pull.
TOTAL DISTANCE 3600

Session 13
Warm-up
400 full – 200 back – 400 full front crawl.
Main set
20 × 75. Recovery 15 secs between. Alternate full stroke and index finger/thumb drill.
Stroke, warm down 400 pull, 2 × 100 kick, 200 'chicken wing', 200 emphasizing long stroke.
TOTAL DISTANCE 3500

Session 14
Warm-up
200 full – 200 pull – 200 full – 200 kick – 200 pull front crawl.
Main set
4 × 500. 1st and 3rd continuous swims, 2nd and 4th rest 10 secs at each 100.
1st and 3rd full stroke, emphasizing long stroke and counting stroke. 2nd and 4th clenched fists. Rest 20 secs.
Stroke, warm down 50 kick, 50 pull, 50 full and repeat four times.
TOTAL DISTANCE 3600

Session 15
Warm-up
400 full – 100 catch up – 300 full – 100 catch up – 200 full – 100 catch up – 100 full – 100 catch up – 100 full.
Main set
20 × 50. Rest 20, 15, 10, 5 secs between, repeat five times. 1–4, 9–12, 17–20 full stroke. 5–8, 13–16 back, breast or fly.
Stroke, warm down 200 crawl with three-point touch, 100 full stroke, repeat three times.
TOTAL DISTANCE 3400

Session 16
Main set
400 full. Recovery 30 secs.
2 × 200 pull (10 secs between 200s), recovery 30 secs after both.
4 × 100 catch up (10 secs between 100s), 30 secs after the 100s.
8 × 50 kick (10 secs between 50s), 60 secs after all 50s. Repeat all above three times.
4 × 50 with 1-min recovery at 90 per cent effort.
TOTAL DISTANCE 5000

Session 17
Warm-up
200, repeat five times: full, finger/thumb, touch other side of back, touch front of head, full. Recovery 10 secs between each.
Main set
2000 straight swim. Alternate each 200 with full stroke and clenched fists.
Stroke, warm down 10 × 50 easy pace. Recover 10 secs between each 50. Odd numbers

down on left arm back on full stroke, even numbers down on right arm back on full stroke.
TOTAL DISTANCE 3500

Session 18
Main set
2000 swim: 400 full – 100 pull – 300 full – 200 pull – 200 full – 300 pull – 100 full – 400 pull. Try to increase pace *gradually*.
Stroke 20 × 50. Four each of 'chicken wing', finger drag, backstroke stretched out, clenched fists. 10 secs recovery between swims.
TOTAL DISTANCE 3000

Session 19
Warm-up
300 front crawl (75 full, 75 fists, 75 catch up, 75 pull), repeat ten times, 15 secs between each.
Main set
30 × 50. Recovery 25, 20, 15, 10 and 5 secs between swims and repeat six times. Try to reduce number of strokes by one on each set of five swims. Try to hold the same time despite reducing rest.
Stroke, warm down easy 600. 100 front crawl, 100 backstroke stretching out; repeat three times.
TOTAL DISTANCE 5100
(*Note*: this session can be quite dragging; prepare mentally to work hard.)

Session 20
Warm-up
1000 straight swim. Over-emphasize body roll and length of stroke.
Main set
400 full stroke, 100 pull. Repeat five times, 15 secs recovery between each swim. Work hard on the pulling, concentrate on full stroke in 400s.
Stroke, warm down, 200 easy backstroke
TOTAL DISTANCE 3700

Session 21
Warm-up
10 × 100 easy swim. 10 secs between each. Alternate full stroke and your choice of drills on each 100.
Main set (*note*: this is a really tough session)
Five sets of 3 × 200. Rest 50 secs on 1st set, 40 secs on 2nd set, 30 secs on 3rd set, 20 secs on 4th set, 10 secs on 5th set.

1st 200 on fist drill, 2nd 200 on pull and 3rd 200 on full stroke in each set.
Warm down. 200 easy swim on any other stroke.
TOTAL DISTANCE 4200

Session 22
Warm-up
Continuous 800. Breathe bilaterally on each alternate 100.
Main set (*note*: another tough session)
10 × 50 recovery 10 secs clenched fists.
5 × 100 recovery 15 secs full stroke.
3 × 200 recovery 20 secs pulling.
1 × 800 recovery 30 secs full stroke.
3 × 200 recovery 20 secs pulling.
5 × 100 recovery 15 secs full stroke.
10 × 50 recovery 10 secs clenched fists.
Warm down. 400 easy pace. Alternate crawl/ choice each length.
TOTAL DISTANCE 5200

Session 23
Warm-up
12 × 50. Alternate finger/thumb, front of head touch, finger drag, 'chicken wing' drills. 10 secs between swims.
Main set
3 × 800. Recovery 1 min between swims. 1st 800 full stroke concentrating on long stroke and counting. 2nd 800 split at each 400 by 20 secs. 1st 400 pull, 2nd 400 full stroke. 3rd 800 split at each 200 by 10 secs, 200 fists, 200 catch up, 200 pulling and 200 full stroke.
Stroke, warm down 4 × 200 easy pace. Recover 10 secs between each 200, 50 each of kick, backstroke, kick, and full stroke.
TOTAL DISTANCE 3800

Session 24
Warm-up
800 swim, 10 secs rest at each 200.
Main set
20 × 100 in four sets of five. 10 secs recovery after each 100, 90 seconds between each set of five.
1st set pulling, 2nd set full stroke, 3rd set pulling, 4th set full stroke.
Stroke, warm down 4 × 100 index finger/ thumb, 4 × 100 fists. Recovery 15 secs between.
TOTAL DISTANCE 3600

February to April/May

The following sessions might be used in the phase from February through to April or May. The times indicated (which relate to a particular athlete) should be treated with caution.

SESSION 1
Warm-up
2 × 400, concentrating on long stroke and emphasizing body roll, 30 secs between 400s.
Main set
4 × 400 on 6 mins 15 secs aiming for 5 mins 30 secs.
16 × 50 on 60 seconds, concentrating on stroke and counting.
12 × 100 plus 15 seconds. Break into 25 easy, 25 increase, 25 drill, 25 swim.
TOTAL 4400

SESSION 2
Note: this is a key session.
Warm-up
3 × 100 swim (10 secs rest between each), 3 × 100 kick (15 secs rest between each), 3 × 100 drill (20 secs rest between each).
Main set
3 × 1000. 1st and 3rd as 200 swim, 200 drill, 200 extend stroke, 200 drill, 200 swim. 2nd 1000 as full stroke, full out and time. 90 seconds between 1000s.
6 × 200 as 50 swim, 50 kick, 100 swim. Recovery 20 secs between each 200.
6 × 150 as 50 swim, 50 drill, 50 swim. Recovery 20 secs between each 150.
TOTAL DISTANCE 6000

SESSION 3
Warm-up
8 × 100 swim, concentrating on long stroke. Recovery 10 secs after each 100.
Main set
5 × 100, 85 secs (10 secs between each).
12 × 25, fast (5 secs between each).
5 × 100, 85 secs (10 secs between each).
12 × 25 fast (5 secs between each).
4 × 200 alternate lengths kick/full (20 secs between each).
8 × 50 pull with paddles.
TOTAL DISTANCE 3600

SESSION 4
Warm-up
8 × 100. Alternate drill/full stroke.
Main set
2 × 1500. First pull with paddles, 90 secs recovery. 2nd full stroke; take times on both.
2 × 200 easy full stroke extending and accentuating body roll.
TOTAL DISTANCE 4200

SESSION 5
Note: this is a key session.
24 × 50 drill (10 secs between each).
24 × 50 full, aim for 40 secs (10 secs between each).
24 × 50 pull with paddles, aim for 42 secs (10 secs between each).
24 × 25 alternate kick and full stroke, untimed (5 secs between each).
6 × 200 alternate full stroke and drill (fists and open), aim 3 mins on full stroke (20 secs between each).
1 × 800 full stroke extended body roll and long stroke.
TOTAL DISTANCE 6200

SESSION 6
Warm-up
12 × 100 on 95, 90, 85 seconds (10 secs between each 100), and repeat four times.
Main set
2 × 100 pull with paddles, aim for 85 secs (10 secs between each), straight into 1 × 200 full stroke, aim for 2 mins 50 secs. Recover for 30 secs and repeat four times.
TOTAL DISTANCE 2800

SESSION 7
Note: this is a key session.
4 × 400, swim 100 backstroke on 4th, 3rd, 2nd and 1st 100 for each successive 400. Recover 30 secs between each 400, aim at 6 mins 15 secs for each 400. Rest 90 secs after 4 × 400 and repeat.
4 × 200 alternate 50 kick/full (15 secs between each).
4 × 200 pull with paddles, aim for 3 mins (20 secs between each).
1 × 200 full, aim for 3 mins 5 secs (25 secs between each), then 8 × 25 pull with paddles fast (5 secs between each); repeat four times.
TOTAL DISTANCE 6400

SESSION 8
Warm-up
6 × 200 alternate full and paddles, recovery 15 secs after each 200, no timing.
Main set
12 × 50 kick (10 secs between each).
32 × 50 on 50 seconds, 9–16 and 25–32 with paddles, recover 60 secs after each eight.
TOTAL DISTANCE 3400

SESSION 9
Warm-up
3 × 200 drill (20 secs between each 200). Different drill for each 200.
Main set
20 × 50 as 25 swim, 25 swim with head out of water (10 secs between each).
2000 time-trial swim. Count strokes each 4th 100. Take time.
TOTAL DISTANCE 3600

SESSION 10
8 × 200. Alternate full stroke (aim for 3 mins 10 secs) and 100 drill/100 full (aim for 3 mins 25 secs). Recovery 20 secs after each 200.
6 × 150, as 50 full, 50 kick, 50 full, with 15 secs recovery after each 150.
10 × 100 pull with paddles.
TOTAL DISTANCE 3500

SESSION 11
Note: this is a key session.
Warm-up
4 × 200. Alternate drill/full stroke, untimed (15 secs between each).
Main set
6 × 100 as kick 50/full 50 with 10 secs recovery between each 100; 60 secs break and repeat as 6 × 100 as full 50/kick 50.
3 × 9 × 100. 1st set and 3rd set pull with paddles (aim for 80 secs/100), 2nd set full stroke (aim for 83 secs/100); recovery 10 secs between each 100, 60 secs between sets.
1 × 400. Alternate 50 back/50 full front crawl.
12 × 50. Alternate odds drill and evens full (15 secs between each).
TOTAL DISTANCE 5700

SESSION 12
1 × 1000 as 400 crawl, 100 back, 300 crawl, 100 back, 100 crawl.

1 × 1,500 as 1000 crawl, 100 back, 400 crawl. Take time.
200 pull with paddles in 2 mins 50 secs, rest for 25 secs then 100 full in 85 secs and recovery 20 secs; repeat three times.
12 × 50, 1–6 full, 7–12 paddles (15 secs recovery between each), aim for 40 secs on all.
TOTAL DISTANCE 4000

Towards the Competitive Season

The sessions above take the triathlete into the start of the competitive season. At this stage, volumes begin to be reduced and the athlete starts to prepare specifically for each individual event. (*See* Chapter 17 on tapering and race preparation.) To avoid boredom, and to introduce even more variety into swim sessions, the following may also be useful.

SESSION 1
Warm-up
3 × 200 stroke, long and smooth (15 secs between each).
Main set
5 × 200 off 2 mins 45 secs to 3 mins.
2 × 1000. 200 full – 200 kick – 200 full – 200 stroke drill – 200 full. 60 secs recovery between.
4 × 200 full stroke, holding long stroke with middle 66 of each 200 with head up and sighting. Recovery 15 secs between each 200.
TOTAL DISTANCE 4400

SESSION 2
Warm-up
8 × 100 drill (four drills × 2). Recovery 10 secs between each.
Main set
20 × 50. 5 full – 5 pull – 5 full – 5 pull with paddles. Recovery 10 secs after each 50, 30 secs after each set of five.
4 × 500. Alternate full and pull (one with paddles) swim and rest. Aim for 7 mins 15 secs.
8 × 100 alternate kick and pull *without* paddles (15 secs between each).
TOTAL DISTANCE 4600

SESSION 3
Warm-up
400. Concentrate on long stroke.
Main set

8 × 50 kick (5 secs between each).
8 × 50 swim easy (10 secs between each).
1 × 3000 straight. Concentrate on stroke. Timed.
1 × 1000. Alternate each length kick/pull/head up/full.
TOTAL DISTANCE 5200

SESSION 4
Warm-up
400. Surge each 3rd length.
Main set
16 × 50. Increase pace: 75 per cent, 85 per cent, 90 per cent, 95 per cent for each set of four (5 secs between each).
Then, 2 × 200 full on 2 mins 45 secs; 1 × 200 kick (15 secs rest); 2 × 200 pull on 2 mins 45 sec, then 200 easy and repeat full set.
20 × 25 (or 16 × 33) hard, with 10 secs recovery after each; breath-hold each 4th length for half of length.
TOTAL DISTANCE 4100

SESSION 5
Warm-up
6 × 200 as 50 drill, 100 kick, 50 swim full (15 secs between each).
Main set
16 × 50 kick (5 secs between each).
12 × 100 as 4 full – 4 pull – 4 full, alternate 95 per cent and long stroke (15 secs between each).
TOTAL DISTANCE 3200

SESSION 6
Warm-up
8 × 100 as 25 drill, 25 kick, 50 full (10 secs between each).
Main set
4 × 200, broken at 50 for 5 secs recovery, on 4 mins; *hard swim*.
4 × 400 on 5 mins 45 sec.
6 × 150 (or 7 × 133) on 2 mins 15 secs. Last length at 99 per cent.
TOTAL DISTANCE 4100

SESSION 7
Warm-up
8 × 100. Alternate free and other stroke (10 secs between each).
Main set

1 × 600 on 9 min.
3 × 3 × 200 on 3 min, 1st and 3rd set full, 2nd set pull with paddles.
10 × 100. Alternate smooth stroke and 95 per cent. Recovery 15 secs after smooth and 30 secs after 95 per cent.
TOTAL DISTANCE 4200

SESSION 8
Warm-up
8 × 200 with middle 50 alternate head up to sight and kick (15 secs between each 200).
Main set
24 × 25 (or 16 × 33) kick (5 secs between each).
40 × 50 on 45 secs: 10 full – 10 pull – 10 full – 10 pull with paddles.
TOTAL DISTANCE 4200

SESSION 9
Warm-up
1 × 2000 on 26 min.
Main set
4 × 200 drill, 15 secs between each.
2 × 800 on 11 min.
2 × 200 full on 3 min.
4 × 100 stroke, 10 secs between each.
8 × 50 pull, 10 secs between each.
TOTAL DISTANCE 5600

SESSION 10
Warm-up
3 × 300. 100 full – 100 drill – 100 pull, recover 20 secs between each.
Main set
10 × 100 kick one length then into full (10 secs between each).
20 × 100 on 90 secs: 10 pull with paddles, 10 full.
TOTAL DISTANCE 900

SESSION 11
Warm-up
3 × 400, 1st and 3rd front crawl, 2nd alternate lengths crawl and choice (20 secs between each).
Main set
1 × 1,500 pull without paddles, legs banded. Take time.
16 × 50 alternate kick and full (recovery 15 secs).
5 × 200 full, long stroke, accelerate final 50 (30 secs between each).
TOTAL DISTANCE 4500

CHAPTER 12
Cycling

'A million miles of whirling wheels.'

Incredible changes and innovations have been seen in cycling over the last decade, with a seemingly entirely new mechanical animal arriving on the scene. The aerodynamics of the bike and the rider's position may have both improved but, according to Olympic gold medallist Chris Boardman, and others, 'It's still what you've got in the legs.' In Dave Scott's

Fig 28. Paul Williams shows excellent aerodynamic form on the aerobars.

view, in triathlon 'the bike section's the equalizer, the longest part of the race.' The swimming is based on technique and the running is fitness and guts, while the cycling is a mixture of both. 'You have to get out there and do it, get some miles in.'

The sport of triathlon has contributed enormously to cycling's advances. In 1987, Glenn Cook caused a furore when he appeared on the front cover of *Cycling Weekly* with his bike fitted with aerobars. Official enthusiasm was muted, and it was not until 1991 that tri-bars were grudgingly allowed. Alf Engers' decade-old record over 25 miles was broken again and again and again. Today, it is more unusual to see a bike in a time trial without tri-bars than with them.

Even with the arrival of tri-bars, discwheels, index shifting gears, clip-in pedals, bikestreams and other add-ons, the basic premise still holds true: get fit and ride faster. A good position leads to good technique, which leads to a good base on which to put the fitness, and then go faster.

Until discussions on drafting are resolved, triathlon is concerned with the time-trialling aspects of cycling. Clearly, if less energy is used to overcome wind resistance, gravity and rolling resistance, there will be more energy available for the essentials – that is, getting you and the bike from the end of the swim to the start of the run as fast as possible and as economically as possible.

THE BIKE

Bike and rider must fit each other perfectly. The riding position has to combine comfort, mechanical efficiency and good aerodynamics.

The rider should be able to alter style, position and technique to compete on a variety of surfaces and gradients, and on courses of different severity and distance.

Fitting and position instructions can only be guidelines, but there are a number of useful starting points. If you have been riding or competing for some time and decide that your position needs radical re-adjustment, you need to make the changes gradually, in stages of a maximum half centimetre each time. This will be far easier on the legs and the backside.

Contrary to popular opinion, the size of the bicycle frame – 21, 21.5 or 22in (52, 54, 56cm) – is not all-important. The adjustments that can be made to the equipment give a lot of leeway. Check the following four major adjustments:

1. Saddle height;
2. Saddle front and rear position;
3. Handlebar height; and
4. Handlebar forward and back position (stem length).

Cycle Inspection

Before starting checks, clean the bike. Check items methodically in the same order.

Frame

Check for cracks around the bottom bracket, head tube, bottom stays and basically around all joints. Sometimes cracks appear around the little holes around the stays.

Wheels

Spin the wheel. Look for obvious signs of buckling or kinks and dents in the rim. If the rim has a big dent or flat spot, or if the rim is really buckled, it is time to replace it. Do this with the tyre off if possible.

If the spinning hub grinds or makes noises, the bearings or cones could be slack. If it runs very unevenly and grinds, there may be dirt in the bearings. This will cause the spokes to work themselves harder and they may snap at the base of the hub. Look for wear on the spokes where they meet the hub.

Take out the quick release and clean it. Lightly grease it and put it back. On the rear hub, check that the spindle on the right-hand side is spinning centrally and that it is not spinning eccentrically. You will need to remove the wheel from the frame to carry out this check.

Tyres

First, look over the tyre tread for cuts or bald patches where the cords are shaving. Some of the smaller cuts can be glued with superglue (make sure the surfaces are clean and dry first). The bigger cuts have probably weakened the tyre structure. If in doubt, consult an expert.

Look at the sidewalls, check that the stitching is not chafed or cut. With the tyre on the rim and pumped up, spin the wheel and look for any bulges or warping in the tyre. A deep cut or a bulge means that the tyre should be changed.

Freewheel (or Block)

Make sure this is kept clean. Clean between the teeth; use an old rag and pull the dirt out. Make sure the freewheel spins freely. If it is dry and has grit on it, it will be tight to move round and will make grinding noises. It may not hold position when you pedal hard and may slip, because some of the parts inside may be seized. A light oil through should normally do the trick.

Setting the Riding Position

1. Set the height of the saddle.
2. Ensure the saddle is level.
3. Set the 'Fore and aft' position of the saddle.
4. Estimate the length of the handlebar stem.
5. Set the 'tilt' of the handlebars.
6. Fix the position of the brake levers on road bikes.
7. The height of the handlebars depends on the type of racing and the physiology of the rider.

Notes:

1. It may be necessary to re-adjust saddle height after Step 3.
2. It is vital to re-assess the riding position of young athletes at regular intervals, as there may be dramatic increases in bone length.

3. Consideration will have to be given to pedalling style when fixing saddle height.

Chain

Make sure the chain is clean and lightly oiled. Look for stiff links and cracks. When the chain is on the bike, it should not be so tight that the derailleur is moved forward or too slack so that it is closed.

Brakes

Check that the brake blocks are not too worn and that you can pull on the brakes and stop. Lightly oil the working parts. Check the cables are not frayed. Make sure the brake callipers are central on the wheel and that one side is not hitting the rim before the other.

Headset

This should turn smoothly. You should get full lock without having to move it with your handlebars. Sometimes the bearings wear inside the headset in one position resulting in a locking effect. It will rest in one position. Check that the headset is not too slack either.

Bars and Stem

Check the bolt is tight and that the bars do not move.

Gears

Check that you can get all the gears available and that the chain does not jump off the sprockets.

Chainwheel and Bottom Bracket

The chainwheel should spin freely. If the bottom bracket is worn or too tight it will stop very quickly. Check that it is not too slack either. There should be no side movement when the crank arms are pushed.

Check that the chainwheel teeth are not too worn. If they are, they will be hooked. Check that the bolts holding the crank arms are tight.

Pedals

Check that the pedals spin freely.

Find a cycle shop that you trust. Whenever you get any work carried out, ask them to explain exactly what they have done and if possible show you as they are carrying out the work. This way, you gradually learn how to carry out various jobs yourself. When you collect the bike, check it before paying; you might even want to take it for a quick spin to see how it works.

POSITION

The body can only transfer energy to the pedals if it is placed in the optimum position on the bike.

The points of contact are:

- saddle;
- backside;
- pedal;
- feet;
- bars; and
- hands.

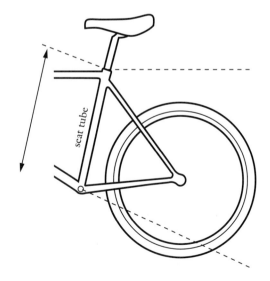

Fig 29. The frame size is measured from the centre of the bottom bracket up the seat tube.

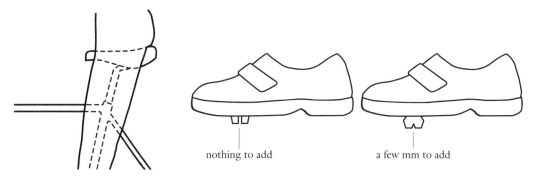

Fig 30. Setting the height of the saddle should take into account the type and size of shoe plates.

With tri-bars, a fourth contact point is added: the forearms (or elbows).

Frame Size

Frame size, measured from the centre of the bottom bracket, up the seat tube to a point level with the top of the top tube, should be approximately two-thirds the length of the rider's inside leg, measured crotch to ground in bare feet (Fig 29).

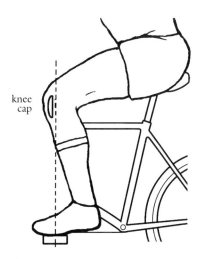

knee
cap

Fig 31. It is crucial that the saddle is adjusted correctly.

Leg Length

Sit on the saddle and place the left crank at the bottom of the stroke in line with the seat tube. Place the heel of the foot (wearing a cycling shoe) onto the pedal. The leg should be straight but not quite locked. Add on the thickness of the shoe plate (Fig 30).

Lateral Position

Check the lateral position with the pedals horizontal, cycling shoes on, and the ball of the foot on the pedal. A plumb line dropped just behind the knee of the forward leg should dissect the ball of the foot, which should be above the pedal spindle. If this is not the case, move the saddle forwards or backwards.

Note 1: any lateral adjustment will alter the saddle height, so re-check the two measurements until you are satisfied.

Note 2: different pedals and shoes will make a significant difference to height and position. If you change types, re-check your position (Fig 31).

Handlebars (Normal)

If you have short arms with small hands, choose a stem that puts your fingertips just level with the back edge of the handlebars. If you have long arms and large hands, choose a stem that puts your hands 2.5–4cm (1–1.5in) behind the bars (Fig 32).

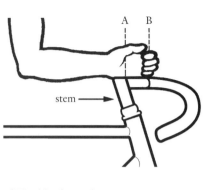

(Above) Fig 32. Stem size is important.

(Right) Fig 33. Handlebars should be approximately 4–6cm below the saddle.

For the rider of average height, the stem should be set at a height of 4–6cm (1.5–2.5in) below the saddle, depending on personal preference. For riders who suffer lower backache (common if there is a lack of fitness, or when cycling in the face of strong headwinds), the bars should be kept at 4cm below the saddle.

The handlebar angle must be comfortable both in the drop position and in the 'tops' position, and it should be easy to reach the brakes. Try to keep the top just under level

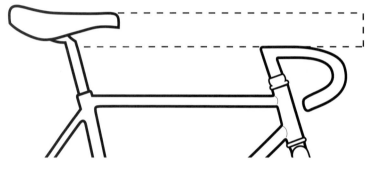

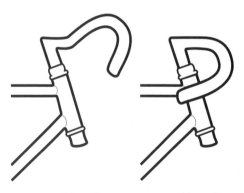

wrong position of bars   correct position of bars

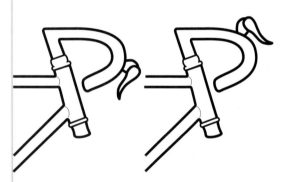

wrong position of brakes

(Above) Fig 34 & *(Right)* Fig 35. The handlebar angle must be comfortable both in the drop position and in the 'tops' position, and it should be easy to reach the brakes.

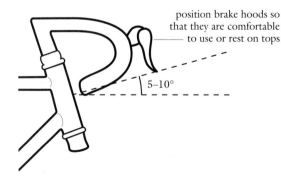

position brake hoods so that they are comfortable to use or rest on tops

5–10°

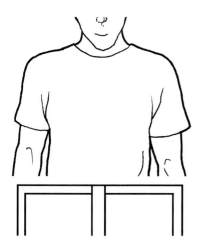

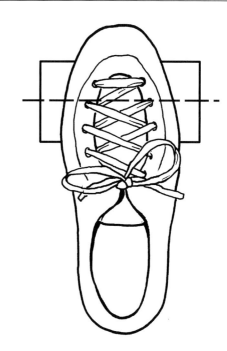

(Above) Fig 36. Handlebars should be approximately shoulder width wide.

Fig 37. Shoe plates and the position of the shoe.

and a 5–10 degree angle on the bottom bend (Fig 35).

The handlebar width should be equal to the rider's shoulder width (Fig 36).

Shoe Plates

The shoe must be square on the pedal and plate and the position must allow the ball of the foot to be above the spindle (Fig 37).

Riding Position with Tri-Bars

The introduction of tri-bars gave rise to many new theories, particularly with regard to the height and forward extension of the bars. With tri-bars, the basic premise of making gradual adjustments still applies. With clip-on extensions, almost all of the advice relating to handlebars (*see above*) remains valid.

The fundamental aim of cycling is to minimize and overcome the forces that resist the cyclist's motion. Of these forces, air resistance is the major factor limiting effective progress. Frictional forces are largely determined by the design and manufacture of the cycle; some of the resistance can be overcome by very high

pressure in tyres or tubulars and use of narrow section types (of 18mm or even less). The cyclist also has to contend with gravity on hills.

Efficiency can be influenced by action and position. What feels best is not necessarily best.

Air resistance (or drag) can be put into three sub-divisions:

1. *frontal resistance* depends on the total frontal area presented to the air; by changing shape, the cyclist can influence this resistance (Fig 38);
2. *air/surface friction* depends on the smoothness of the surface the air flows over; baggy tops and shorts, and uncontrolled hair can influence the effect of resistance in this case;
3. *turbulence* depends on aerodynamic force and is probably the most influential of the three factors. The cyclist should try to keep the whole shape 'smooth', like the downhill ski racer's 'egg' shape (Figs 39 & 40).

Before the tri-bar, cyclists would try to make their position aerodynamic by achieving an increasingly low position, without radically changing anything else. The theory of the

Position: Problems and Solutions

Problem	*Possible causes*
Pain in crotch, groin	Saddle too high; saddle tilted; too many rpm; irregular or infrequent training; saddle too wide, too narrow, too hard
Pain in shoulders, arms, neck	Wrong stem length; stem too low; weak lower back; not tilting head to one side; saddle tilted down; unaccustomed to crash-hat
Pain in hands	Too much weight on arms; staying too long in one position
Knee pain (not from accident)	Pedal cadence too fast; wrong saddle height; using too big gears too soon; cleat angle wrong; pronation or structural problems; old injuries; cold air on uncovered legs
Hitting inside of ankle on crank arm	Excessive pronation; cleat rotation
'Bouncing' in the saddle at high rpm	Incorrect saddle height; tense upper body; poor pedal stroke
Bunched-up feeling	Top tube or stem too short
Frequently shifting position on saddle	Saddle too high or tilted incorrectly
Tight calf muscles	Fore–aft cleat position incorrect; rigid ankles; overly pointed toes
Saddle sores	Irritated tissues; infection from dirty clothing; *see also* 'Pain in crotch' *above*

frontal   friction   turbulence

Fig 38. Air resistance can be frontal, frictional, or due to turbulence.

tri-bar is well demonstrated in ski racing. A wide position is not competitive, creating a hole catching air that works like a parachute to slow the skier down.

Ski racers also keep the hands very close to the face. If the hands are lowered, a second parachute effect is created into the chest.

Taking their cue from the ski racers, cyclists now aim to go narrow and to put the bars in such a position that the head is close to the hands. When tri-bars were introduced, it was feared that the rider's breathing might be impaired. In fact, if anything, breathing is more comfortable in the new position. The advantages gained from a narrow riding position are significant.

approx. area: 0.6m²   approx. area: 0.45m²   approx. area: 0.3m²

Fig 39. The less body area presented to the wind, the less the resistance.

Fig 40. The tri-bar position helps the rider to get both lower and narrower.

(Left) Fig 41. Double world champion Spencer Smith low on his aerobars.

KIT

Shoes and Pedals

Once the triathlete has progressed from the introductory stage of wearing training shoes on the bike section, there is a choice of three main types of pedals and shoes:

1. Toe-clips and straps, with cleats on soles of shoes;
2. Clipless pedals, with a step-in ski-type shoe binding;
3. 'Thompson' type – the pedal has an elongated flat, solid platform fitted to it so that the pedals rather than the shoes are rigid. This enables the triathlete (or, more usually, the duathlete) to compete in the cycling section wearing running shoes without loss of power, and to save time in the transition areas.

These days, traditional toe-clips and straps are less popular than the click-in type pedals and shoes inherited from ski racing.

It is essential that shoes fit properly. The correct fit and match-up will increase pedalling efficiency and power transfer to the wheels, and help pedalling technique. Good shoes will also reduce the possibility of injuries, and the pain and decreased performance that go along with them.

The ball of the foot should be set above the pedal axle and the cleat or click-in should be adjusted to ensure this. If it is too far forward, the rider may suffer calf and toe cramping; if it is too far back, this will create an uneconomical, up-and-down pedal action.

For many triathletes, a major advantage of the clipless pedal system is that it avoids the numbness sometimes associated with the traditional toe-clip system. When the feet were held almost rigid in the early clip-in pedals, local soreness in hips and knees was a problem. This has been largely overcome with the newer pedals, which allow a certain amount of lateral movement in the feet and shoes.

However, toe-clips are still popular with many triathletes and cyclists, and as an added advantage they are small, medium and large, according to shoe size.

What to Wear

First, *get a crash-hat*. In competition you will be disqualified without one; in training, you will just be a mug without one.

During races, most athletes wear the minimum – a swimming costume, vest or maybe a trisuit. Don't be tempted to wear just that in training. Often, you will be cycling more slowly, so you'll need to keep your top warm. Take pity on your crotch! A decent pair of cycle shorts with a chamois or padded insert gives the greater comfort that you'll need when you are out training for a long time.

Other Items

Campagnola make *brake levers* in two sizes, to cater for people with particularly small hands.

A woman's pelvis is wider than a man's, so women may find a slightly wider *saddle* more comfortable.

Crank lengths should be as follows: 175–180mm for long legs, big gears, riding on dual carriageways (also time trialling); 170–172.5mm for normal undulating conditions (also road racing, touring, time trialling); 165 mm for track cycling and riders with very short legs.

PEDALLING

Gears and Cadence (Pedalling Speed)

Gravity, rolling resistance and wind resistance all contrive to stop the cyclist going faster. Good aerodynamic form is essential if at least two of these are to be overcome. Once the rider's aerodynamic form is close to perfect, there are other ways of increasing speed. The obvious one is fitness, but this is useless without the correct choice and use of gears and cadence. The secret of fast cycling is finding the perfect trade-off between the size of the gear used and the speed of pedal revolutions. The two classic mistakes at either end of the spectrum are either electing too big a gear and being forced to pedal so slowly against the high resistance that fatigue is almost immediate; or 'overspinning', that is, selecting so small a gear that, however high the cadence, you will make little progress.

For detailed information on choosing the correct gearing, *see* Chapter 15. It is worth noting that taking into account cadence, speed, heart rate, perceived effort, fatigue and ability to run off the bike, there is no single correct cadence for every athlete.

The following are important points to consider:

- the use of high gears tends to be a strength exercise;
- the recovery rate on low gears is faster than on high gears;
- the constant use of high gears in time trials may restrict the cyclist's ability to compete successfully in triathlon;
- the use of low gears, from a young age, tends to develop suppleness and flexibility in a rider;

Use of Gears in Particular Racing and Training Circumstances

110in plus	Downhill; open dual-carriageways; wind-assisted
90–108in	Steady fast pedalling on open, flat roads in good conditions; wind behind; triathlon, time trial
86–94in	Road racing, some training; triathlon/time trial on undulating roads; track work
70–85in	Road racing (sitting in bunch, coasting); summer/spring, and all hard training
60–65in	Winter; fixed gear for commuting, training, 'getting the miles in', touring; while racing, used for most uphills
50–60in	For steep uphills (1-in-10 or steeper)
50 or less	Very steep slopes

- in time trials, fast rides have been done by some riders using high gears, and these riders have developed an appropriate technique for this purpose; however, triathletes must consider the run afterwards; and
- when in doubt, it is always better to under-gear to start with.

Research on economical cadence (particularly Hagberg, in 1981) has demonstrated a most economical efficiency of between 90 and 100 revolutions per minute (rpm). However, each triathlete is an individual; just because 90 to 100rpm is the norm or median, it is not necessarily appropriate for everybody. Triathletes also have to be able to run when they get off the bike.

During the Tours de France from 1987 to 1993, observers of legendary cyclists Lemond and Indurain – the best in the world at their peak – observed a cadence of 120rpm during the time-trail stages. The results are likely to be more than just coincidence.

One rule of thumb may help individuals to determine their best cadence: if the heart is pounding, the revs are too high; if the leg muscles are crying out for relief, the gear is too big and the revs are too low.

Note: Gear size (in inches) = number of teeth on chainring *divided by* number of teeth on sprocket *multiplied by* size (27in diameter is usual)

For example: 42 *divided by* 14 *multiplied by* 27 = 81in

Training gears are almost always lower than racing gears, to teach quick pedalling. It is preferable (and kinder to knee joints) to use medium gears and pedal quickly than to use large gears and pedal slowly.

It is worth experimenting with the gears. Try a higher gear occasionally, to find out if you can cope with it at the same cadence. It is also worth knowing what speed you are riding at in a particular gear and a particular cadence. For example, in a gear of 42 × 15 at 110rpm, you will be travelling at the same speed (approximately 25mph) as in a gear of 52 × 15 at 90rpm. Similarly, a gear of 52 × 15 at 80rpm gives a speed of just over 22mph, as does 52 × 17 at 90rpm. Experiment and find out what suits you best.

Determining Speed (mph) by Cadence (rpm) and Gearing				
Gear	*Pedal Revolutions per Minute*			
	80	90	100	110
42 × 17	15.9mph	17.9mph	19.9mph	21.9mph
42 × 16	16.9	19.0	21.1	23.2
42 × 15	18.1	20.4	22.6	24.9
42 × 14	19.3	21.7	24.1	26.5
52 × 17	19.8	22.2	24 7	27.2
52 × 16	20.9	23.6	26.2	28.8
52 × 15	22.4	25.2	28.0	30.8
52 × 14	23.8	26.8	29.8	32.8
53 × 16	21.1	23.8	26.5	29.1
53 × 15	22.6	25.4	28.3	31.1
53 × 14	24.3	27.3	30.3	33.4
53 × 13	26.2	29.5	32.7	36.0

(Below) Fig 42. Indication of force output through each phase of the pedal circle. From Hellemans and Baker, *The Winning Edge* (Heinemann 1988).

Pedalling Technique

Novices in cycling and triathlon tend to use a 'piston-type' up-and-down pedalling action. They should persevere in trying to achieve a smoother circular action, which will bring into play the hip flexors and hamstrings rather than relying purely on the quadriceps (front of the thighs) and the gluteal muscles (backside). The onset of fatigue in the quads and the glutes will be delayed, and this is particularly important for triathletes who have to run immediately after getting off the bike.

This technique does not mean that equal pressure will be applied at all times, nor that the return will be equal from each phase of the pedal circle. Figure 42 demonstrates the contribution of propulsive forces from the four main phases of pedalling.

If the athlete is to obtain the maximum from the pedalling technique, a smooth transition between each phase is essential. This will come with experience, from the melding and synchronization of the relevant muscle groups.

Although steep hills will require you to get out of the saddle to climb, relatively easy hills should be attempted by shifting down one or two gears and trying to maintain the same revolutions. Experience will determine when it is better to stand up and work.

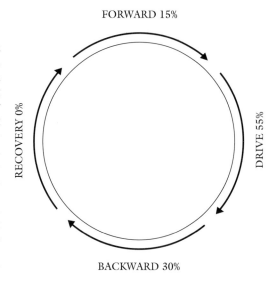

FORWARD 15%

RECOVERY 0%

DRIVE 55%

BACKWARD 30%

OTHER TECHNIQUES

Braking

Normally, both brakes should be applied together and with the same pressure. However, applying the brakes while cornering may make the rear wheel slip away – the action of cornering causes tyre (surface) traction to be reduced and braking and slowing will exaggerate this.

Cornering

It is important to learn good cornering – the less you slow down, the less speed you will need to pick up after the corner. Experience and confidence will help, but the following training tips may contribute to progress:

- if the corner is severe enough to make you stop pedalling, straighten the outside leg and bring the inside foot up;
- keep the weight on the outside pedal, as this will give good friction and traction from tyre to road;
- lean your body and bike into the turn and maintain that position to stop the bike drifting outwards;
- keep the body relaxed (but not so relaxed that you lose control!);
- take extra care in wet or slippery conditions, especially over metalled roads or when rain

over grease has caused very 'slick' conditions; watch out for gravel or loose stones or sand on the road, too;

- the straightest possible line affords the quickest exit and keeps the bike more upright and less likely to slip;
- brake or adjust speed before the bend; braking while cornering, especially if the bike is at an angle to the road, leads to wheel-slip and a possible fall; and
- if there is a sudden uphill just past the corner, change down gear on the approach to the bend and pedal, not at the bottom of the hill.

Climbing Hills

It is better to stay down in a good aerodynamic position on 'easy' climbs, but some hills will cause the rider to get out of the saddle the whole time and some will be 'in-between' (Fig 46).

OPEN ROADS

Fig 43. Go wide before a corner or bend to minimize distance and angle through the corner.

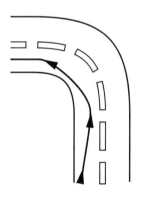
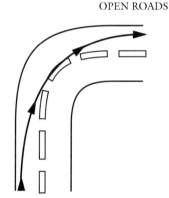

CLOSED CIRCUIT

Fig 44. Similarly on a closed road, go wide before a corner or bend to minimize distance and angle through the corner.

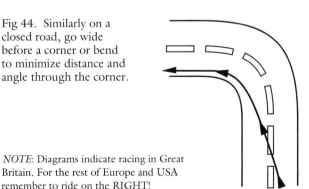
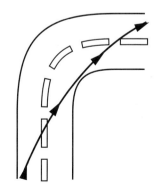

NOTE: Diagrams indicate racing in Great Britain. For the rest of Europe and USA remember to ride on the RIGHT!

Fig 45. Sîan Brice demonstrates clear control and concentration on cornering in a World Cup event.

(Below) Fig 46. One technique for climbing hills is the in and out of the saddle method.

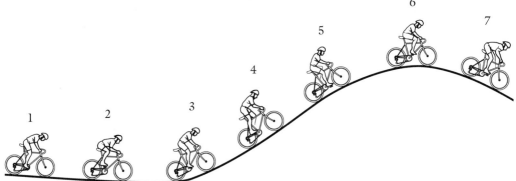

To get up the 'in-between' hill (too easy for the all-out, but too steep to stay in the saddle):

1. approaching the hill, change down to a gear that is suitable for the first part of the hill; continue pedalling;
2. as the bottom of the hill is reached, get out of the saddle and really pedal that gear, to get the bike started up the hill;
3. stay out of the saddle, pushing and pulling pedals round, developing a steady rhythm and breathing correctly;
4. if the hill is long, change down (if needed) and sit well back in the saddle, pulling on handlebars for extra leverage, pushing and pulling pedals;
5. a final out-of-the-saddle spurt will see you over the crest of the hill;

Fig 47. Excellent climbing technique, out of the saddle.

6. take a breather, in the saddle, up a gear, to get your breath back;
7. on the descent, adopt a seated low position, and continue pedalling, changing up a gear where necessary.

TRAINING FOR CYCLING

Cycle training has been slow to adopt new technology and new ideas. There are still many cyclists whose training consists solely of club runs and who rely on racing alone to get themselves fit for more racing. There is some method to this seeming madness. The foundations are laid with the long, steady club runs and, as the time trials and the early-season road races start, riders gradually get fitter and faster purely by racing.

This may be a winning formula, but it is worth looking at it again – some formulae are better than others. For swimming training, the year can be broken up in phases; in running, the different aspects of different types of running training are considered. Amalgamate the two into cycling training by looking at the periodization aspects and technique work of swimming, and breaking down the specific sessions similarly to running.

The training histories of many sports – particularly swimming and running – and the cross-fertilization of ideas have been essential to developments, particularly in cycling. Many cyclists as well as triathletes have recently adopted and adapted the system made popular by Chris Boardman and his coach and mentor Peter Keen, which makes use of a heart rate monitor. Different levels (one, tempo, two, three, four and, occasionally, five) of effort are used to set against heart rates which have been deduced from the respective ramp/increasing demand tests. (Tempo sessions take in a largish range of HRs.)

The table (*see* page 96, top) shows the winter phase of training of a female cyclist. The heart rates and levels of training are appropriate to her; levels and training sessions can be adapted to the heart rate of any athlete.

Having established the guidelines and evaluated the strengths and weaknesses of this particular female athlete, a five-week programme was set (*see* table, page 96 bottom). This phase was towards the end of the off season but, with the first race taking place in the first weekend in March, it may well be viewed as a pre-season phase. After the five-week period, a further session would be added on Thursdays. Mileage would tend to decrease at weekends, but the majority of the programme would remain largely similar, depending upon racing schedule.

Heart Rates and Levels of Intensity

Intensity	Heart Rate Range	Purpose
Level 1	Below 135bpm	Short rides for recovery. Very long aerobic-type, fat-burning sessions.
Tempo	135–165bpm	Development of economy and efficiency with high-volume work. The wide zone is useful for long sessions but the majority of time should be spent below 155bpm.
Level 2	155–165bpm	Development of aerobic capacity with moderate-volume work at a controlled intensity. Normally done alone or with a small group. Can be done on the turbo but there is a risk of boredom.
Level 3	170–180bpm	Raising anaerobic threshold and acclimatization to race speed. Can be done: on a turbo; for controlled periods within a shortened tempo session; or in a 10- or 25-mile time trial.
Level 4	180bpm plus	(Should only be done when rested and recovered.) High-intensity interval training to increase maximum power and improve lactate tolerance. Most conveniently and safely done on a turbo trainer. Heart rates are not necessarily the best accurate guide for this type of intensity work. The training should rely more on perceived effort with the heart rate being used and monitored for feedback.

Pre-Season Phase of Training

Week 1

Monday	Recovery day
Tuesday	35 sprints on turbo
Wednesday	1 hour 45 mins, Level 2 ride (alone or in group)
Thursday	Recovery day
Friday	30 mins continuous Level 3 (turbo or track)
Saturday	3-hour tempo ride (in group)
Sunday	4-hour tempo ride (in group)

Week 2

Monday	Recovery day
Tuesday	40 sprints on turbo
Wednesday	2 hours, Level 2 ride (alone or in group)
Thursday	Recovery day
Friday	30 mins level 2, 15 mins Level 3, 5 mins Level 4, on turbo
Saturday	3-hour tempo ride (in group)
Sunday	4-hour tempo ride (in group)

Week 3

Monday	Recovery day
Tuesday	40 sprints on turbo
Wednesday	2 hours, Level 2 ride (alone or in group)
Thursday	Recovery day
Friday	35 mins continuous Level 3 (turbo or track)
Saturday	3-hour tempo ride (in group)
Sunday	4-hour 30-mins tempo ride (in group)

Week 4

Monday	Recovery day
Tuesday	40 sprints on turbo
Wednesday	2 hours, Level 2 ride (alone or in group)
Thursday	Recovery day
Friday	30 mins Level 2, 15 mins Level 3, 5 mins Level 4, on turbo
Saturday	3-hour tempo ride (in group)
Sunday	5-hour tempo ride (in group)

Week 5 (recovery week)

Monday	Recovery day
Tuesday	1 hour, Level 1
Wednesday	1 hour, Level 1
Thursday	Max test or recovery day
Friday	10 mins continuous Level 3
Saturday	1-hour 20-mins tempo ride (in group)
Sunday	3-hour tempo ride (in group)

CHAPTER 13

Turbo Training for Triathlon

'At some point in training or in a race, suddenly the pain is there and for the first time (since the last time) you remember how hard it can be and how much it is going to hurt.'

Although most triathletes would prefer to train outside all the time, there may be occasions when the weather is too inclement, and it is safer to train indoors on a cycle. The turbo trainer (usually referred to as the turbo, and sometimes called a 'wind load simulator' or 'wind-trainer') is a valuable training tool. Sensible use will pay dividends. One advantage is that there can be no distractions when doing a quality, interval-based training session.

The technology of turbo trainers has improved immensely over the last ten years. A state-of-the-art model may cost over £2000. It will measure everything that can be measured – speed, power output, calories burned – and be able to provide extra resistance to simulate hill climbing. At the other end of the spectrum, a perfectly adequate model may be as little as £50. You usually get what you pay for and not everyone will be able to make best use of the expensive models.

TESTING MHR

When training using a heart rate monitor, your calculations of maximum heart rate (MHR) rate and resting heart rate (RHR) must be accurate. Use either of the following methods for finding MHR on a turbo trainer; alternatively, a flat-out 10- or 25-mile time trial should leave you at MHR. Other methods of calculating MHR are outlined in Chapter 7, Training with a Heart Rate Monitor.

Self-Testing Procedure (Basic Equipment)

(*Note*: this test is extremely demanding and exhausting. Do not attempt it if you are unwell or very unfit. It is much better to have a friend or coach monitor the test with you.)

1. Warm up until heart rate (HR) is constant. Go into big ring and bottom (easiest) gear (e.g. 52 × 22), and pedal at 95rpm for 2 minutes. Note HR at beginning and end of the 2 minutes.
2. Progress up through the gears every 2 minutes. Note HR at beginning and end of every 2 minutes.
3. Eventually, the HR will level out after having risen constantly (although not necessarily consistently) throughout the test. This is probably not MHR.
4. Carry on by getting out of the saddle until exhaustion (this is where you need the friend or coach.)
5. Note down max HR as accurately as possible.
6. Warm down (spin) in easy gear and note HR recovery.

Self-Testing (or Monitored by Exercise Physiologist) Procedure (Using Equipment with Power Output)

1. Warm up until heart rate (HR) is constant.
2. Set and monitor power output at around one-half to two-thirds of what you believe is your maximum; for the purposes of this example the workload is 150 watts. Note HR.

3. Increase the wattage load by 20 every 4 minutes (opinions differ on the timing of each increase). Note HR throughout, as before.
4. Continue until exhaustion.
5. Note down max HR as accurately as possible.
6. Warm down (spin) in easy gear and note HR recovery.

Results

The table below shows the results of an actual testing procedure performed on MEL, an 18-year-old female athlete. Her best time for 25 miles (not in a triathlon) was just outside 1 hour.

The test provided a wealth of information, making it possible to formulate a training schedule that made best use of MEL's strengths and addressed her weaknesses. Her fractional utilization of VO_2max was approximately 65 per cent, VO_2max was 57, and max HR 191bpm. For her cycling HR zones of 140–150 were used for base endurance and 165–170 for her threshold work. This very basic outline paid dividends, resulting in an upward shift in fitness, an increase in fractional utilization and a significant improvement in times over 10, 25 and 50 miles.

SESSIONS USING A HEART RATE MONITOR

In the sessions outlined without using a heart rate monitor, each stage is a progression from the previous stage. Improvements are initiated in either time, repetitions, resistance or time of each individual repetition. Each stage may last a week or a month depending on the individual capability and standard of each triathlete. The starting point will depend on individual fitness. The sessions set out in each stage should be discussed before progressing to the next stage.

Notes: All sessions are based on the assumption that the gearing is a front chainring of 52/42, and a 7-speed rear selection of 13/14/15/16/18/20/22. All training sessions presuppose a warm-up before, and a warm-down at the end of the hard work phase.

Session 1: Lactate Tolerance

This is a 'classic' session given by every triathlon and cycling coach to their athletes. It is close to a time trial on the roads, requires great concentration from the athlete and closely relates to a race situation.

1. Warm up steadily to 80–85 per cent of MHR.
2. Hold this percentage for 40 minutes with 90–110rpm. You will almost certainly need to change gears to maintain this heart rate.

Session 2: Anaerobic Threshold

This demanding session pays dramatic dividends for athletes who persevere with it. It teaches tolerance of discomfort and a return

Example Testing Procedure and Results					
Time (mins)	0–4	4–8	–12	–16	–20	Max –24
Workload (W)	150	170	190	210	230	250 (plus)
Blood lactate (mmol/l)	1.18	1.32	2.01	2.35	3.49	10.20
Heart rate (beats/min)	147	155	161	168	173	191
VO_2 (l/min)	2.08	2.28	2.53	2.74	3.04	4.25
VO_2 (ml/kg/min)	28.5	31.0	34.3	37.3	41.3	57.8

to that discomfort. Using this session, a drop in time of over 10 minutes for a 25-mile time trial has been seen with 'novice' cyclists and triathletes from one season to the next.

1. Warm up to 75 per cent of MHR.
2. Ease back 10 beats per minute (bpm).
3. Go into the large chainring and hold 100rpm until bpm gets to 85 per cent of MHR.
4. Hold at this rate for 30 seconds.
5. Change into small ring until HR drops to 70 per cent of MHR.
6. Repeat 10 times or until HR will not return to 70 per cent of MHR in less than 3 minutes.

Session 3: Progressive Resistance/ Increasing Demand

Hurt … and then hurt a little bit more. Similar to Session 2, but can be even more demanding.

1. Warm up to 75 per cent of MHR, ease back to 70 per cent.
2. Go into large chainring (assume 52 teeth) and 20-tooth sprocket assuming 13/14/ 15/16/18/20/22.
3. Stay in this gearing at 90–100rpm until HR is 80 per cent of MHR.
4. Go into small chainring until HR drops to 70 per cent of MHR.
5. Go into 52 × 18 at 90–100rpm until 80 per cent of MHR is reached.
6. Recover to 70 per cent of MHR.
7. Go into 52 × 17 at 90–100rpm until 85 per cent of MHR is reached, then recover as before.
8. 85 per cent of MHR in 52 × 16.
9. 90 per cent of MHR in 52 × 15.
10. 90 per cent of MHR in 52 × 14.
11. 95 per cent of MHR in 52 × 13.

Session 4: Speed Endurance/Increasing Demand

This session, perhaps even more than Session 1, can simulate the feelings, hurt and discomfort of a road time trial. Many athletes never really dig deep into their reserves; this session teaches them very quickly! It gives an appreciation of just how much more is there after superficial levels of effort have been reached.

1. Warm up to 70–75 per cent of MHR.
2. Go into large chainring; pedal at 80 per cent of MHR for 25 minutes in the appropriate gear at 90–100rpm.
3. Without resting, go up one gear and hold for 20 minutes at 85 per cent MHR.
4. As before, go up one gear and hold for 15 minutes at 90 per cent MHR.

Session 5: Hills (With or Without Heart Rate Monitor)

If the turbo trainer has the facility to add resistance and/or to simulate hills, it may be more appropriate to set the resistance rather than choose the biggest gear. (For instance, the setting may be at about 5 per cent gradient with the gearing set at 52 × 19. This gives rpm of between 60 and 80 for most athletes.)

Many triathletes and cyclists are weak on hills, sometimes because of the terrain where they live or sometimes because they do not relish hillwork outside on the road. Either way, the athlete who is weak on hills is at a distinct disadvantage.

The increasing time spent out of the saddle on each succeeding repetition is far more difficult than working for, for example, ten sets of 1 minute with a minute recovery.

1. Warm up.
2. Go into 52 × 13 and pedal flat out for 1 minute, out of the saddle.
3. Recover for 1 minute in easy gear.
4. As before in 52 × 13 but hold for 2 minutes, recover for 1 minute.
5. Repeat for 3, 4, and 5 minutes.

These sessions provide a starting point; others are available. Triathletes will quickly work out their weak and strong points and add or subtract from the training sessions accordingly.

TURBO SESSIONS WITHOUT A HEART RATE MONITOR

When using these sessions, it is essential to be realistic about the gearing needed. The gears suggested are only examples. You need to find the correct starting point – perhaps 22 or 18 rather than 20 – and progress from that starting point.

The sessions below have been used with a great deal of success with a number of triathletes of very different standards and abilities, particularly in the latter part of the winter going into the early season (January to April/May). Each stage lasts between two and three weeks and is best used in conjunction with one or more long outdoor rides and the HRM sessions. A senior élite triathlete used these sessions for a period of six months before the inaugural world triathlon championships in Avignon, France in 1989, and was rewarded with a top-five cycle split time and a top-twenty placing in the élite women.

The entire philosophy – not necessarily innovative – behind these sessions is that of increasing demand. A huge number of

triathletes and time-trial cyclists have not exploited their potential because they have never tried such basic interval work.

In an endurance sport like triathlon, a strictly restricted interval of rest and recovery between efforts is important. The recovery interval here is mostly 1 minute, rarely more. Where it is longer, athletes will certainly have earned it. Work effort times range from 1 minute to 18 minutes. Individuality remains paramount: not every athlete has to achieve this; nor is it expected that all athletes will stay on a particular stage for the same amount of time before moving on to the next.

All the sessions can be done on the road, and most active cyclists and triathletes would probably prefer this. However, the conditions existing on all but the most rural of roads mean that turbo training is here to stay. When athletes are self-monitoring their training efforts, looking down and checking heart rates, speed, leg cadence and power output, the open road is not the best place to be.

All training sessions presuppose a warm-up and warm-down.

Progressive Turbo Sessions

STAGE 1 (Introductory)

Session 1
5 reps of 52 × 20 for 1 min, aim for 100rpm
Recovery: 42 × 20 for 1 min at 60rpm

Session 2
7 reps of 52 × 20 for 1 min, aim for 100rpm
Recovery: 42 × 20 for 1 min at 60rpm

Session 3
10 reps of 52 × 20 for 1 min, aim for 100rpm
Recovery: 42 × 20 for 1 min at 60 rpm

Session 4
5 reps of 52 × 20 for 2 mins, aim for 100rpm
Recovery: 42 × 20 for 1 min at 60 rpm

STAGE 2

Session 1
5 reps of 52 × 18 for 2 mins, aim for 100rpm
Recovery: 42 × 18 for 1 min at 60rpm

Fig 48. Gary Gerrard drinking during a turbo session.

Session 2
10 reps of 52 × 18 for 1 min, aim for 100rpm
  Recovery: 42 × 18 for 1 min at 60rpm

Session 3
7 reps of 52 × 18 for 2 mins, aim for 100rpm
  Recovery: 42 × 18 for 1 min at 60rpm

Session 4
5 reps of 52 × 20 for 3 mins, aim for 100rpm
  Recovery: 42 × 20 for 1 min at 60rpm

STAGE 3

Session 1
7 reps of 52 × 16 for 2 mins, aim for 100rpm
  Recovery: 42 × 16 for 1 min at 60rpm

Session 2
15 reps of 52 × 18 for 1 min, aim for 100rpm
  Recovery: 42 × 18 for 1 min at 60rpm

Session 3
4 reps of 52 × 20 for 2 mins, aim for 100rpm
  Then straight into 52 × 18 for 2 mins, aim
for 100 rpm
  Recovery: 42 × 20 for 1 min at 60rpm after
each 4-minute effort

Session 4
3 reps of 52 × 20 for 2 mins, aim for 100rpm
  Then straight into 52 × 18 for 2 mins, aim
for 100rpm
  Then straight into 52 × 16 for 1 min, aim
for 100rpm
  Recovery: 42 × 20 for 1 min at 60rpm after
each 5-minute effort

STAGE 4

Session 1
3 reps of : 52 × 18 for 3 mins, aim for 100rpm
  Then straight into 52 × 16 for 2 mins, aim
for 100rpm
  Then straight into 52 × 15 for 1 min, aim
for 100rpm
  Recovery: 42 × 20 for 1 min at 60rpm after
each 6-minute effort

Session 2
12 reps of 52 × 16 for 1 min, aim for 100rpm
  Recovery: 52 × 22 for 1 min at 60rpm

Session 3
3 reps of 52 × 20 for 4 mins, aim for 100rpm
  Then straight into 52 × 18 for 3 mins, aim
for 100rpm
  Then straight into 52 × 16 for 2 mins, aim
for 100rpm
  Recovery: 42 × 20 for 1 min at 60rpm after
each 9-min effort

Session 4
10 reps of 52 × 18 for 2 mins, aim for 100rpm
  Recovery: 42 × 18 for 1 min at 60rpm

STAGE 5

Session 1
2 reps of 52 × 22 for 2 mins, aim for 100rpm
  Then straight into 52 × 20 for 2 mins, aim
for 100rpm
  Then straight into 52 × 18 for 2 mins, aim
for 100rpm
  Then straight into 52 × 16 for 2 mins, aim
for 100rpm
  Then straight into 52 × 15 for 2 mins, aim
for 100rpm
  Then straight into 52 × 14 for 2 mins, aim
for 100rpm
  Recovery: 42 × 22 for 2 mins at 60rpm after
first set of 12 mins effort

Session 2
15 reps of 52 × 16 for 1 min, aim for 100rpm
  Recovery: 52 × 22 for 1 min at 60rpm

Session 3
3 reps of 52 × 20 for 3 mins, aim for 100rpm
  Then straight into 52 × 18 for 3 mins, aim
for 100rpm
  Then straight into 52 × 16 for 3 mins, aim
for 100rpm
  Recovery: 42 × 22 for 2 mins at 60 rpm
after each set of 9 mins effort.

Session 4
8 reps of 52 × 16 for 2 mins, aim for 100rpm
  Recovery: 52 × 22 for 1 min at 60rpm

STAGE 6

Session 1

1 rep of 52 × 20 for 4 mins, aim for 100rpm
  Recovery: 52 × 22 for 1 min at 60rpm

1 rep of 52 × 18 for 4 mins, aim for 100rpm
  Recovery: 52 × 22 for 1 min at 60rpm

1 rep of 52 × 17 for 4 mins, aim for 100rpm
  Recovery: 52 × 22 for 1 min at 60rpm

1 rep of 52 × 16 for 4 mins, aim for 100rpm
  Recovery: 52 × 22 for 1 min at 60rpm

1 rep of 52 × 15 for 4 mins, aim for 100rpm
  Recovery: 52 × 22 for 1 min at 60rpm

1 rep of 52 × 14 for 4 mins, aim for 100rpm
  Recovery: 52 × 22 for 1 min at 60rpm

Session 2
15 reps of 52 × 15 for 1 min, aim for 100rpm
  Recovery: 52 × 22 for 1 min at 60rpm

Session 3
3 reps of 52 × 17 for 4 mins, aim for 100rpm
  Then straight into 52 × 16 for 4 mins, aim
for 100rpm
  Then straight into 52 × 15 for 4 mins, aim
for 100rpm
  Recovery: 52 × 22 for 2 mins at 60rpm after
each set of 12 mins

Session 4
8 reps of 52 × 15 for 2 mins, aim for 100rpm
  Recovery: 52 × 22 for 1 min at 60rpm

STAGE 7

Session 1
1 rep of 52 × 18 for 8 min, aim for 100rpm
  Recovery: 52 × 22 for 2 mins at 60rpm

1 rep of 52 × 17 for 8 min, aim for 100rpm
  Recovery: 52 × 22 for 2 mins at 60rpm

1 rep of 52 × 16 for 8 min, aim for 100rpm
  Recovery: 52 × 22 for 2 mins at 60rpm

1 rep of 52 × 15 for 8 mins, aim for 100rpm
  Recovery: 52 × 22 for 2 mins at 60rpm

1 rep of 52 × 14 for 8 mins, aim for 100rpm
  Recovery: 52 × 22 for 2 mins at 60rpm

Session 2
15 reps of 52 × 14 for 1 min, aim for 100rpm
  Recovery: 52 × 22 for 1 min at 60rpm

Session 3
3 reps of 52 × 17 for 6 mins, aim for 100rpm
  Then straight into 52 × 16 for 6 mins, aim
for 100rpm
  Then straight into 52 × 15 for 6 mins, aim
for 100rpm
  Recovery: 52 × 22 for 2 mins at 60rpm after
each set of 18 mins

Session 4
10 reps of 52 × 14 for 2 mins, aim for
100rpm.
  Recovery: 52 × 22 for 1 min at 60rpm

ADVANCED SESSIONS

In addition to the turbo trainer sessions
above, a number of 'exploratory/advanced'
sessions have proved successful with experienced triathletes. These may be used when:

- triathletes have been invited to compete
  out of season and have been unable to get
  in sufficient quantity and quality work outside on the road due to bad weather;
- triathletes have been unable – however
  hard they think they are working – to raise
  their heart rate to that which they think is
  commensurate with the amount of work
  they are putting in; or
- (with experienced triathletes of a high standard only), when athletes have been away
  from training for whatever reason, but
  need to get back to a good standard of fitness very quickly in order to fulfill racing
  commitments.

Health Warning! The following sessions are
not recommended for inexperienced triathletes and are not a short-cut to success. As

Fig 49. David Giles leads a group turbo session.

with any aspect of training, trying to do too much quality too soon, without sufficient basework, can lead to injury. However, the sessions can add variety to training and may also be used when the weather means that outside road riding is dangerous or impossible for a significant amount of time.

Session 1

1. Warm up, going through gears progressively for 2 mins each: 42 × 22 for 2 mins, 42 × 20 for 2 mins, 42 × 18 up to 42 × 13, then change to 52 × 22, and repeat up to 52 × 13. This in itself is a good hard session for many triathletes.
2. Spin 5 mins.
3. 7 sets of 52 × 13 for 1 min followed by 52 × 14 for 2 mins.
4. 1 min recovery only between each 3-min effort.
5. Spin for 10 minutes.

Session 2

1. Warm up with 10-min spin.
2. 10 reps of 52 × 13 for 1 min (recovery is 1 min between effort).
3. 3-min spin followed by 10 mins at 52 × 15.
4. 3-min spin followed by 1 min at 52 × 13 (1 min recovery).
5. 2 mins at 52 × 13 (1 min recovery).
6. 3 mins at 52 × 13 (1 min recovery).
7. 3-min spin.
8. Repeat above.
9. Spin for 10 mins.

Session 3

1. Warm up – 10-min spin, then 5 sets of 1 min right leg only, 1 min both legs, 1 min left leg only, 1 min both legs.
2. 4 sets of 52 × 15 (1 min), 52 × 14 (2 mins), 52 × 13 (3 mins); total 6 mins.

3. Allow 2 mins recovery between each 6 mins effort.
4. Spin for 10 mins.

Session 4

1. Warm up by going through the gears progressively for 2 mins each.
2. Spin for 5 mins.
3. Prolonged hill session, all done in the hardest gear that can be handled (usually 52 × 13); if the turbo trainer has percentage hill resistance, use it accordingly.
4. 1 min out of the saddle followed by 1 min sitting.
5. 2 mins out of the saddle followed by 2 mins sitting.
6. 3 mins out of the saddle followed by 3 mins sitting.
7. 4 mins out of the saddle followed by 4 mins sitting.
8. 5 mins out of the saddle followed by 5 mins sitting.
9. Spin for 10 mins.

Session 5

1. Warm up by going through the gears progressively for two mins each, on small ring (42) only.
2. 52 × 22 for 1 min.
3. 52 × 20 for 1 min. Recovery 52 × 22 for 1 min.
4. 52 × 18 for 2 mins. Recovery 52 × 22 for 1 min.
5. 52 × 16 for 3 mins. Recovery 52 × 22 for 1 min.
6. 52 × 15 for 4 mins. Recovery 52 × 22 for 1 min.
7. 52 × 14 for 5 mins. Recovery 52 × 22 for 1 min.
8. 52 × 13 for 6 mins. Recovery 52 × 22 for 1 min.
9. 52 × 13 for 1 min. Recovery 52 × 22 for 1 min.
10. 52 × 14 for 2 mins. Recovery 52 × 22 for 1 min.
11. 52 × 15 for 3 mins. Recovery 52 × 22 for 1 min.
12. 52 × 16 for 4 mins. Recovery 52 × 22 for 1 min.

13. 52 × 18 for 5 mins. Recovery 52 × 22 for 1 min.
14. 52 × 20 for 6 mins. Recovery 52 × 22 for 1 min.
15. Spin for 10 mins.

Session 6

Both this session and Session 7 are used to try and adapt experienced triathletes to pushing big gears, while trying to maintain a reasonable cadence so that they are still able to run efficiently off the bike.

1. Warm up 10 mins at 100rpm.
2. 52 × 13 for 1 min at 43–45kph (27–28mph) or max HR less 20 beats; straight into 1 min at 110rpm in whatever gear is needed to maintain speed or HR.
3. Straight into 52 × 13 for 2 mins at 43–45kph or max HR less 20 beats; straight into 2 mins at 110rpm in whatever gear is needed to maintain speed or HR.
4. Straight into 52 × 13 for 3 mins at 43–45kph or max HR less 20 beats; straight into 3 mins at 110rpm in whatever gear is needed to maintain speed or HR.
5. Recover 2 mins and repeat once or twice.

Session 7

1. Warm up 10 mins at 100rpm.
2. 52 × 13 for 5 mins at 43–45kph or max HR less 20 beats; straight into 1 min at 110rpm in whatever gear is needed to maintain same intensity
3. Recover for 2–3 mins.
4. Then 5 mins at 110rpm at 43–45kph or max HR less 20 beats; straight into 52 × 13 for 1 min at the same intensity.
5. Recover for 2–3 mins.
6. Then repeat 2, 3 and 4.

There are literally hundreds of different combinations that can be used to make up turbo sessions. The above examples have proved successful; they are mostly very demanding, both physically and mentally.

MORE VARIETY

The five sessions below have been used with triathletes of very different standards, particularly in the off season and when there is a need for a slight change in emphasis or to alleviate boredom. The emphasis here is on smoothness and 'supplesse'. Think 'smooth as silk'.

Session 1

1. Warm up 10 mins.
2. 30secs/40/50/60/1.10mins/1.20/1.30/1.40/1.50/2 mins and then come back down at five HR beats below anaerobic threshold, all at 100–110rpm.
3. Take 20 seconds spin in between.
4. Warm down 10 mins.

Session 2

1. Warm up 10 mins.
2. Single legs, right at 30 secs, then left at 30 secs, then right and left at 60 secs, 1 min 30 seconds, and 2 mins all with 1 min in between, and then come back down.
3. Warm down 10 mins.

Session 3

1. Warm up 10 mins.
   Alternate 1 min only at whatever gear you can hold 130rpm, with your biggest gear (52 × 13?), smoothly and sitting down.
2. Take 1 min recovery between reps and repeat 6 times on each gear.
3. Warm down 10 mins.

Session 4

1. Start in your smallest gear (42 × 21/23?) and work for 8 mins at 110rpm.
2. Go straight into the next gear up (42 × 19?) and work for 7 mins.
3. Then go into 42 × 18 for 6 mins, right up to 42 × 13.
4. Try to maintain at least 100rpm right the way through.

If you are feeling like a superstar, come back down again.

Session 5

1. Start in your smallest gear (42 × 21/23?) but work for 2 mins only at 110rpm.
2. Then go straight into the next gear up (42 × 19?) and work for 2 mins again.
3. Then go into 42 × 18 for 2 mins, right up to 42 × 13.
4. Try to maintain at least 100rpm right the way through.
5. Then go into the big chainring and start again at 52 × 23.
6. Warm down 10 mins.

POWER AND SPRINT SESSIONS

The above turbo sessions are geared towards standard-distance triathlon or 10-, 25- or 50-mile time-trial cycling, so none of them includes any periods of work of less than one minute. However, there are situations where extreme power and breakaway-type sprint speed are required. In draft-legal races, power to get away from the pack is needed; in non-drafting races, with large numbers of athletes and bunching at the start, race marshals will be looking for misdemeanours, and you need to break away from a potentially precarious situation.

Session 1: Short Sprints

Short sprint sessions will improve ability and efficiency to increase speed quickly when necessary. After warming up and gradually increasing speed to around 65 or 70 per cent of max HR, go into a big gear of between 52 × 13 and 52 × 17 (as appropriate for the individual athlete) and go flat out for 5 seconds only. Recover for 10 seconds only and repeat the effort.

After three or four sprint efforts, HR should be at approximately 85 per cent of max and will remain constant at this level. If HR rises significantly higher than this, increase the recovery time. Equally, if HR does not reach 85 per cent of max, decrease the recovery period. The sprint efforts must remain at 5 seconds only, and under no circumstances should exceed 8 seconds.

Fig 50. World junior silver medallist Lesley Paterson.

1. Warm up.
2. Sprint flat out (big gear) for 5 seconds.
3. Recover 10 seconds only.
4. Repeat the above ten times.
5. Easy recovery for 1 min.
6. Repeat all above, so that 40 × 5-second sprints are done.

Although the efforts are very short, this is an extremely demanding session as the HR does not have very much time to decrease in the 10-second recovery intervals. Beginners may wish to start with 5 × 5 seconds and repeat 3 times or similar.

Most accurate efforts and recoveries are achieved by using a pre-set interval timer set at the appropriate times.

Session 2: Longer Sprints

1. Warm up and then select the gear that is slightly 'too big' (feel as if you are having to make an effort to handle the gear).
2. Sprint flat out for 15 seconds.
3. Recover to 70 per cent max HR.
4. Repeat 5 to 10 times.

For both sprint sessions, as efforts are analactic/anaerobic, the HR will continue to rise after 5- and 15- second efforts for a short time. This should not be a matter for concern.

Turbo training is one of the most significant tools for both cycling and triathlon and has played an important role in the recent rise in standards in the sport. It is one of the most worthwhile investments that the athlete can make.

CHAPTER 14

Running

'If you can fill the unforgiving minute, with 60 seconds worth of distance run, yours is this world and everything that's in it.'

Many aspiring triathletes come into the sport from a running background; indeed, almost everybody has run at some time in their lives. Of the three disciplines, running is the least complicated, *but* the sensation of putting one foot in front of the other after having swum and then having cycled for an hour only remotely resembles the smooth flowing action previously experienced in single-sport running. The circular motion of cycling, with the blood pooling in the cycling muscles, is not the best warm-up for a 10-km run. The fatigue that triathletes bring into a run may often be severe. The ability to overcome that fatigue and to run fast and efficiently can be a major factor in successfully completing an event in an acceptable time.

'There's a lot of great runners humbled when they get off the bike.' (Dave Scott, six-time Hawaii Ironman winner)

There are no short-cuts to becoming a good triathlon runner. Technique, speed, strength, and mobility training, together with an awareness of the specific requirements of triathlon running, will lead to longer and faster performances.

SPEED

'If speed is the name of the game, don't get too far away from it.' (Peter Coe, Coach to Olympic gold medallist runners)

When triathletes with similar levels of aerobic and anaerobic endurance compete against each other going into the final discipline, it is usually their basic running speed that decides the outcome. Speed is an essential attribute for any endurance event and it is as important to develop this aspect of fitness as it is to develop stamina.

Running speed is related to how fast the legs move and how much distance is covered with each stride:

Speed = stride length × stride rate

Clearly, an increase in length of the stride will lead to increased speed, provided that the rate

Fig 51. World University Champion Jodi Swallow maintains her form in the final stages of a race.

of striding does not slow. Alternatively, an increase in cadence will have the same result, provided that the stride length remains constant (*see also* Chapter 15). Success in improving this will be largely governed by range of movement in the joints and strength in the running muscle groups.

TECHNIQUE

Running is the most simple of the three disciplines, but it is the only discipline in which the athletes carry their own body weight and remain relatively unprotected from the forces of gravity. These forces are quadrupled when we are running and will by necessity increase the likelihood of injury with the strains and stresses on the bones, tendons, muscles and joints of the legs, hips and feet.

The technique of endurance running is a modification of sprinting. As relaxation and saving energy are so important in triathlon, the action of running has to be more compact in order to eliminate unnecessary expenditure of energy.

As with the arms in swimming, there is a propulsive phase and a recovery phase with the legs in running. The propulsive phase starts as soon as the foot makes contact with the ground during a running stride. The whole of the body weight is carried by the foot as the hips and trunk pass over the foot, and the hip, knee and ankle stretch out to push the runner forwards.

The recovery phase begins with the foot breaking contact with the ground. The foot is pulled upwards to the backside and the thigh swings forward and through until it is parallel, or nearly parallel, to the ground. The lower part of the leg then comes forwards as the thigh begins to move downwards. The whole leg then sweeps backwards and downwards until the foot strikes the ground again.

The upper body remains upright or leaning slightly forwards. The arm action is often forgotten, but it should match the leg action, with the left arm coming forward at the same time as the right leg and vice versa, in an equal and opposite action and reaction. The arm movement should be kept relaxed and rhythmic, moving backwards and forwards in a

Fig 52. Sami Williams shows excellent rear leg lift.

straight line with the hands loosely cupped and the thumbs resting on the fingers. You will almost certainly feel tight and stiff at some point during the run. Rolling the neck and the head around from time to time, and shaking out the arms may overcome this.

SKILLS AND MOBILITY

Running at a good speed has to be learnt if it is to be done efficiently. Millions of people may run every day, but running is still a skill that can be improved by attention to detail. A complex movement, it cannot be learnt in one piece, just by running fast – that would simply reinforce existing faults.

Drills

Drills designed to develop the running action are commonly used by sprinters. Triathletes are not sprinters but, in order to run fast in races, they should explore every possible advantage that can be gained. Good execution of drills requires co-ordination and balance; the actions may have to be learnt initially by working through each one separately in slow motion. Drills isolate and concentrate on only one aspect of running at a time and are carried out for very short distances, usually between 40 and 100m.

Some fundamental learning principles have to be observed and a tired, stiff or injured triathlete should not be embarking upon new drills.

The most important components of the running action are the following:

- high lift of the thigh;
- paw down and back of the lead leg;
- full extension of the rear leg;
- full and straight range of arm movement; and
- high kick back.

Many track runners at all distances will incorporate the following drills into their warm-up in order to try to establish the above components.

1. *Long rear leg:* make a singular effort to push the ground away and to leave the foot in contact with the ground a fraction longer than usual.
2. *High knee action:* pull the knees higher than usual while still trying to maintain an erect body position.
3. *Leg reach out:* as the lower leg reaches forward, push it slightly further and then consciously pull the foot back to strike the ground.
4. *Bounding:* exaggerate the entire running action and slow it down, lifting high between steps and floating between foot-plants.
5. *High arms:* exaggerate the forward lift of the arms; the opposite leg will follow and lift higher.
6. *Rear arms:* as you run down the track, pull the elbows backwards and upwards without lifting the shoulders.
7. *Close arms:* keep the elbows close to the sides of the body while running, with the arms swinging backwards and forwards.

Most or all of the above drills are done at the start of track running sessions.

It is possible and, indeed, advisable sometimes to do a running session just concentrating on these drills. This might perhaps be a series of $8 \times 100\text{m}$ repetitions concentrating on just four of the drills, and repeating each one twice. A coach might set the occasional session with 60×100 repetitions, broken down into sets of 10 or 20, and playing around with combinations of drills and flat-out sprinting, and allocating the rest and recovery intervals accordingly.

Many triathlons are won and lost on the running phase, not through a lack of stamina but rather because of an inability to accept the challenge of another athlete running past. Every athlete must be prepared to accept that challenge, and must learn during training sessions how to cope with the sensation of increasing speed when tired.

Mobility

Strength and mobility play an important part in the length and speed of the stride when running. With a busy training schedule, some aspects – usually mobility – can easily be neglected. Triathletes have an advantage over pure runners as their more complex schedules in three separate sports do give greater mobility. However, it should be remembered that mobility naturally decreases from the late teens unless remedial action is taken. Mobility work should be done at every training session during the warm-up and warm-down.

The degree to which triathletes can develop their running action will depend to some extent on their mobility through a wide range of movement. Without sufficient mobility in the joints that are used in running, a shortened stride length and a poor technique are likely. A good running technique involves the flexion and extension of the ankle, knee, hip and elbow joints, and some rotation in the joints. Poor mobility inhibits this flexion and extension and can also increase the likelihood of damage to muscles, tendons, ligaments and other connective tissue as the athlete attempts to exceed the normal range of movement. Stresses can also accumulate as extra work is placed on muscles, in order to accommodate a lack of mobility.

Good mobility is particularly important for triathlon, as it encourages efficient movement in the last discipline of a race when cumulative fatigue is being felt by the competitor. A good level of mobility will reduce energy demands.

Mobility work can be divided into active exercises (when athletes stretch their own muscles) and passive exercises (when athletes allow a partner to stretch their muscles for them). For passive stretching, the partner must be aware of the dangers of forcing a muscle to stretch too far. Swinging and bouncing warm-up exercises are not recommended, as they can actually cause injury rather than prevent it. When performing stretching exercises, the athlete should slowly stretch out as far as possible and then hold that position for a count of 10 seconds before slowly relaxing and then repeating.

Experienced athletes in many sports are able to concentrate on relaxing the muscle even while stretching it. Mobility exercises will feel more comfortable if they are performed after an easy jog, which will raise the temperature of the body.

Fig 53. Joanna Hinde maintains form during a gruelling training session.

SHOES

A good pair of shoes is essential to avoid injury. Some studies might claim that barefoot running is the most natural and the best way to avoid injury, but it is too late for people who have worn shoes since childhood.

The correct running shoe for each athlete is a matter of individual choice and correct fit. Shoes are straight, slightly curved and curved. Curved shoes tend to give better mobility to the foot while straight shoes tend to give better support.

The shoe will be board-lasted (normally the heavier training shoes), slip-lasted (normally the lighter racing shoes), or a combination of both, with the board-lasting from heel to mid-foot. Triathletes who do most of their running training in a heavier shoe should beware of

Requirements from Running Training

- Oxygen uptake: using more oxygen from the air breathed in
- Oxygen debt tolerance: being able to keep running fast after the oxygen requirements have exceeded the oxygen intake
- Technique: an economical technique (with economy of movement) reduces oxygen requirements
- Speed: the ability to sprint/run fast/up the pace
- Using fat as a fuel as well as/rather than carbohydrate
- Endurance: the ability to keep going

What Affects Speed?

- Leg strength
- Range of leg movement (mobility)
- Stride length
- Cadence (leg speed)
- Training
- Body fat

Types of Running Training

- Steady state running – short, medium, long distance
- Fartlek – structured, unstructured
- Intervals – short, long. What rest?
- Repetitions – short, long. What rest?
- Hills – slope, distance, recovery
- Tempo running – surging
- Differentials – increasing speed, zig-zag runs
- Time trials – what distance?
- Resistance running – hills, weighted, water, sand
- Triathlon running – is there a difference?

racing in a lighter, slip-lasted shoe without having worn them in training. There can be a significant difference in foot-plant with a new shoe, and differences in weight and construction may well slow down the novice triathlete.

New runners should also work out whether they are pronators (the ankle pushing inwards on the foot-plant), neutral runners (straight on the foot-plant), or supinators (the ankle pushing outwards on the foot-plant). While the majority of runners and triathletes are pronators or neutral runners, it is worth finding out whether orthotics are appropriate to correct excessive foot motion. Most good sports shops will take time and trouble to ensure that you are fitted properly according to your needs. Properly fitting shoes are essential to make running enjoyable and to avoid injury.

BUILDING A PROGRAMME

For the novice triathlete with little experience of competitive running, the initial progression must be made slowly; this may be frustrating, but it will lessen the chance of injury. It takes months and years rather than days and weeks for the body to become accustomed to the jarring impact of hard running. Increase each week's training gradually, but be prepared to put in both easy and rest weeks. Accept that you are an individual. Listen to your body for early warning signs of injury and back off. If you do get slightly injured, treat it as a potential major injury and you will recover more quickly.

The following sample programme is suitable for the new runner/triathlete (assuming some fitness from swimming and/or cycling). It should not be followed blindly (*see* provisos above).

Weeks 1 and 2
3 easy runs of 6.5km (4 miles) or 30 minutes

Weeks 3 and 4
2 easy runs of 6.5km or 30 minutes, 1 run of 9.5km (6 miles) or 45 mins

Weeks 5 and 6
2 easy runs of 6.5km or 30 minutes, 1 run of 13km (8 miles) or 60 mins

Weeks 7 and 8
3 easy runs of 6.5km or 30 minutes, 1 run of 9.5km or 45 mins

Fig 54. Annelle Rabie, hill training above Stellenbosch, South Africa.

Testing for 10km Speed Requirements

Run for 15 mins as hard as you can – on a running track if possible.
Record the exact distance covered (for example, 3000m).

The Programme
1. Run twice the distance recorded (for example, 6000m) in double the time plus 10 per cent or 3 mins (33 mins). Aim to reduce this by 1 min every six weeks. This session should be done twice within each phase of training.
2. Run half the distance (for example, 1500m) in 7.5 mins with 1 min rest between the three efforts. You may need to take more rest to begin with on this programme. Aim to reduce the time or increase the distance by 15–20 seconds or 70–100m every six weeks.
3. Find pace from the timed run (for example, 2 mins for each 400m). Halve this (60 seconds) and take off another 8 seconds to find 200m pace (52 seconds). Run a series of 200m in 52 seconds with reducing rest. Start at 90 seconds, then 75, 60, 45, 30, 15 seconds; start again at 90 seconds and keep going until you cannot maintain 52-second pace.
4. Run overdistance: start at 10km (6 miles) plus a third (13km or 8 miles) and gradually work up to double the distance (20km or 12 miles). Do not run hard.
5. Hills/resistance and strength work. Run 10km with half of the distance (5km) up hills. If this is not possible, do hill repetitions. Work hard on the hills and jog the recovery.

With two runs on the first session, there are six sessions in all before the phase is repeated. For example, if the athlete runs three times each week, the entire programme is repeated three times before re-testing is done at the end of a six-week period.

Weeks 9 and 10
3 easy runs of 6.5km or 30 minutes, 1 run of 13km or 60 mins

Weeks 11 and 12 (recovery weeks)
3 easy runs of 5–6km (3 or 4 miles)

Weeks 13 and 14
3 runs of 6.5km, 1 run of 16km (10 miles)

Weeks 15 and 16
2 runs of 6.5km, 1 fast 6.5km run, 1 run of 16km

Weeks 17 and 18
2 runs of 6.5km, 1 fartlek 6.5km run, 1 run of 16km

Weeks 19 and 20
2 runs of 10km, 1 run of 16km, first structured interval-type session; after warm-up, 6 × 2-min efforts with 1-min jog between

Weeks 21 and 22
2 runs of 10km, 1 run of 19km (12 miles), second structured interval-type session; after warm-up, 8 × 2-min efforts with 1-min jog between

Weeks 23 and 24 (recovery weeks)
3 easy runs of 30 mins each week

Weeks 25 and 26
2 runs of 10km (one easy, one fast), 1 long run of 19km plus third structured interval-type session; after warm-up, 6 × 3-min efforts with 90 seconds jog between

Don't do too much too soon!

In the above schedule (a real example, used by a cyclist-turned-triathlete), the triathlete progresses from 19km (12 miles) of easy running per week to around 48km (30 miles), with a mixture of speed, easy runs, effort and endurance. It takes six months to achieve this and includes two periods of recovery running. It should be achievable by most reasonably fit people, but the time factor will be extremely variable.

Once a base programme has been established, some running fitness gained, and per-haps some weight lost, triathletes will want to be more specific to their individual needs and start to build some structure into their programme. After the initial steady state running of building up a base distance, the essential ingredients will be steady running at near to race pace, hill running, long (overdistance) runs, and some form of interval or repetition running.

The requirements of triathlon, with its three disciplines, may mean that fitting in all aspects of running within one week's schedule is nearly impossible for most people. You may need to plan your training programme over ten days, two weeks or even a month. However, having stated all that, it is satisfying to know that every day of the week does have fixed requirements for training, for example every Tuesday evening is hill repetitions.

The specific, testing programme below has been used in the run-up to the racing season with some success. It seems to work particularly well over a six-week period.

Triathletes beginning to experiment with interval-type training should see the table on page 114 for the sort of recovery interval times they should be aiming at. Recovery times may seem very short to begin with, but triathlon is endurance-based. The running element comes at the end of the race and recovery times for all but speed work should be restricted. The times given are merely examples, but the ratio between efforts and resting intervals are the important thing.

FIVE-PACE TRAINING

Many triathletes believe that they do not need to vary running training sessions. Their theory is that, as running is the final discipline, the ability to keep going is more important than speed. This may be true at entry level, but at a more competitive level, varying the sessions and including a variety of paced efforts spread through the training cycle will not only make you faster, but it will also help to offset the fatigue experienced during the run. The better the athlete's 10-km time, the better the times over 800m, 1500m, 3000m, 5000m, 10 miles and the half-marathon should be.

Pace and Recovery Times for Interval and Repetition Running Training

Pace of Repetition	Distance of Repetition	Time (mins)	Recovery Jog	Recovery Time
5000m	4 × 1600m	5.10	200m (eighth)	1 min (fit); 90 secs (unfit)
3000m	6 × 1000m	3.05	250m (quarter)	75 secs (fit); 2 mins (unfit)
1500m	6 × 600m	1.40	300m (half)	90 secs (fit); 2 mins (unfit)
800m	4 × 400m	1.05	400m (same)	2 mins (fit); 3 mins (unfit)
400m	8 × 200m	0.30	400m (double)	2 mins (fit); 3 mins (unfit)

These times were attempted by a senior male athlete over a 5-week period in May/June before a major race. He had previously run a low 34-minute 10km, but he seemed to be capable of 2 to 3 minutes faster, with the appropriate training. It is worth examining this principle further.

The essentials are:

1. to race the distances; and
2. to train at those speeds on a regular basis.

Using the examples in the table above, and the advice on equivalent times for equivalent distances (*see* page 116), it is possible to make significant increases in speed in one season.

The schedule below works very well, but it should not be attempted by anybody who does not have a good background, is fit, and is prepared to suffer. There are twelve training sessions during each cycle of training; a four-times-a-week runner can attempt this over a three-week cycle, a three-times-a-week runner over four weeks.

Session 1
19km (12 miles) steady pace.
Session 2
10km pace. 3 × 5km (2 miles) with 200m jog (90 seconds to 2 mins recovery). Increase to four repetitions when you hit the target pace.
Session 3
13km (8 miles) fast pace.
Session 4
5km pace. 3 × 1.5km (1 mile) with 200m jog (90 seconds to 2 minutes recovery). Increase to four repetitions when you hit the target pace.
Session 5
16km (10 miles) easy pace.
Session 6
3km pace. 5 × 800m with 200m jog (90

seconds to 2 minutes recovery). Increase to four repetitions when you hit the target pace.
Session 7
19km (12 miles) steady pace.
Session 8
1500m pace. 6 × 500m with 250m jog recovery (2 mins to 2 mins 30 seconds recovery).
Session 9
13km (8 miles) fast pace.
Session 10
800m pace. 16 × 200m with 200m jog recovery (90 seconds to 2 mins recovery).
Session 11
16km (10 miles) slow pace.
Session 12
400m pace. 8 × 100m at sprint pace with 200m jog/walk recovery (90 seconds to 2 mins).

Running programmes are not only for the speed merchants. The three-week programme below was followed by a senior male athlete one month before his first-ever standard-distance (1500m, 40k, 10k) triathlon. He was also fitting in three cycle sessions (two on the turbo trainer) and two swimming sessions per week. His pre-triathlon background was swimming.

Week 1
1. Easy 8km (5-mile) run.
2. Steady 10km (6 miles) including 8 × 30 secs striding with 60 secs jog recovery between.
3. Steady 8km.
4. 45-min run made up as: 10 mins warm-up,

2 × 10 mins fast stride with 5 mins easy jog recovery, 10 mins jog warm-down.

Week 2
1. Easy 10km run.
2. 45-min run made up as: 10 mins warm-up, 10 × 60 secs fast stride with 2 mins easy jog recovery, 5 mins jog warm-down.
3. Steady 10km made up as: warm-up, 3 × 5 mins fast stride with 4 mins easy jog recovery, 10 mins jog warm-down.
4. Easy 13km (8-mile) run.

Week 3
1. Easy 8km (5-mile) run.
2. Steady 10km including 12 × 60 secs striding with 90 secs jog recovery between.
3. Steady 10km, gradually increasing pace over the second 5km (3 miles).
4. Easy 15km (9-mile) run.

This male triathlete finished his first standard-distance race with a 10km run split of 49 minutes 22 seconds.

POINTS TO REMEMBER

There are a number of points to bear in mind as you are preparing and carrying out a training programme, whatever your current standard of running.

- Running off road, on grass or other soft surfaces is kinder to your legs than pounding away on roads or tartan tracks all the time.
- Even if you don't consider yourself a fast runner, don't forget speed sessions at 10km pace or a little faster, even in your steady or long runs.
- On some of your steady runs, try to run the second half faster than the first half. This will prepare you for 'digging in' when the going gets tough in races.
- Resting weeks and easy weeks are essential, to give your body a chance to recover from hard training.
- If you are going to improve, sometimes you are going to have to hurt yourself in training. Don't be afraid to train with people who are a little better than you are.

Fig 55. The ability to hold technique when tired and under pressure is essential.

- Build flexibility into your training programme. If Emma Carney turns up at the track just as you are setting off on your steady run and asks you to join in the interval session, do it! You might learn something.

BEATING YOUR PERSONAL BEST

In every sport, there are some athletes who lack the imagination to make the most of their potential. Unable to see more than the tiniest upgrade past the level at which they are currently training or competing, they do not 'dare to dream'. The 30-minute 10km for men and 33-minute for women are regarded with awe; perhaps rightly, since they are better than the efforts of the majority. However, when the distance is broken down, are such times still unachievable?

Much of the philosophy behind training, particularly behind running training, and even more so for triathlon running training, is to start slow and get faster. This means that for many years, the athlete will not experience the sort of speed required to compete at world level (or whatever level is appropriate). Backing away from this speed, it is easy to think that it will never be attainable.

Compare the breakdown of intermediate times of the runner who is capable of 39 minutes for 10km and of a 30-minute 10km runner:

Comparative Running Times and Speeds		
30-min *10km* *Runner*	*Distance*	*39-min* *10km* *Runner*
30.00	10km	39.00
15.00	5km	19.30
3.00	1km	3.54
1.12	400m	1.34

The differences are significant. However, the differences at 10km and 5km are greater than the spread at 400m, which is just 22 seconds. For the 39-minute 10km runner, running a 15-minute 5km would be impossible, but running 400m in 72 seconds is certainly achievable; with a reasonable jog recovery in between, these times can be repeated.

The most important factor in this is that it is essential in the long-term training pro-gramme to build in the appropriate speed work, at race pace and faster than race pace, over less than the racing distance.

PROGRESSION IN TRAINING

Simple progression in training can be achieved via the following:

- continuous running/cycling/swimming for a longer time;
- training for the same time but at a higher speed;
- lifting heavier weights; and
- doing the same amount of work in a shorter time.

Think DIRTY! *D*istance-*I*nterval-*R*epetition-*T*ime-*Y*ou

Starting Schedule

Start with a fairly simple training session: four repetitions of 1.5km (1 mile) to be complet-ed in 6 minutes each, with a resting interval of 4 minutes between each repetition.

Distance: 1.5km
Interval: 4 mins rest
Repetition: 4 reps
Time: 6 mins

Any of the DIRTY factors can be improved/bettered by increasing or reducing the num-ber involved:

- increase the number of repetitions;
- increase the distance of the repetitions;
- decrease the resting time between the rep-etitions; or
- decrease the time taken for completing the repetitions.

First increase
Distance: 1.5km
Interval: 4 mins rest
Repetition: 4 reps
Time: 6 mins

Second increase
Distance: 1.5km
Interval: 3 mins rest
Repetition: 3 reps
Time: 6 mins

Third increase
Distance: 1.5km
Interval: 4 mins
Repetition: 4 reps
Time: 5 mins 40 secs

Fourth increase
Distance: 2km
Interval: 3 mins rest
Repetition: 4 reps
Time: 7 mins 5 secs (the pace for each 400m is 5 secs faster)

FACTS, FIGURES, FORMULAE AND FALLACIES

Self-Testing for Oxygen Uptake

1. Run as far as possible in 15 minutes;
2. record the distance covered (in metres);
3. divide total distance by 15 to find speed in metres per minute;
4. compute maximum oxygen intake using this formula: speed minus 133, then multiply by 0.172, then add 33.3.

Example 1: top triathlete Monica Humblebum covers 4000m in the 15 minutes. This is 267m per minute. Subtracting 133 from this gives 134. $134 \times 0.172 = 23.048$. $23 + 33.3 = 56$. Accepting this formula's accuracy, Monica has a VO_2 max of 56. A level of 40 is a minimum standard of everyday fitness. The two quickest ways to improve are increased aerobic training and lowering body fat.

Example 2: international triathlete Bert Glormsdyke covers 5000m in 15 minutes, or 333m per minute. $333 - 133 = 200$. $200 \times 0.172 = 34.4$. $34.4 + 33.3 = 67.7$.

The Karvonen Test: Finding the Right Level of Aerobic Training

Improvements are controlled by the amount and type of exercise that you take. Physiologists estimate that aerobic capacity can be improved by up to 30 or 40 per cent through training regularly, continuously, at the right intensity and for sufficient time.

For a rough indication of this level:

1. Find your maximum heart rate – 220 minus your age (preferably test); and
2. train at between 70 and 85 per cent of this.

For example, a 30-year-old triathlete would work at between 70 and 85 per cent of 190 (220 minus 30), in other words, 133 to 162.

Karvonen attempts to indicate the level more accurately by using the resting heart rate (and therefore the present level of fitness), thus (using the same 30-year-old male triathlete as an example):

1. Find maximum heart rate; 220 – 30 (his age) = 190;
2. subtract resting heart rate (say, 60) = 130;
3. find 70 or 80 per cent of this; 70 per cent = 91, 85 per cent = 110;
4. then add resting pulse (60), 70 per cent = 151, 85 per cent = 170; this gives a lower level of 151 and an upper level of 170 to aim for.

Hopefully, the athlete will get fitter and eventually reduce his resting heart rate to 40. Applying the same formula, he will then have limits of 145 (lower) and 167 (upper). The fitter he is, the lower the pulse he will have to work at to maintain this.

Equivalent Times for Different Distances

The *potential* for speed is more important than *present* speed.

The formulae below are about 90 per cent accurate. They become less accurate with very fast or very slow runners. The computations are based on male athletes of a reasonable standard; the equivalents for female athletes are in brackets. Slower male athletes are advised to use the female figures; faster female athletes are advised to use male figures.

Using the mile as a starting point:

- to find your best half-mile time, halve your mile time and deduct 11 seconds (13 seconds for women);
- to find your best time for 400m, halve your time for 800m and deduct 5.5 seconds (6.5 seconds);
- to find your best time for 2 miles, add 20 seconds (24 seconds) to your mile time and double it;
- to find your best time for 3 miles, multiply your mile time by 3 and add 75 seconds (90 seconds);
- to find your best time for 6 miles, double your 3-mile time and add 75 seconds (90 seconds).

NB: conversion from 3 miles to 6 miles will be inaccurate if endurance training is insufficient.

Example 1: Said Aouita has a best mile time of 3 minutes 46 seconds. Using the equivalent tables this would indicate a 3-mile time of 12 minutes and 18 seconds, giving him a 5000m time of 12 minutes and 48 seconds. His world record for 5000m was actually 12 minutes and 58 seconds.

Example 2: top British triathlete Hugh Jarmpitt is very unhappy with his running form, which has been letting him down in triathlon events. In an individual 10km race, he has averaged about 39 minutes. He works hard all winter on improving his speed and maintaining his endurance work. In March, he runs 4.40 minutes for a mile race in an open event. What could he hope for in a 10km?

$4.40 \times 3 = 14$ mins

14 mins + 75 secs = 15.15 mins for 3 miles

Fig 56. Sîan Brice leads a pack of runners at a European Cup Final race.

Conversions from miles/yards to km/m

880 yards to 800m	Deduct 0.7 seconds
1 mile to 1500m	Deduct 18 seconds (men), 20 seconds (women)
2 miles to 3000m	Deduct 40 seconds (men), 50 seconds (women)
3 miles to 5000m	Add 30 seconds (men), 35 seconds (women)
6 miles to 10,000m	Add 60 seconds (men), 72 seconds (women)

Points to Remember

1. Endurance. The 20-minute effect. Long run versus repetitions.
2. Ten-day effect.
3. Destruction testing.
4. Intensity – running/cycling/swimming.
5. Macro-/micro-cycle of training.
6. Five-phase effort.
7. Don't be a 'I'm not a ... type triathlete'.
8. Very few athletes in any sport are extraordinarily talented. Mental tenacity, strength, willpower, will to win – whatever you want to call it – is perhaps the most important factor in separating the good athlete from the great athlete.
9. Triathlon is a sport in its own right.

$15.15 \times 2 = 30$ mins 30 secs
$30.30 + 75$ secs $= 31.45$ mins for 6 miles
$31.45 + 60$ secs $= 32.45$ mins

It's a healthy anticipated improvement!

Style/Technique

When you are at the point of exhaustion during a race, or perhaps during a very taxing training session, learn to concentrate on technique. Think about the following points while you are running:

1. Knees pointing forward.
2. Roll heels forward.
3. Arms balance your legs; move them slightly across the body.
4. Do not roll your shoulders.
5. Do not push your elbows out.
6. Every time you turn round to check who's behind you, you lose approximately half a second, or roughly 3m.
7. Running in a triathlon is at least 80 per cent aerobic, even in short sections. It makes good sense to train predominantly at an aerobic level, or to *attempt to raise your aerobic threshold*.
8. Coming back from injury, it is often a temptation to accentuate speed work. Injury beckons ...

Implications for Triathlon Training

1. Triathlon is an aerobic activity, even at the shorter distances (1500m swim, 40km bike, 10km run). The majority of training should be endurance-based.
2. Endurance training alone is not enough to succeed at the highest level. Speed work also has to be done, but should not be done without sufficient endurance work.
3. Training should be specific if it is to have maximum effect.
4. Fatigue must be endured in training to enable the athlete to cope with it in races; in other words, sometimes training will hurt. It is possible to cope with some fatigue, but not with all types. Compensated fatigue is brought into a training session from previous sessions. There will always be a point of failure at the limit of your physical and mental ability; however, appropriate, progressive and specific training will enable you to push the point of failure further away.
5. Improving your speed will make it easier to 'cruise' at a faster pace.
6. The amount of training is important; equally important is how that training load is made up.
7. What you do in the lead-up (6–8 weeks prior) to an important race will determine how well you do. What you do before the lead-up will determine how much you can do in the period before the race. A solid background established during the winter and early spring is essential.
8. Of the three disciplines, running training brings with it the most likelihood of injury. Even minor injuries should be regarded as potentially major. Water- or aqua-running may go some way to help avoid injuries.

CHAPTER 15
Spin, Stroke and Stride

'Be brave and focus.'

Having established the rudiments of the three disciplines (*see* Chapters 9, 12 and 14), the triathlete can examine further the trade-off between speed of action and power/strength of all three.

CYCLING

Pedalling Efficiency

Triathletes understand that swimming involves a lot of technique and skill work in training, certainly for beginners, but sometimes fail to recognize that significant gains can be made by examining the skills in the other two disciplines. In order to cycle at maximum efficiency, it is necessary to learn the right technique.

Pedalling is not a simple up-and-down action. Cyclists know that the majority of power will be exerted on the down thrust, when the large propulsive muscles are mostly brought into action, and that the recovery phase will be on the upstroke. The phases at the top and bottom of the circular action are, however, little emphasized and likely to be neglected.

To become more efficient during the recovery phase it is necessary to pull the foot back towards the end of the downward stroke rather than to continue to push downwards, rather like a horse bringing its hoof back when pawing at the air. To work on the top of the stroke, emphasize a straight, forward push rather than initiate the downward movement. It may help here to think of bringing the lower leg forward as the knee is at the top of the circle.

This sounds simple, but it needs work.

Dead Spots and Single Legs

The following two testing drills are best carried out on a turbo.

Dead Spots

After warming up, move upwards through the gears until your cadence is at around 80rpm – the trade-off point between strength and suppleness. While pedalling, look down at your chain (this is why a turbo is best). If there are any dead spots in your pedal action, you may notice a brief time when the chain ceases to be just a blur, when you will be able to see – just for an instant – the individual links. This will almost certainly occur at the top or the bottom of the pedal stroke action.

Single Legs

For a quick, efficient self-test, pedal with each leg individually while resting the other on a chair. Single-leg pedalling, which leads to quick fatigue, will magnify any faults and immediately show up any discrepancies in strength between the two legs.

It may take time to sort out dead spots and leg inequalities, but it is worthwhile. By studying gearing and cadence charts it is immediately obvious just how much faster you will be able to ride by upping your cadence by, say, 5rpm.

Strength and Power

Even a small increase of force applied to the pedals during the power phase of the stroke will produce a substantial increase in speed. In triathlon, although sudden increases in force

Fig 57. Marsha Wessells demonstrating to youngsters.

– to win a sprint or break away from a bunch of riders – may sometimes be necessary, the aim is to apply this increased force over the whole period of the cycling discipline.

It makes sense to strengthen the specific muscles that are used during the power phase. Weight-training is the easiest way of doing this, focusing particularly on half-squats, leg presses and extensions, lunges (with caution) and leg (hamstring) curls. The key muscles exercised will be the quadriceps, gluteals and hamstrings. Do some of the leg exercises on each leg in turn, as this will show up any discrepancies in strength and will serve as an indication of likely cadence differences when working on single-leg drills.

Triathletes with good leg strength may wish to utilize this to its best effect by changing (with caution) their crank length. Lengthening the cranks will allow the triathlete to apply greater muscle force to the pedals, but the fitness and conditioning must be there in order to benefit from the change (as well as the necessary leg length, of course). Any increase in crank length will bring about a drop in cadence but will increase pressure on the hip joints and the leg muscles. The legs will travel further, longer and higher in the pedal circle, which will lead to the extra pressure on the knee joints.

If you have short legs, don't be tempted to lengthen the cranks. Remember, you have to run after finishing the cycle section.

SWIMMING

Distance per Stroke, Rate of Stroke

It is easy to tell within minutes of the start of a race which triathletes have a swimming background. They seem to have all the time in the world, with a slow and unhurried stroke. How can non-swimmer triathletes compensate for their lack of experience? The stroke drills in Chapter 9 will help, but for adult learner swimmers there will always be a gap.

One way to reduce the gap is to consider the ratio of turnover and distance per stroke and to make the most of your own strengths rather than accentuate your weaknesses.

In swimming, although the hands seem to move through the water, in fact, the idea is to fix the hand on the water and to move the body over and past the hand. There is a tendency for the hand to 'slip' through the water, with a corresponding reduction in distance per stroke. In any group of swimmers or

triathletes, the faster and better swimmers will be using fewer strokes.

In order to swim faster, you need to do the following:

1. increase the distance per stroke by applying force correctly and by streamlining (reducing the force that will work against this);
2. increase stroke rate – the rate at which you cover that distance per stroke.

The greater the force you can apply to the water to give forward propulsion, the faster you will swim. However, if this force is misdirected due to poor technique, the effort will be wasted and there will be a reduction in speed. Increasing the distance per stroke is achieved by concentrating on stroke technique.

Stroke rate depends on the number of muscle fibres in the body and on the rate at which those fibres contract. These factors are best improved in the weights area, or in the swimming pool with speed/sprint work.

To measure a swimmer's speed, stroke rate and distance per stroke, time them over a measured distance of 10m during a maximum-speed 25m sprint:

Velocity (in m/sec) = distance divided by time

To determine stroke rate, time the athlete for completing ten arm cycles:

Stroke rate (arm cycles per minute) = 10×60 divided by time (in secs)

Therefore, distance per stroke is:

Distance/stroke = Velocity $\times$ 60 divided by stroke rate

Dividing 100m by the athlete's velocity gives the athlete's time for that distance. These calculations do not take into account starts and turns, or fatigue; the results for a fit triathlete are unlikely to correspond with those of an equally fit, specialist swimmer.

(Right) Fig 58. Glenn Cook coaching swimming.

Example 1
Athlete's personal best time for 100m = 81.9 seconds
Test velocity 1.21m/sec
100 divided by 1.21 = 82.6 seconds
A difference of just 0.7 seconds

Knowing the athlete's stroke rate and distance per stroke, it is possible to work out his or her velocity:

Stroke rate $\times$ distance per stroke = Velocity (in m/sec)
Velocity (m/sec) = Velocity (in m/min) divided by 60

This information is useful to athletes and coaches because, if either the stroke rate or the distance per stroke can be increased, it is possible to increase speed.

Example 2
Female athlete's test results: Velocity = 1.45 m/sec; Stroke rate = 53 arm cycles/min; distance/stroke = 1.64m/stroke
100m divided by 1.45 = 68.9 seconds

This athlete's distance/stroke is poor compared with her stroke rate, tending to indicate that her stroke technique is not good. The athlete needs to work hard on technique while maintaining her stroke rate, so that her distance/stroke goes up to 1.69m/stroke:

New velocity = 53×1.69 = 89.57 m/min
89.57 divided by 60 = 1.49 m/sec
100m divided by 1.49 = 67.01 secs

The improvement in stroke technique, and the increase in distance covered per stroke of about 5cm, gives an improvement of 1.89 seconds over 100m – an immediate improvement of 30 seconds over 1500m without any increase in fitness. It is actually likely to be more significant than this, as the improved stroke technique is maintained better with the onset of fatigue as the swim progresses. Similarly, an increase in stroke turnover, perhaps through working on strength, will pay similar dividends, assuming that stroke length is maintained. The moral of the story is: *work on your weaknesses*.

RUNNING

Stride Length and Turnover

Running may seem to be the most simple of physical activities, but is it? Some people attempt to overcomplicate it, and even a cursory glance at a group of runners reveals that some make the activity look so much easier than do others. This is because their economy of movement, and thus speed, is so much better.

Simplistically speaking, the action of running is twofold: pushing off the ground and landing again. What happens between these two actions is largely determined by the actions themselves.

Stride Length

The stride length is the distance between each landing of the foot. One part of running faster is covering more distance with each stride; this entails pushing off harder and reaching out further. Many runners, especially triathletes, claim that as they run faster they shorten their stride. In fact, they have probably pushed off harder but not extended their stride forward, giving the impression of a shorter stride. Usually, the length has been maintained or even extended. It would seem that the push-off is more important for stride length than forward extension.

To understand the foot-plant, compare the landing of a four-hour marathon runner with that of a top-class 800m or 1500m runner at full flight coming into the home straight. The marathon runner will be landing on the heel of the foot while the fast runner will be landing almost on the ball of the foot. A 100m runner will come down almost on the toes. The slower runners who land each time right on their heels will be almost pushing the foot forward after the first plant has been made and will be using extra energy *and* slowing the foot down before it goes into the next phase of pushing off.

A distance runner's shoes and a sprinter's spikes show exactly where the foot lands each time. There is, of course, a trade-off. The energy used by a sprinter has to carry the athlete through 10 seconds; for a triathlete, it's 40 minutes, after 90 minutes of effort already.

Note: you should not try to run with such a long stride that you are actually slowing yourself down. Stride length is governed by mobility, and an unnatural increase in stride length (overstriding) may create a braking effect. Work on your mobility.

Turnover

If you cannot stride that much longer, you have to stride faster. Do the following simple test to demonstrate the importance of leg turnover. First, run 200m at 8-minute mile pace (200m in 60 seconds) and count the number of strides. Have an adequate recovery and then run the 200m again at 7-minute mile pace (200m in 52 seconds), at 6-minute mile pace (200m in 45 seconds) and finally at 5-minute pace (200m in 37 seconds). Your stride length will increase but far more significant will be the number of strides that you take to cover the same distance; particularly if you take into account the shorter time you take to run each succeeding repetition.

Drills

There are a number of drills that you can do to improve your running efficiency. The two below will pay the quickest dividends:

1. Run down a hill as fast as you can (choose a hill where you will not lose balance). If you go too steep, you may find increased stiffness and soreness on the first few occasions.
2. Run up the hill as well – you will be forced to push off that much harder in order to maintain momentum and improve strength.

It is also worth doing occasional track sessions with a middle-distance group. The realization that you *can* run faster – and, just as importantly, how good you feel running really fast – will pay dividends. Every middle-distance/distance runner, from distances of 400m to 10,000m, will occasionally compete on the track at 800m, just to remind themselves of two things:

1. how good it feels to run fast; and
2. how much it hurts.

That philosophy might not be such a bad one for triathletes either.

CHAPTER 16

Endurance Training and Competition

'For I have promises to keep and miles to go before I sleep.'

Completing an Ironman event involves swimming 2.4 miles, cycling 112 miles, and running 26.2 miles non-stop, within a time limit imposed by the event organizers. This chapter is a guide to the training and nutritional requirements specific to the Ironman and to the other triathlon endurance events.

PREREQUISITES

A full medical check-up is the first essential task of the potential Ironman triathlete, to find out whether he or she is fit enough to begin the training required. The athlete should have competed in at least two full seasons over the Olympic distance (1.5km swim, 40km cycle, 10km run) and should also have completed two long-course races (2.5km swim, 90km cycle, 20km run) in the two-year period. This kind of base allows the athlete to experience and adapt to the unique demands that Ironman events place on the body.

Apart from the specific physical preparation, the races over the two years will help the athlete to gain confidence, as well as providing the experience of extreme fatigue, and demonstrating that everything does not go always according to plan: goggles are knocked off at the start, bike tyres get punctures, the body may suffer from dehydration and/or glycogen depletion.

Triathletes who know that they can cope with potential setbacks efficiently will have a greater chance of success. Efficiency is vital if you are to cross the finish line of an Ironman.

There are so many things that can go wrong that preparation for every eventuality is essential.

NUTRITION

The correct diet is vital to the Ironman competitor. In 1989, Mark Allen 'blew up' in the Hawaii Ironman on the run section, primarily because he was totally depleted of energy supplies. At the Dutch Open that year, Ben Van Zelst (1991 European Ironman Champion, and the man who achieved the fastest recorded marathon – 2 hours, 39 minutes – during an Ironman event) put a poor run down to the fact that he was unable to absorb his electrolyte drink, which caused his stomach to become cramped and upset. (*See* Chapter 18 for information on nutrition for the general triathlon event. The information below is directed more specifically at athletes aiming to compete over endurance and Ironman distances.)

The aim of the triathlete is to replace glucose burned in supplying energy, and electrolytes lost through sweat. The replacement of glucose – through an intake of carbohydrates and electrolytes (normally through a performance drink) – will increase the triathlete's endurance ability.

The majority of carbohydrate feeding through solid foodstuffs should take place on the bike, partly because the relatively static position of the upper body makes digestion easier. The other reason is that glycogen stores are severely depleted during the swim, which lasts, for the majority of Ironman triathletes, for an hour to an hour and a half. The glycogen stores from the outset would have been supplying a higher percentage of energy than the fatty acid stores for the swimming muscles to burn. Only as the race goes on does the energy supplied by fatty acid stores increase.

This process was seen in the following study, conducted on an athlete running a three-hour marathon.

Progressive Comparison of Carbohydrates and Fatty Acids Used		
Hour	*Carbohydrates Burned*	*Fatty Acids Burned*
1	85 per cent	15 per cent
2	71 per cent	29 per cent
3	62 per cent	38 per cent

With a 112-mile cycle ride and a marathon run to be done after the swim, it is essential to replenish some of the glucose already used. Complex and easily digestible carbohydrates are recommended. They are absorbed by the stomach more quickly than any other food source and will be available for energy before the race finishes. Such foods include bananas, kiwi fruit, figs and nutritional sports bars that are designed to enhance endurance. Every triathlete should experiment in training with different foods, to see what works best for them.

Fluid Intake

Fluid is another essential component to success. It should be taken straight after the swim; after this, a gap longer than 15 minutes without any fluid is undesirable. Taking fluid little and often allows the body to absorb it more easily. Fluid intake will also help maintain core body temperature, which can overheat due to energy output and the air temperature.

Water mixed with a small solution of electrolytes (sodium chloride) and glucose will be absorbed better within the small intestine than plain water, but overly sugared solution will be retained in the stomach. The optimum amount is around 2–3g of glucose per 100ml of water. Again, experiment in training with different types of sports drinks and mixtures, to see what works best for you.

Note: if you lose only 3 per cent or more of your body weight through fluid loss, dehydration will set in.

Nutrition for Recovery

After the race and after training sessions some kind of complex carbohydrate intake (such as fruit) must take place immediately. This intake will speed up the recovery from the race or session, as the body's absorption rate is increased after exercise. Failure to do this can lead to a slower recovery rate; later training may be missed, or completed with overuse symptoms, leading to possible illness.

TRAINING

Developing Aerobic-Endurance Capability

The objective of training for an Ironman is to improve the body's aerobic-endurance capability, through Ironman-specific fitness training.

A training programme based on ever-increasing miles is not a recipe for success. A successful programme should be based on establishing an optimum mileage, at any given state of fitness. To determine mileage, carry out regular body checks (*see* below). Once you have found an optimum training mileage for the Ironman, at your level of fitness, you can begin to increase the speed and intensity of these miles until a plateau is reached. With the levelling out, impose a slight increase in mileage again. In this way, the progression towards your ultimate training and racing potential continues.

With the above theory in mind, the table opposite shows a basic mileage guide for an 'average' triathlete (with no major weaknesses in any discipline) building up to a first Ironman.

One way to check your daily recovery is to monitor your resting heart rate. If it is elevated, you may need to reduce training to allow for a longer rest interval. Other checks include weight, sleep patterns and general disposition (perhaps irritability). Any changes may indicate overtraining.

The crux of fitness training for an Ironman will be aerobically based. Aerobic sessions do not have to be the same week in, week out. Every Monday, triathlete Chris Ray does a 100-mile steady cycle; every Wednesday, a 20-mile run; and every Saturday, a 100-mile

Mileage Guide for Building up to an Ironman

Week	Swim (m)	Cycle (miles)	Run (miles)
1	7000	130	36
2	8000	150	40
3	6500	170	44
4*	7000	150	40
5	8000	170	44
6	9000	190	48
7	6500	200	50
8*	9000	160	42
9	10,000	200	50
10	8000	180	40
11	6000	130	36
12	Race	Race	Race

*Weeks 4 and 8 are slight recovery weeks.

cycle followed by a 20-mile run. For him, this is fine, but it is not recommended for others. This kind of regime may well lead to staleness and boredom. Use some imagination when planning a weekly training programme.

With this in mind, the generalized programme in the 12-week mileage guide could indicate the training programme for Week 3 and Week 7 shown overleaf.

The Week Before

In the week prior to the Ironman event, emphasis should be placed on stretching and relatively light training, to keep the muscles active. Time that was spent training in previous weeks should now be directed towards sorting out race organization. This aspect of race preparation is often forgotten; according to the Gatorade Ironman World Championship information, contestants have brought bikes to check-in with loose spokes, loose brakes, loose headsets and stripped cables, and did not have the tools and equipment to make the adjustments. After weeks of preparation, don't risk having to withdraw from the race because of a mechanical failure that could have been prevented or mended.

Finally, increasing time should be devoted to getting into the positive frame of mind that is essential to success in an Ironman. (*See* Chapter 22, on mental attitude.)

Overtraining

Ironman athletes often go into training overload, pushing the body to, or near, its physiological limit for a specified period of time, to improve fitness. They are also prone to overtraining, when the body shows symptoms of chronic fatigue, leading to undesirable physiological and psychological changes.

Take your heart rate daily, ideally first thing in the morning. Take your pulse in a lying position and then immediately afterwards in a sitting position. The gap between the two heart rates should remain relatively constant. An unexpected increase in the gap could mean that the body is run down. If this is the case, you must rest. Continued training may lead to illness.

The triathlete's body weight has great importance. With all the LSD (long, slow distance) workouts, some glycogen and fluid depletion will inevitably occur, so you should weigh yourself regularly, preferably every morning, and after any LSD work. After LSD work, drink an electrolyte drink, and then weigh yourself.

For example, an 11-stone man who is more than 2lb underweight should drink electrolytes, and eat complex carbohydrates frequently, until

Sample Endurance Training Programme

Week 3	am	pm
Mon	Rest day	
Tue	Swimming club	Run 10 miles (off road)
Wed	Run 4 miles	Cycle 10-mile time trial (with ups and downs)
Thur	Swimming club followed immediately by 6 miles tempo run	
Fri	Run 5 miles steady	Cycle 60 miles (hilly course)
Sat	Run 20 miles steady (10 miles off road, 10 miles on road)	
Sun	Cycle 40 miles + 2000m open-water swim + Cycle 40 miles	

Week 7	am	pm
Mon	Swimming club	Cycle 1 hour (concentrate on rpm)
Tue	Run 1 hour (including some 1- to 2-min stride-outs with the wind)	Cycle 2 hours steady (undulating course)
Wed	Run 3-mile time trial (2 miles with ups and downs)	
Thur	Cycle 2 hours steady or run 5 miles steady (some efforts with the wind)	
Fri	Cycle 5 hours (efforts on the hills) + 5-mile run steady	
Sat	Rest day	
Sun	Cycle 20 miles fartlek + Run 20 miles steady (5 off road, 15 on road, 35-mins steady run to begin with) (Sunday is a key back-to-back session with a short gap of 15 mins to 1 hr between sessions. Speed up as the session goes on.)	

The time trials are used to gauge improvement and to set new short-term goals. The 'efforts' during the aerobic runs and cycle rides push the body near to its aerobic capability. This will improve aerobic-endurance fitness, and also help adapt the body to the kind of stress it will under during competition.

his body weight returns to within 2lb of its norm. This kind of process allows quicker recovery from LSD sessions, and avoids illness that may occur during training while depleted.

RESTING AND RELAXING

Rest and relaxation are of vital importance to the triathlete, to allow the body to adapt to the stresses of training. The commitment to attaining training goals at three separate disciplines will inevitably lead to tiredness and fatigue. Many professional triathletes will strive for 9 to 12 hours' sleep a day. After a few nights' disturbed sleep, the resting HR of some athletes will become elevated, motivation will be harder to achieve, and training sessions will become more difficult.

The ability to relax is a vital ingredient in success. You can relax by watching television with a glass of wine, trying meditation or yoga, or mixing with a social group who will not be talking about the latest set of tri-spoke wheels on the cycle market.

Rest and relaxation can stop the infamous 'burn-out effect' that is suffered by athletes doing too many miles, with little or no time out away from their sport. They are continually tired, and are likely to suffer from injury and/or illness. This can add up to poor race results that do not reflect the training effort they have put in. This in turn leads to disenchantment with the sport.

On the physiological side, resting coupled with stretching enhances the training effect. Muscles will be given a chance to recover from workouts and will eventually grow stronger, in preparation for the next overload. (*See* Chapters 20 and 24 on stretching and relaxation.)

A NEED FOR SPEED?

An endurance event – even a standard-distance triathlon – is, in a way, a question of survival. In an ultra-endurance event, the survival element becomes even more significant. Getting through an Ironman will take a minimum of six months of specific and regular training. *Racing* in an Ironman requires significantly more than that. Yet even triathletes with full-time jobs and families have achieved magnificent times in Ironman-distance races. The secret, if there is one, is to be absolutely specific in training.

A number of sessions have proved to be crucial in preparing for Ironman and other ultra-distance events. It is possible to finish an Ironman event on around 10 hours' training (six sessions) per week – with difficulty, discomfort, and not a little pain. Doubling the amount of training time to around 20 hours will enable the novice Ironman to finish with much less distress.

Doubling the amount of time does not mean doubling the amount of sessions; for

Fig 59. Sîan Brice reflects on how tough but rewarding a discipline triathlon is.

ultra-distance training, some of the sessions must be long. For this type of event you must educate the body to store and use glycogen efficiently; running and cycling (swimming is less important) need to make up a significant portion of the total week's mileage. The serious athlete with restricted training time may

---

Points to Remember

- Every potential Ironman triathlete should go through a thorough medical examination to determine whether he or she is medically fit to participate in an ultra-endurance event.
- A fit triathlete needs the right daily diet, high in carbohydrates. Practise eating certain carbohydrates during training so that you are able to consume and absorb food during the race, enhancing your endurance ability.
- Build distance slowly, and incorporate the miles into an imaginative weekly training programme.

- Avoid overtraining by checking your HR and weight regularly. This can help prevent possible illness. Symptoms of overtraining include sleeplessness and irritability; they need to be recognized straight away, and acted upon with rest.
- Rest also helps the 'training effect' by allowing muscles to recover and grow stronger.
- Being able to relax away from training is vital for mental and physical reasons. Athletes who have learned to relax between training sessions are less likely to 'burn out', and give up training and racing altogether.

work up to running 20 miles or more and cycling 90 miles. These distances are undoubtedly long, but a professional cyclist might easily ride that far on six days a week during a heavy build-up period or while racing in a big tour. A marathon runner, or even an experienced 10km runner might cover the distance in two or three sessions each week.

For the majority of working people, a day job takes priority over triathlon. A number of triathletes have adapted marathon running schedules to include cycling, and have used them to work on pace for endurance events, with quality becoming an integral part of ultra-endurance scheduling. The running schedules are based on projected times for the marathon (as a single discipline rather than at the end of an Ironman) and the conversion times and pace for half-marathon, 10km, 5km and 3km. The cycling schedules are based on projected times for 100–112 miles (again, as a single discipline) and their conversion times and pace for 50 miles, 25 miles and 10 miles.

The sample schedule below has been used (with the appropriate adjustment in times and pace) for would-be Ironmen trying to fit in training schedules with full-time work and family commitments. This schedule assumes a good state of basic fitness and background aerobic training work.

Endurance Training Programme

Week 1

RUN
11 miles at 6.40-min mile pace or slower. What is comfortable?
13 miles as 15 mins easy, 15 mins steady, remainder (1 hour?) hard run
Warm up, then 3 × 2 miles at 5.55-min mile pace; 90 secs recovery

CYCLE
60 miles at 20mph

30 mins easy twiddle, 30 mins steady, 2–3 hours steady/hard ride
Warm up, then 3 × 20 or 4 × 15 mins at 25mph, 300 watts or best 25-mile time trial pace; 60 or 90 secs recovery

Week 2

RUN
12 miles at 6.40-min mile pace or last week's pace
4 × 1 mile in 5.40 mins, 90 secs recovery between
Warm up, then 16 × 400m at 77–80 secs pace; 45 secs recovery

CYCLE
60–65 miles at 20mph

16 × 2 mins (60 recovery) at just sub max HR?
Warm up, 5 × 10 or 4 × 12 mins at 27mph, 340 watts or best 10-mile time trial pace; 60 or 90 secs recovery

Week 3

RUN
13 miles at 6.40-min mile pace or last week's pace
2 × 10km at 6.10-min mile pace; 60 secs recovery between; on an out and back course

Warm up, then 24 to 30 × 400m as straight run with each consecutive 400 alternating between 85 secs and 1 min 35 secs

CYCLE
65–70 miles at 20mph

Similar to run; after warm-up, 2 × 25 miles (out and back) as two hard straight rides; 5 mins recovery between
Warm up, then similar to run (on turbo if necessary) with alternating 3 mins at 25mph and 21–22mph. Go through 15 to 20 times – if you can bear it!

CHAPTER 17
Tapering

Little less least = much more most

Like many other sports, triathlon has legions of athletes who are superb in training, but never quite manage to produce the goods on race day. They never seem to finish as well as they should, according to their capabilities. A number of clichés are used to describe this phenomenon:

'He's left it all on the poolside.'
'Training's more important than racing to her.'
'He just doesn't have what it takes.'
'She falls apart when it comes to racing.'
'A bundle of nerves.'
'No bottle.'

Athletes *do* suffer from nerves, they *do* train too hard, they *do* consider training very important, but perhaps a poor racing performance can be put down to just one major factor: preparation.

Poor pre-race preparation might include the following:

- incorrect food;
- lack of sleep;
- rushed travel;
- insufficient knowledge of the course;
- wrong kit and equipment.

These are things that usually go wrong on the day of or just before the event. One other important factor of race preparation is much misused, much maligned and mostly misunderstood: tapering. What can you do to maximize your race results? Longer, harder, shorter, faster training? Complete rest? Eat more or less? Stop weight-training? Start weight-training? You do training to make you race faster, otherwise it's not worth the time or effort, but the real trick is how to *peak* for the best possible performance.

THE THEORY OF TAPERING

Working hard in the endurance and pre-competition phases of training consistently adds a series of stresses to the body, on top of the stresses of everyday living. Athletes in training find themselves in a fairly constant state of fatigue. Adding extra training sessions will add further stress, unless the body has become accustomed to handling the current workload. Eventually, stressed and exhausted, you take a day away from training and lose some of the fatigue and stress. If you can cope with the guilt and take more than one day off, more of the stress and fatigue disappears. So, if you take a few days off training, will you perform brilliantly? Is it that simple?

Theoretically, tapering for the major competition of the season requires you simultaneously to maintain your fitness at as high a level as possible while bringing your fatigue level as low as possible. Achieving this will improve your chances of a personal best performance. In normal circumstances, this is likely to occur in the later stages of the racing season, when you have trained hard throughout the year and you rest/taper going into the race.

Four areas require careful analysis if you are to produce your personal best:

1. increased glycogen levels;
2. maximum blood volume levels;
3. maximum muscular strength; and
4. maximum aerobic capacity (VO_2max).

Just resting will not look after these. You will need to set out final training sessions that will work together to bring you to a peak on race day.

The general principle is as follows:

'Do less, go faster, recover fully.'

Training in the final few days must be less in pure bulk and in actual time (not including resting time between efforts) spent doing the sessions. The intensity of the sessions will necessarily be higher. The amount of recovery between the efforts will be longer. It is also necessary to increase both carbohydrate and water intake. In pure mileage terms you should be aiming for a maximum of 66 per cent of your normal training load; for most athletes, 50 per cent or less would be optimal.

Triathletes tend to be obsessed with maintaining fitness and training and the thought of actually doing *less* is anathema to them. Visions of fatness and lethargy may assault you, but you *must* taper for an important race.

TYPES OF TAPER

There are several different ways of tapering, all of which have been tried with varying degrees of success. The three most widely used are:

- rest-only taper (ROT);
- low-intensity taper (LIT); and
- high-intensity taper (HIT).

Rest-only taper is exactly as it sounds: some time (whether 24 hours, 48 hours or a week) before the race, the athlete stops training and rests only.

Low-intensity taper: the athlete stops doing any quality training and continues with easy swimming, cycling and running without any intensity.

High-intensity taper: the athlete continues to train hard but, a number of days before the important event – sometimes as much as 10 days – the amount of time spent training is reduced. However, the athlete continues to maintain, or even increase, the intensity of the training.

Indications are that LIT type makes little or no difference to a race performance than no tapering at all, and that ROT will actually reduce race performance. The HIT-type taper tends to be the most successful.

A high-intensity taper might look something like this:

5 days before race: 8 × 400m in 80 seconds (with 1 min rest between)
4 days before race: 6 × 400m in 70 seconds (with 2 mins rest between)
3 days before race: rest
2 days before race: 4 × 400m in 64 seconds (with 3 mins rest between)
Day before race: 2 × 400m in 60 seconds (with 4 mins rest between)

It may be a simplistic example but it does hold true. The principle is as follows:

1. Increase intensity;
2. reduce total amount of work;
3. increase recovery; and
4. go into race fast but rested.

A number of other types of taper are used. The two most common are the *race through taper* (RThT), in which no taper and little or no race preparation is done. This is frequently used for minor or early-season races or when an athlete is using a race merely for training purposes or as a fitness indicator.

The other type is the *panic taper*, which is perhaps used more frequently than most athletes would like to admit! An athlete finds a race looming and realizes that sufficient training has not been done. Panic sets in and the athlete goes out and tries to fit two weeks' training into the three days before the race. You can imagine the outcome.

JUST PRE-RACE

The final 48 hours before the race are often the most worrying for triathletes. The generally accepted philosophy is that you do nothing before a race, certainly for 24 hours, and perhaps for as much as 48 hours. However, it is important to keep the speed element going right into a race. It is better to rest completely two or even three days before a race, and then do some fast efforts in the preceding day or two days, to remind the fast-twitch muscles what they are expected to do on race day. Resting up for a whole day just pre-race encourages lethargy and this will not help you perform to the best of your ability. It is particularly important to get in the water and swim, even if only for a few minutes. Many athletes find that they quickly lose their 'feel' for the water.

Do have the courage to experiment with your pre-race preparation, perhaps before a less important race. Incorporate lots of stretching, flexibility and mobility.

Just before a race, be aware of your food. During those endless pre-race hours, it is easy to eat more than you normally would, or drink too much coffee, hanging around socializing and 'killing time'. Don't try to justify this by excusing it as 'carbo-loading'. If you have eaten and prepared properly, an excess of junk food will not help you race better.

Examples of Sessions in the Taper Phase

Swimming
1. 10×50m on 90 seconds, then into $5 \times$ 100m on 3 mins, then into 1×500m. All done at faster than race pace.
2. 2×400m on 10 mins, then into $2 \times$ 200m on 8 mins, all at 100 per cent.

Cycling
1. 10-mile time trial (start flat-out, accelerate in the middle, and sprint to the end).
2. 30-mile steady ride with 5×1-mile full-out efforts between mile 5 and mile 25; full recovery in between single-mile efforts.

Running
1. 1×600m, 500m, 400m, 300m at 95 per cent with 5 mins easy jog or walk in between efforts.
2. 4-mile run with 1 mile in the middle at 95 per cent effort.

All the above sessions presuppose a very relaxed and adequate warm-up.

OTHER FACTORS

Super-Adaptation and Overcompensation

Many triathletes work so hard, so often that they are constantly tired. When the amount of training is severely restricted, the body will continue to overcompensate at the same high level, even though the high stress level has been removed. A best competition performance may well occur.

Some research indicates that overcompensation works best over a period of ten days. An exhausting training session ten days prior to a major event may lead to super-adaptation for the event itself. Athletes must experiment with this. If you are just one day out in your calculations, things can go disastrously wrong.

Travel

Don't arrive at the start line just five minutes before you are due to dive into the water. Try to have enough time to reconnoitre, to see the ins and outs of the transition area, to pick up helpful landmarks and to look at the particular anomalies of a particular course. Give yourself enough time to prepare mentally for the race. Consider writing a list of what you intend to do immediately before the start and have a countdown to getting on the start line. This sort of activity can take the uncertainty out of preparation, even if it is just a little.

Food

Try to stay with your normal food as much as possible. If you are a burger and chips person, making a radical adjustment to a plate full of pasta the night before the race will not make a difference. Travelling and racing abroad can put pressure on diet – some years ago, for example, racing in one Eastern European country meant a staple diet of pasta with apricot jam. If in doubt, take enough of your own food to be able to cook or at least snack on.

Accommodation

Although a good night's sleep is not essential to a good day's racing, it does help to make you feel more confident. If you have to stay over the night before a race, try to get an idea of the suitability of the accommodation. Take account of noise. If you find yourself sleeping above an open-air disco, demand to be moved.

Equipment and Clothing

Have the right stuff. If you are racing in mountains, a discwheel with a straight-through block of 13–18 is not wanted. If the race is due to take place in freezing-cold water, pack a wetsuit. Use your common-sense. If you don't know, ask.

Poor Pre-Race Preparation

- Incorrect food.
- Lack of sleep (strange room, insufficient ventilation).
- Rushed travel.
- Wrong kit.
- Lack of knowledge of the course.
- Wrong equipment.

POINTS TO REMEMBER

- Tapering will be of little benefit to athletes who have not trained hard. It is necessary to have experienced the feeling of training-enduced fatigue before being able to reap the benefits when that fatigue is gone.
- Decide which races are important. You do not need to taper for 'unimportant' races.
- The same type of taper will not work in the same way for everybody. Experiment with different tapers, sessions and combinations before less important events.
- Successful tapering results from good judgement and careful planning. Lucky athletes may find that a similar taper works before every event, whatever the distance, but it is more likely that different tapering will yield better results for different types of event.
- The athlete's reaction to pre-race nerves and anxiety will also determine the right kind of taper for each individual.
- Mental preparation is at least as important as physical tapering.
- Triathletes with a full season of races ahead should be sparing with their tapering if they hope to peak properly for major championships. Early-season and less important races should be 'raced through', without cutting back significantly on training load.
- The taper that works one season may well not be as effective the next season if fitness, training load, mental attitude have changed significantly. This is particularly the case with younger athletes.
- Veteran triathletes may need a longer tapering period than younger triathletes.
- Some research indicates that larger, more muscled triathletes will need a longer taper than those with a smaller build.
- It is possible to taper too much and to have lost a certain amount of conditioning thereby not performing as well as anticipated in a major race.

Tapering

How best to do it? Longer training? Harder training? Complete rest? Shorter? Faster? Eat more? Eat less? Stop doing weights? Start doing weights? IMPORTANT: do you let other athletes influence you? So... Training = Stress! Are you *always* a little bit tired? Take a day off?! What happens? = GUILT!

Tapers

ROT: rest-only taper.
LIT: low-intensity taper.
HIT: high-intensity taper.
PT: panic taper – worry about how little training you've done and go out and train the night before.
OPT: over-preparation taper – taper too much and lose form.
RThT: race-through taper – no taper at all (for little races).

Do less. Go faster. Recover fully.
Extra: carbohydrate and water.
Absolute max work = 66 per cent.
For most = 50 per cent.

Part III

The Extras

Fig 60. Tim Don takes an energy supplement on the run.

CHAPTER 18

Nutrition for Triathlon

'You are what you eat.'

The amount and intensity of training undertaken by a triathlete is the main influence on that individual's fitness, but diet can also significantly influence performance. A carefully planned diet before, during and after training and competition will maximize the athlete's potential.

Proper nutrition is critical for optimal physical performance. Conversely, a poor diet can adversely affect performance. A triathlete has to know how to plan the right diet that will allow the completion of hours of training each day, and also what to eat and drink before, during and after races.

THE BASICS

A Healthy Diet

With the vast range of foods and preparations available today, what is a basic healthy diet? Endurance sportspeople do have some special dietary needs, the guidelines for a healthy diet – less sugar, fat, salt and alcohol; increased amounts of complex carbohydrate and fibre – should form the basis of any nutrition plan. In the triathlete's diet there will be a greater emphasis on increased calories, and on increased carbohydrate intake within this larger calorie intake. Calories can be increased up to 5000 per day for men and 4000 for women (compared with general recommendations of 3000 and 2000 calories per day respectively), depending on the frequency and duration of training sessions. In the optimum diet for endurance sports, carbohydrate should contribute 60–70 per cent of the total energy intake and protein about 12 per cent, with the remainder coming from fat. The diet also needs to satisfy vitamin, mineral and fluid requirements.

Energy Systems

A basic knowledge of the body's energy systems can help to maximize dietary advantages. Energy from food eaten is converted into a form that the body can use. Exercising muscles rely on carbohydrate and fat as a main source of fuel; protein is used as a fuel only when the carbohydrate and fat sources run out.

Carbohydrate, fat and protein are converted into glucose, fatty acids and amino acids respectively and it is these that are used by the body for muscle contraction.

Glucose can be stored in the muscles and liver in the form of glycogen. The glycogen in the muscles is used as fuel, while liver glycogen is used to maintain normal blood glucose supplies to the brain. Muscle glycogen storage capacity increases with increased training but is still limited, and in relatively high-intensity exercise over a long period of time, such as a middle- or long-distance triathlon, or even during daily training, stores of muscle glycogen are depleted. There is no danger of complete energy depletion as plenty of fat can be stored in the body, but energy produced by fat will allow the normal individual to work only at about 50 per cent of maximum exercise capacity; a very well-trained triathlete may be able to maintain up to 70 per cent using fat as fuel. If the muscle glycogen levels are low because of a low carbohydrate intake, depletion will occur quickly, and as fat becomes the more prominent fuel, the pace of exercise slows.

During an event the triathlete uses a mixture of both fat and carbohydrate fuels. If both are available, fat is used in preference to carbohydrate for up to 50 per cent of the athlete's energy needs. This allows the body's limited carbohydrate stores to be eked out. In endurance races, almost all participants slow down as the race proceeds, and the winner is usually the one who slows down least. Slowing down allows fat to provide a greater proportion of energy.

A triathlete performs most of the race at 80 per cent of maximum effort, which would mean, for example, 8-minute miling for the run. During the swim and the cycle, fat and carbohydrate contribute equally as fuels but, halfway through the run, carbohydrate runs out. As a result, power output falls to 40 per cent of maximum effort, producing a speed of 16 minutes per mile. This explains why some non-élite triathletes may walk in later stages of the run, despite efforts to keep running. This phenomenon is known as the 'wall' by marathon runners and as 'bonking' by cyclists. It would be unusual for élite triathletes to experience this in a competition, as their muscles can use fat more efficiently allowing the limited carbohydrate stores to be eked out and finishing the event without 'running out' of carbohydrate.

DIETARY COMPONENTS

The raw materials for the energy-producing system are the food and drink consumed by the individual. The groups to consider are carbohydrates (including fibre), protein, fats, vitamins and minerals, and fluids.

Carbohydrates

Carbohydrates represent the main source of energy in a triathlete's diet and should form the basis of each meal. Most carbohydrate foods contain significant amounts of essential vitamins and minerals and, in an unprocessed state, fibre. Carbohydrates may be starches (complex carbohydrates) or sugars (simple carbohydrates). The body breaks down the complex carbohydrates to form simple sugar (glucose). The glycaemic index, which compares the characteristics of different carbohydrates, is generally determined by the rate at which the carbohydrate eaten is made available for fuel (it is a function of gastric emptying time).

Using this system it is possible to have both simple and complex carbohydrates that are easily absorbed and have, therefore, a high glycaemic index. For example, baked potatoes and maltodextrin starches produce glycaemic responses that are identical to the response of glucose – in other words, they are quickly absorbed – whereas the rise in blood glucose after eating the simple sugar fructose is less than for bread or cornflakes.

When carbohydrates are required quickly, athletes should ingest those that are easily absorbed and have a high glycaemic index. A number of the newer 'athletic' nutrition products are labelled in this way.

Endurance athletes who need to increase their carbohydrate intake should eat starches (complex carbohydrates). These, which include potatoes, rice and corn, are less energy-dense (containing a small number of calories per gram) than simple sugars and a greater quantity can be eaten in order to obtain the equivalent number of calories.

Complex carbohydrates are also high in fibre and other nutrients and are digested slowly so that absorption into the body takes place over a long time. This slow digestion encourages the storage of carbohydrates as glycogen. A greater intake of fibre is beneficial in many ways – an intake of more than

Carbohydrate Foods	
Cereals and grains	Bread, rolls, crackers, breakfast cereals, porridge, pasta, rice*
Beans	Lentils, soya beans, kidney beans, baked beans
Vegetables	Roots such as potatoes and carrots as well as the green leafy varieties
Fruit	All varieties
Sugar	A high-energy food that does not contain any other essential nutrients

*Wholemeal varieties contain greater quantities of fibre, vitamins and minerals

Fig 61. Pasta party the night before a race or training session.

30g a day decreases the risk of bowel disease, constipation, diverticulitus and colon cancer. Increasing fibre intake by eating wholegrain foods is preferable to taking bran additives.

Carbohydrate is the most important nutrient in the triathlete's diet because it is the only component that can fuel intense exercise for prolonged periods. However, its stores within the body are relatively small and triathletes are often undernourished with respect to carbohydrate. Those who train intensely several times a day can suffer from daily glycogen depletion, which has an adverse effect on training and performance. Increasing carbohydrate intake can speed up recovery from such heavy training and can also improve performance during competition. Individuals must ensure that their diet contains a sufficient quantity. For athletes engaged in heavy training, the daily carbohydrate requirement may be as high as 9–10g per kg of body mass per day. This should guarantee adequate carbohydrate prior to and during exercise, and allow full recovery of reserves afterwards.

After each training session or competition, athletes should take some carbohydrate immediately – preferably 1g of high glycaemic index carbohydrate per kg of body weight within 30 minutes – to start replenishing the glycogen stores. This can be provided by easily absorbed high-carbohydrate snacks (*see* table, page 140). Athletes who do not feel like eating solids after heavy exercise can drink fluids containing glucose, sucrose or maltodextrins (*see* 'Fluids', page 146).

Protein

Protein foods include red meat, fish and chicken; milk, cheeses, yoghurt and eggs; legumes, nuts and seeds. Foods contain different amounts of protein: by dry weight, spinach is 40 per cent protein, soya beans 35 per cent, eggs 50 per cent and lean meats and fish 75 per cent.

Proteins are made up of amino acids. All body cells are partly composed of these so an adequate protein intake is essential for building and repairing body tissues. Different combinations of amino acids are needed for different growth and repair mechanisms. Twenty-two amino acids have been identified, and proteins consist of anything from eight to eighteen of these bonded together in various amounts and combinations. The bonding is broken down by digestion, which allows the amino acids to be absorbed into the blood and utilized by the body cells.

The amino acids that are provided preformed in food are termed *essential*. In reality all amino acids are essential, but more than

Carbohydrate Snacks

- Carton of UHT semi-skimmed or skimmed milk, fruit juice
- Can of diet drink
- Plastic bottle (500ml) UHT low-fat flavoured milk
- Canned fruit in natural juice, in ring-pull tin
- Fresh fruit – banana, orange, pear, apple, grape, melon

- Dried fruit – raisins, dates, figs, prunes, apricots
- Teacake, currant bun, maltloaf (no butter or margarine), swiss roll, scone
- Pot of UHT rice pudding or custard (preferably low-fat variety)
- Low-fat UHT fruit flavoured/plain yoghurt (with added muesli if desired)
- Rice cake, crispbread with jam, honey

The following individual items will provide 50g of carbohydrate:

Vegetables and Pulses
150g baked potato
180g parsnip
60g instant mash
450g can baked beans
½ of 440g can chickpeas
½ of 440g red kidney beans
430g can cannellini beans
400g can sweetcorn

Breakfast Cereals
2 average helpings porridge
(made with water)
3 Shredded Wheat
4 Weetabix
1½ average helpings Shreddies
2 average helpings Fruit 'n'
Fibre
6 tbsps Alpen
2 average helpings bran flakes
14 tbsps Rice Krispies
10 tbsps cornflakes
9 tbsps grape nuts
(quarter pint of low-fat milk will
add 6g)

Sugars and Preserves
10 tsps granulated sugar
7 tsps honey
8 tsps jam
(all teaspoons are level)

Puddings
425g can low-fat rice
2½ 200g pots of Mullerice
300ml low-fat custard
1½ average helpings jelly
2 × 150g pots fruit-flavoured
low-fat yogurt
2 average helpings crème
caramel

Cereal Bars
3½ Trackers
3 Jordans Crunchy
2½ Jordans Fruesli

Fruit
4–5 medium apples
3 medium bananas
125g dried apricots
4–5 medium pears
4–5 medium oranges

8 tbsps raisins
410g tin of fruit in natural
juice

Grains and Cereals
75g uncooked rice
70g uncooked wholewheat
pasta
Half a 9in pizza base (thick)
425g canned spaghetti in
tomato sauce

Confectionery
8 boiled sweets
1½ Milky Way bars
1 standard-size Mars bar
70g Liquorice Allsorts

Drinks
850ml (1½ pints) 6 per cent
carbohydrate sports drink
1060ml (2 pints) diluted
orange juice (1:1)
Diluted orange squash (1:5 =
175ml squash in 875ml
water = 1050ml/1½ pints)
475ml (1½ cans) Coca-Cola

one-half of them can be made within the body. The number of essential amino acids present in a protein food determines its 'biological value'. For example, meat, fish, eggs and cheese all contain a relatively large number of essential amino acids and thus have a high biological value. For comparative purposes, the World Health Organization classifies the proteins in milk, meat and hens' eggs as '100 per cent'. Using this ranking system, soya beans are also given a 100 per cent value, with green vegetables as 70–90 per cent, potatoes 76 per cent, brown rice 66 per cent and peanuts 62 per cent.

Protein foods also contain essential vitamins and minerals and may serve as a source of energy if required.

Athletes have a slightly higher requirement for protein than the general population, but high-protein foods are often high in fat. High-protein foods also take longer to digest and can cause discomfort for a triathlete attempting to undertake a number of training sessions each day.

The amount of protein needed for the body to function optimally depends on the amount of active tissues an individual has, so protein requirements are expressed as an amount per unit of body weight. A protein intake of 10–15 per cent of total energy or 1.5g per kg body weight is adequate, perhaps increasing up to 2.5g per kg body weight for triathletes building up their training, adolescents and those training more than three hours per day. This intake can be met through a normal diet, as most triathletes will already consume sufficient protein as a consequence of their increased energy intake.

Protein Content of some Common Foods

Animal proteins (g protein per 100g)
Tuna 28.0
Cheese 25.4
Pork sausages 22.0
Beef 14.8
Eggs 11.9
Milk 3.3

Vegetable proteins (g protein per 100g)
Peanuts 28.1
Peas (dried) 21.5
Bran Flakes 11.5
Wholemeal bread 9.6
White bread 8.3
Baked potatoes 2.0

It would appear that taking protein supplements and eating high-quality protein foods does not improve a triathlete's performance. Excess protein cannot be stored and, if not used by the body, is simply excreted in urine. Triathletes should primarily concentrate on eating a diet high in carbohydrate, and maintain an adequate protein intake. By eating mostly vegetable proteins, triathletes can maintain the recommended high-carbohydrate and low-fat training diet with an adequate intake of protein.

Triathletes who choose not to eat red meat need not lose out on proteins, as fish and poultry actually have a slightly higher protein content than red meat. While the trend to increase protein from vegetable sources (such as legumes, nuts and seeds), with a moderate contribution from animal protein, is healthy, eating lean meat does also contribute the essential nutrients of iron and zinc (*see* page 142, Vitamins and Minerals).

Fat

Fat is the most concentrated source of food energy (calories). Each gram of fat supplies about 9 calories, compared with about 4 calories per gram for protein or carbohydrate, and 7 calories per gram for alcohol. In addition to providing energy, fat aids in the absorption of certain vitamins and provides insulation. Foods containing fat have a high satiety value and are appetizing and full of flavour.

Butter, margarine, lard and oil are obvious sources of fat, along with fatty meats, poultry skin, whole milk, cheese, ice cream, nuts, seeds, salad dressings and some baked products.

Different types of fat commonly discussed are the following.

Cholesterol

Cholesterol is not needed in the diet, and high blood cholesterol levels tend to increase the risk of heart disease. Cholesterol is present in all animal tissues, meat, poultry and fish, in milk and milk products and in egg yolks. Cholesterol is not found in foods of plant origin such as fruits, vegetables, grains, nuts, seeds and dried beans and peas.

Saturated Fatty Acids

Saturated fats raise blood cholesterol levels. They are found in large proportions in fats of animal origin. These include the fats in whole milk, cream, cheese, eggs, butter, meat and poultry. Saturated fats are solid at room temperature. They are also found in large amounts in coconut and palm oil.

Monounsaturated Fatty Acids

Monounsaturated fats may have a beneficial effect on lowering blood cholesterol levels. They are found in fats of both plant and animal origin, particularly olive oil and peanut oil. Most margarines and hydrogenated vegetable shortenings also tend to be high in monounsaturated fatty acids.

Polyunsaturated Fatty Acids

Polyunsaturated fats can help to lower blood cholesterol levels. They are found in largest proportions in fats of plant origin and are soft or even liquid at room temperature. Sunflower, corn, soya-bean and safflower oils are vegetable oils that usually contain a high proportion of polyunsaturated fatty acids. Some fish are also a source of polyunsaturated fatty acids.

Note: all fats, whether they contain mainly saturated fatty acids, monounsaturated fatty acids, or polyunsaturated fatty acids, provide the same number of calories.

Fat is a very efficient fuel for storage as it produces more energy per gram than carbohydrate, it is not stored with water like carbohydrate and the body has a large reserve. The one disadvantage of fat is that it can only be used as fuel aerobically whereas carbohydrate can be utilized both with and without oxygen.

For most people, fat intake is far in excess of their needs. A high fat intake can lead to obesity because of the large number of calories, and can contribute to heart disease. Fat intake from animal origins (butter, cream, full cream milk, cheese and meat) should be reduced. An endurance athlete's diet should contain only 25–30 per cent fat, allowing for a higher carbohydrate and adequate protein intake. Cutting down on fat intake may be the only major change triathletes need to make to their normal diet.

Take the following steps to decrease fat intake:

- minimize the use of butter and margarine on bread; alternatively, use a low-fat substitute;
- minimize the use of fats (butter, margarine, oil) in cooking, choosing instead such methods as grilling, baking, steaming, boiling and microwaving, or stir fry in minimal amounts of oil;
- use lean cuts of beef, lamb and pork and remove the skin from chicken;
- eat fish, fresh or canned (such as tuna or salmon in water or brine);
- use low-fat milk products such as skimmed or semi-skimmed milk, low-fat yoghurt, cottage cheese, quark or fromage frais (hard cheeses have a high fat content);
- avoid the following foods on a regular basis: cream, sour cream, mayonnaise, cream cheese, high-fat salad dressings, cakes, pies, pastries, chocolate, chips and crisps, fast foods and ice cream.

Vitamins and Minerals

Some researchers claim that a balanced diet adjusted for calorie needs will provide all the athlete requirements in terms of vitamins and minerals; others believe that nutritional supplements are essential.

Vitamins play an important part in the formation of red blood cells, utilization of oxygen in the cell and in carbohydrate, protein and fat metabolism. Minerals are also involved – calcium in neuromuscular activity, iron in oxygen transport. Of the minerals and trace elements essential for health, particular attention should be paid to iron and calcium. Iron deficiency is fairly common among endurance athletes.

Generally, supplements should not be necessary for an athlete eating a diet adequate in both quality and quantity. Supplements need only be taken if a triathlete is on a very restricted diet (fewer than 1200 kcals per day) or on a junk-food diet. A low-dose, broad-range nutritional supplement may then be beneficial, but it will not make a poor diet good. Large doses are not recommended because of toxicity.

Figures for a Recommended Daily Allowance (RDA) have been devised for the main vitamins and minerals and these may be shown on food labels. The requirements depend on a person's age, gender and activity level. For simplicity, a single value for each nutrient has been chosen; this value represents the *highest* requirement for a normal adult. For example, the iron figure is based on the RDA for women under the age of 55, whose iron needs are greater than those of men or older women.

Vitamins

Vitamins must be present in the daily diet because they cannot be synthesized by the body at a sufficient rate to satisfy its needs. Vitamins occur widely in many foods and are easily provided in a properly prepared mixed diet containing fresh fruits and vegetables. Although the therapeutic effects of vitamin supplementation are dramatic in a deficient person, it does not follow that the same improvements will occur if large doses of vitamins are ingested along with a normal, balanced diet.

Vitamin requirements are not increased before or during strenuous exercise and the body cannot be loaded as most vitamins are not stored; the excess is rapidly excreted. All of the fat-soluble vitamins (A, D, E and K) can be stored, primarily in the liver, but extra amounts of these vitamins are either inactive and therefore of no benefit, or toxic, producing serious symptoms.

A healthy triathlete eating a well-balanced diet will receive adequate amounts of all the essential vitamins. Supplements will not improve performance, but vitamin deficiencies of all kinds will be damaging to performance. How long performance can be maintained when one or more vitamins are omitted from the diet will vary according to the individual's tissue reserves of the particular vitamin, and the role of that vitamin in exercise. Because of their participation in metabolism, lack of the B vitamins will probably have the most

immediate effects; lack of thiamine is evident in a few days or weeks and the symptoms appear earlier in active individuals. On the other hand, the effects of vitamin A deficiency may not appear for months in previously well-nourished subjects.

Although there is no evidence that exercise increases vitamin requirements, increased activity does increase calorie requirements and, subsequently, the requirements for the B complex vitamins thiamine and niacin, which are involved in energy release. Some diets may be below recommended levels of thiamine (B1) if the large energy intake of the athletes is taken into account.

Chemical and physical changes occur in food as a result of preparation. Storage in light and air reduces the vitamin content of most foods. Cooking procedures are also important. Vitamin C is the least stable and is partially destroyed in water and readily destroyed in air. Between 50 and 70 per cent of vitamin C in fruit and vegetables is lost during cooking. This loss is reduced if the skin is left intact.

Vitamin A is fat-soluble and locked inside the cell walls of vegetables. Cooked in the correct way (steaming or microwaving), diced carrots can provide more than three times the vitamin A of raw carrots.

Milling of cereals such as wheat and oats results in a loss of nutrients. Wholegrain (unrefined) products have a much higher nutrient value. Some cereal products are labelled 'enriched' or 'fortified', meaning that the vitamins lost during milling have been added back. These nutrients are usually thiamine, riboflavin, niacin and the mineral iron. This process of enrichment returns the important nutrients, so there is no great difference between the nutrient value of wholegrain and enriched products.

Minerals

Minerals are used by the body in complex ways and interrelate with each other to perform different functions. For example, calcium is directly related to the development of healthy bones and teeth but is also utilized by the body to regulate the heartbeat and to exert a balance between sodium and potassium in maintaining muscle tone.

Generally, minerals provide the substance for bones and teeth and are present in soft tissues and fluids enabling cells to function properly (allowing body fluid balance, muscle contractility, nerve response and blood clotting). Minerals can be effective as performance enhancers only if an athlete is deficient, usually as a result of a poor diet. Calcium, magnesium, zinc, iron and copper are of the most importance to endurance athletes, who often show deficiencies in iron and zinc. With the possible exceptions of calcium and iron, any deficiencies can easily be corrected by the establishment of a well-balanced diet. Minerals ensure good health rather than enhancing performance.

Iron (RDA = 10mg for men, 18mg for women)
(Found in liver, baked beans, potatoes, bread, peas, fresh green vegetables; 80g split peas provide 1.2mg.)

Iron deficiency is fairly common among endurance athletes and occurs more in women, vegetarians and those on low-energy diets. Once a deficiency has developed it cannot be reversed by diet alone and iron supplements become necessary. If iron stores are depleted, less iron is available for haemoglobin formation (haemoglobin is a substance in the blood essential for carrying oxygen around the body), and the concentration of haemoglobin decreases. The oxygen-carrying capacity of the blood depends on haemoglobin concentration and low levels are associated with a decrease in maximum oxygen uptake and therefore in physical working capacity.

Iron-deficient (anaemic) individuals show symptoms of early fatigue, breathlessness and headaches. To remain in iron balance, the iron absorbed from the diet must equal the amount of iron lost by the body. In normal circumstances, men and non-menstruating women lose approximately 1mg of iron per day through urine, faeces, sweat and cell breakdown. Menstruating women with normal cycles lose an average of 1.5mg per day. A balanced western diet would easily contain enough iron to replace these small losses, but only 10 per cent of the dietary intake of iron can be absorbed into the body; the remainder is excreted.

To help prevent iron deficiency an adequate dietary intake is essential. Dietary iron comes from two sources: foods containing 'haem iron' and foods containing 'non-haem iron'. Haem iron is present in meat, offal, poultry and fish and is well absorbed. Non-haem iron is found in pulses, grains, cereals, and vegetables and is poorly absorbed. Vitamin C enhances iron absorption, and meat, fish and poultry increase the absorption of non-haem iron. Absorption of iron is adversely affected by the tannin in tea and coffee.

Iron balance can be achieved if men take in 10mg of iron per day and women 18mg per day. In a normal, balanced diet there will be approximately 6mg of iron per 1000kcals ingested. This makes the 10mg target for men fairly easy to attain, but a woman eating the same diet would be deficient . It is common for women to take in only 10–12mg per day.

The following will maximize your dietary intake and availability of iron:

- eat lean red meat (beef, lamb, pork) approximately three times a week;
- include liver in your diet once a fortnight;
- have fish and poultry regularly;
- include non-haem iron foods such as wholegrain bread, and cereals, pulses, green leafy vegetables and dried fruits;
- include a source of vitamin C at each meal (orange juice, fruit or vegetables) as this aids absorption; and
- avoid drinking tea and coffee with meals

Iron supplements have been found to be effective in improving the performance of iron-deficient individuals. However, increased haemoglobin levels and improvements in performance have generally only been shown in subjects who were initially deficient. Triathletes should have their iron status evaluated annually; iron supplements should be taken only if a deficiency is reported. There is a danger of iron toxicity if large amounts of iron supplements are used.

Calcium (RDA = 800mg)
(Found in milk, cheese, carrots, leafy green vegetables; 30g cheddar provides 205mg)

Vitamin and Mineral Summary

Vitamin	Source	Functions
Vitamin A	Liver, carrots, dark green vegetables, fish, liver oil, eggs, butter, margarine	Helps to fight infections; prevents bacteria and viruses from entering the body by keeping the cell walls strong; good for the skin and necessary for vision in dim light
Vitamin B group: Thiamine (B1), Riboflavin (B2), Niacin, Folic Acid (B12)	Milk, meat, fish, fruit, vegetables, cereals, eggs, nuts and bread	Helps the breakdown of carbohydrate, protein and fat to release energy; essential for the functioning of nerves; so a daily supply is important
Vitamin C	Fresh and frozen fruit and vegetables; products fortified with vitamin C	Needed to fight infections; helps absorption of iron and promotes healthy skin; cannot be stored so daily supply necessary
Vitamin D	Produced by the body; also in liver, fish oil, eggs, fortified breakfast cereals, butter and margarine	Formed mainly by the action of sunlight on the skin; helps the body to absorb and use calcium and phosphorus for strong bones and healthy teeth
Vitamin E	Many foods, especially vegetable oils, eggs, green leafy vegetables	Helps to protect the cells
Vitamin K	Produced by the body; also in green leafy vegetables, liver	Plays a vital role in the blood-clotting mechanisms

Mineral	Source	Functions
Calcium	Milk, cheese, fish, beans, dark green vegetables	Forms the structure of bones and teeth; in constant demand, so a regular supply is vital
Iron	Meat, liver, dark green vegetables, peas, beans	Needed for the formation of red blood cells, which help to transport oxygen round the body
Phosphorus	Liver, fish, poultry, eggs, cheese, milk, wholegrain cereals, nuts	Helps build bones and teeth and to regulate many internal activities of the body

Trace elements – zinc, selenium, sodium, potassium, iodine, chlorine, copper, manganese and magnesium – are needed in tiny amounts and perform a variety of functions. They are found in a wide range of foods and deficiency is very rare.

The body contains more calcium than any other mineral, mostly in the bones and teeth. Its presence in soft tissues and fluids is also essential. If there is a calcium deficiency, muscle spasms may occur and bone density may be lost, but if too much is present it may be deposited in the muscles and organs, impairing function.

A very low calcium intake is thought to contribute to the bone-wasting condition of osteoporosis. In women, osteoporosis is generally caused by a drop in the level of the hormone oestrogen due to menopause or ammenorrhoea (lack of menstrual periods) and possibly by low intake of calcium and an inactive lifestyle. While female triathletes are unlikely to suffer due to inactivity, one of the strongest predictors of osteoporosis is long-term ammenorrhoea. Medical experts recommend that such women consume 1500mg of calcium per day.

Salt (Sodium) Some salt is needed by the body, but the average western diet contains considerably more salt than required; an excess leads to high blood pressure. Although sodium is lost from the body through sweating, the kidneys increase their retention of sodium and other electrolytes during exercise and for this reason sodium loss is slight.

As triathletes have a high calorie intake, salt intake is likely to be high, unless it is consciously restricted. Adding salt to food is only necessary if there is a combination of intense daily endurance training, a hot environment and a low-sodium diet.

Fluids

Fluid intake is very important to the triathlete during both training and competition. Large amounts are lost through perspiration during exercise, especially in a hot, humid environment. If this is not replaced, dehydration occurs, stressing the body and leading to a decrease in performance, and overheating.

Water is the most suitable fluid to drink and at least 5 litres should be incorporated into the daily diet. Drink plenty before a training session and also during long bike rides and runs. Any weight loss noted when weighing before and after a training session will reflect the amount of fluid lost from the body during that session; this needs to be replaced. For every kilogram lost, 1 litre of water should be drunk. Exercise performance is impaired by the plasma volume decreases that accompany dehydration and a loss of as little as 2 per cent of body weight can have a marked effect.

Drinking in training will help you build up a tolerance for taking essential fluids while racing. Fluid intake should not be based on thirst, as this is not a reliable indicator of fluid needs. Urine colour is a good indicator; with good hydration, it will be the colour of pale straw.

Fluid ingestion during exercise aims to supply water, replacing losses incurred by sweating and to provide a source of carbohydrate fuel, supplementing the body's limited stores. There may also be a need to replace the electrolytes lost in sweat. If using a fluid containing carbohydrates, the composition of drinks taken will be determined by the relative needs to supply fuel and water. This in turn depends on the intensity and duration of the exercise task, on the ambient temperature and humidity and on the characteristics of the individual.

Increasing the carbohydrate content of drinks will increase the amount of fuel that can be supplied to muscles, but tends to decrease the rate at which water can be made available. High concentrations (more than 10 per cent for simple sugars and more than 15 per cent for glucose polymers) of carbohydrate may delay gastric emptying, reducing the availability of the fluid, while very high concentrations may increase the likelihood of dehydration, as water has to be secreted in to the intestine. Where provision of water is the first priority, as in prolonged events at a high ambient temperature, the carbohydrate content of drinks should be low. Carbohydrate depletion may result in fatigue and a reduction in exercise intensity, but this is not normally a life-threatening situation. However, disturbances in fluid and electrolyte balance and in temperature regulation have potentially more serious consequences; as such, the majority of triathletes should be emphasizing the maintenance of proper fluid and electrolyte balance.

The *type* of carbohydrate in the drink does not appear to be critical for performance; glucose, sucrose and long-chain glucose polymers are all readily used by the muscles. Fructose is best avoided because of possible gastrointestinal upset. Instructions on the packaging should be followed. Drinks should have a pleasant taste to stimulate consumption – remember that flavours taste stronger when exercising. The temperature of the beverage is not important as long as it is palatable.

Electrolyte replacement may not be necessary in an Olympic-distance race, but triathletes may suffer from salt depletion when performing in ultra-distance events in a very hot environment. Salt depletion occurs more in the unfit athlete. In Ironman races, electrolytes are important; competitors taking large amounts of low-sodium fluids have shown symptoms of hyponatraemia or water intoxication (body fluid dilution), which are potentially life-threatening. Adding electrolytes to fluids may help prevent this. The addition of small amounts of sodium also stimulates sugar and water uptake from the gut.

Alcohol

For the serious triathlete, alcohol consumption should be restricted. Alcohol has a dehydrating and blood sugar lowering effect, which combined with exercise can cause problems. If you are serious about your training only take alcohol in small quantities and avoid consumption completely for two days prior to a race and immediately after a long distance race.

ERGOGENIC AIDS

An ergogenic aid is an aid to improve athletic performance that aims to substitute or augment training. Beware of advertiser's claims – the most potent ergogenic aid is effective training itself. There is no good evidence to support the use of alternative nutritional supplements, including those commonly assumed by athletes to have ergogenic effects, such as bee pollen, caffeine, carnitine, and creatine.

Bee pollen is a mixture of various vitamins, minerals, amino acids, and other organic compounds. There is no research to show how bee pollen aids recovery or contributes to any improvement in recovery times.

The IOC allow the use of *caffeine* in limited amounts as it occurs naturally in the diet. Caffeine is a stimulant. Its psychological effects are to increase arousal, attention, motivation and concentration. Its physiological effects act in a similar way to adrenaline (a hormone produced by the body), increasing muscle blood flow and the level of free fatty acids in the blood. In theory, this increases the use of fat as an energy source, sparing glycogen.

Studies have shown improvements in endurance capacity but only with high doses of caffeine (well above the banned level). The effect of caffeine appears to be more psychological than physiological. Everyday consumption of caffeine leads to a tolerance and benefit will be seen only after abstinence from caffeine

A Few Sports Drinks					
Product	Type	E	Cb	Sodium	Type
Isostar	Powder/drink	27	6.6	40	Fluid and carbo replacer
Lucozade Sport	Drink	26	6.9	55	Fluid and carbo replacer
Ultrafuel	Drink	40	22.5	Nil	Carbo replacer
Maxim (or High 5)	Powder	40*	10.7*	Nil	Carbo replacer
Isostar Light	Drink	17	3.8	Trace	Fluid replacer
Low-Calorie Lucozade Sport	Drink	3	0.7	30	Fluid replacer

(*made with 4 scoops/750ml)

for at least 4 days. A high-carbohydrate diet will blunt the effect of caffeine and may stimulate the release of the hormone insulin, which inhibits the releases of free fatty acids.

Some coaches recommend taking one or two cups of strong black coffee an hour before a middle- or long-distance race where glycogen-sparing is an issue. However, this is not very practical. Large intakes are illegal and not healthy. Caffeine also has unwelcome side-effects. It is a diuretic and increases the basal metabolic rate and heat production, causing problems when competing in hot countries.

Carnitine is found in most cells in the body. Its major function is to act as a carrier to facilitate the transport of fatty acids into the mitochondria of the cells, where they are broken down to produce energy. In theory, increasing the levels of carnitine would supply more fatty acids for energy production, sparing glycogen. The limited research so far suggests no improvement in performance, however, with carnitine supplementation. Currently, its use is legal. It is important to use the L-carnitine rather than the D- or DL-forms, as the latter have a greater potential for toxicity.

Creatine is found naturally in the diet and therefore in the body. When the body begins intense work quickly, for example, at the start of a sprint, it uses a reserve of energy that is present in the muscle; this is creatine phosphate. Creatine phosphate provides energy for just a few seconds before other energy systems come into play.

The theory behind creatine supplementation is that creatine phosphate stores in the muscle will be increased, allowing the explosive energy store to last longer. Investigations have shown that such supplementation does increase the creatine phosphate content of muscles, and that exercise performance is enhanced. However, the benefits are only seen in sprinting and in multiple-sprint type activities, like football. It would seem that there is little benefit for the endurance triathlete, except perhaps when doing high-intensity speed work in training.

Any adverse side-effects have yet to be documented. At the time of writing, creatine supplementation is not a banned practice.

VEGETARIANISM

If a triathlete chooses a vegetarian diet, a basic knowledge of nutrition is essential. It is easy for fat intake to become high and protein low as plant protein generally has a lower biological value than animal protein. Combinations of plant protein foods can be taken in a meal to ensure complete protein intake. The following are suitable combinations:

- grains and legumes (baked beans on toast; lentil soup and bread);
- grains and nuts (peanut butter sandwich; nuts sprinkled on rice or pasta salad); or
- the addition of a glass of milk or some cheese to a meal.

Depending on the type of vegetarian diet, intake of the following nutrients may be inadequate:

- protein (only if the diet is poorly planned); vitamin B12 (only if dairy products are excluded as well as meat, fish and chicken);
- calcium (especially when dairy products are excluded); tahini is a good source;
- iron (although plant foods contain iron, this is poorly absorbed and supplementation may be required);
- zinc; in most vegetarian diets, zinc intake is low and supplementation may be required; and
- vitamin B2 (only if dairy products are excluded).

IDEAL BODY WEIGHT

One area of concern for triathletes is body weight. Being either under- or overweight can have an adverse effect on strength, endurance and speed, and thus on athletic performance. If you are carrying excess weight when taking up training, your weight will usually drop to the right level automatically after a period of endurance training accompanied by a suitable training diet. However, your diet should be adjusted if too much weight is lost, as this indicates a breakdown of muscle tissue.

Body-weight information needs to be interpreted correctly. Athletes carry a higher ratio of muscle bulk than non-athletes and may be heavier. Normal 'weight for height' charts are not applicable. Body fat measures may be more useful to the triathlete. Percentage body fat can be assessed using skin-fold callipers to measure skin-fold thickness in different sites on the body. Desirable fat percentages for the normal population are 13–15 per cent for men and 20–25 per cent for women. For élite triathletes, appropriate levels range from 6–12 per cent for men and 10–18 per cent for women. The wide range indicates that successful triathletes come in a variety of shapes and sizes. Excess body fat results from either a large number of fat cells, or from very large fat cells. The number of fat cells remains constant from adolescence.

The best way to lose body fat is simply to reduce the amount of fat taken in the diet. As fat is very high in energy (calories), a reduction in fat intake should lead to a decrease in energy intake. It is important that energy intake (calories taken in food) does not exceed energy expenditure (calories burnt up during activity), as any excess of carbohydrate or fat is stored as fat. As fat is very energy-dense, decreasing energy intake need not mean small meals; if complex carbohydrates are chosen in preference to fat, less than half the calories are consumed for the same weight of food. Eating a low-fat diet should not cause any nutrient deficiency.

To reduce fat intake, choose foods that contain a relatively low proportion of fat. The amount of fat in poultry and meats is quite variable depending on the feeding conditions and age of the animal. Young animals are relatively low in fat. Shrimp, oysters, crab and many fishes (tuna, halibut) are very low in fat (1–2 per cent of cooked weight). Fatty fishes such as herring and mackerel have 13–16 per cent fat. Chicken eggs have about 11 per cent fat, all in the yolk, which is one-third fat. Milk varies in fat content, with whole milk being marketed at about 3.3–3.7 per cent fat. Milk fat is also present in cheeses, which range from a low of 4 per cent fat in cottage cheese to 30–35 per cent fat in Cheddar types.

Some plants store fats in fruits, seeds, or nuts, and common vegetable oils such as olive, coconut, soya-bean, corn and palm oil are obtained from these. Most common nuts contain 50–70 per cent fat, and soya beans about 30 per cent. Avocados and olives range from 11–20 per cent fat; whole cereal grains have 2–6 per cent fat.

Much of the fat eaten in the daily diet is invisible and added to foods in such a way that it becomes part of the product. Fat is added for texture and flavour, and a low-fat food may become a high-fat food when prepared for eating. For example, potatoes have only traces of fat, but crisps are 40 per cent fat.

If you wish to lose body fat without compromising your training or performance, follow the guidelines below:

- do not follow a crash diet, as these are severely restricted and lack vital nutrients, which can affect performance and health in general; extreme diets frequently lead to bingeing;
- although calorie intake needs to be reduced, it is important to take adequate amounts of complex carbohydrates, protein, vitamins, minerals and fluids.

The main avenues for cutting down are to reduce fat intake, avoid refined carbohydrates (sugar and sweet foods), avoid alcohol and aim for a gradual weight reduction (0.5–1kg per week maximum).

SPECIFIC DIETS

The Training Diet

Day-to-day eating patterns should be based on the basic healthy diet with a high calorie intake (at least 5000 calories for men and 4000 for women triathletes) consisting of a high percentage (60–75 per cent) of carbohydrate. If your body weight is appropriate and stable, this – and appetite – can act as a guide to requirements.

Triathletes working and training may find it difficult to eat adequate amounts of quality food. Try to have at least three well-balanced meals a day, interspersed with smaller meals or snacks if you are training twice a day or more. It is usually not advisable to eat immediately prior to a hard session but a slice of toast or cereal with low-fat milk is usually tolerated by most people prior to a steady cycle or swim.

Of the 60–75 per cent carbohydrate in your diet, most should be complex – wholemeal bread, cereals, rice, potatoes, pasta, vegetables and fruit. Intake of refined carbohydrates such as sugary, sweet foods should be moderate, although these can be an easy way of consuming extra calories without eating too much bulk, especially when energy needs are high (when training exceeds 3 hours per day).

High-Carbohydrate, Low-Fat Meals and Snacks

Breakfast
- Wholemeal toast with minimal or no butter, margarine or low-fat spread with marmite or jam, honey, banana, cottage cheese, tomato, boiled or poached egg.
- Wholegrain cereal (muesli, Shredded Wheat, puffed wheat, Weetabix, Bran Flakes, porridge) with low-fat milk and fruit. Check the labels on cereal packs, as some products contain a high percentage of added sugar and fat.
- Drink low-fat milk, fruit juice, water or tea and coffee if desired.

Lunch
- Wholemeal bread sandwiches or rolls with low-fat spread. Suitable fillings include tuna, chicken (skin removed), lean meat, cottage cheese, egg, peanut butter*, cheddar cheese*, marmite, banana or salad items.
- Baked potatoes and salad.
- Baked beans, spaghetti or egg (poached or scrambled) on toast.
- Rice or pasta with low-fat sauce such as tomato or mushroom and yoghurt.
- Fresh fruit.
- Drink skimmed milk, fruit juice and water.

(*Caution: high fat content)

Dinner
- Lean meat or fish, chicken (skin removed), eggs, pulses, tofu, and so on.

- Steamed or baked potatoes, rice, pasta, or bread.
- Variety of vegetables cooked or raw, including some green leafy varieties.
- Fruit salad or low-fat yoghurt, skimmed-milk pudding.

Snacks
- Sandwiches.
- Fresh or dried fruit.
- Crackers or crispbread with cottage cheese, marmite, tomato, and so on.
- Low-fat yoghurt.
- Milk shake with low-fat milk and fruit.
- Low-fat baking such as fruit bread, malt loaf, scones, etc.
- Nuts and seeds (high in fat, so moderate amounts only).

Drink lots of extra glasses of water during the day.

Competition Diet

The objective is to ensure that you are optimally prepared to enhance performance. In the days prior to a race, it is important to ensure that the right foods are being eaten and sufficient fluids taken. Avoid unfamiliar foods and do not have alcohol for at least two days before the race.

For middle- and long-distance triathlons, a carbohydrate-loading regimen may be followed. The object of this is to superload the muscles with glycogen in an effort to maximize the body's energy stores and delay the onset of fatigue. With increased glycogen stores a certain race pace can be maintained for a longer period before fatigue slows the pace. This will improve overall performance time. Research has shown clearly the benefits of carbohydrate-loading; on a practical level, triathletes will have their own opinions and ideas.

Carbohydrate-loading is most appropriate for the highly competitive or motivated triathlete. Combining the loading with a suitable taper in training requires knowledge, discipline and practice, but the results can be worth it. Even if your main aim is simply to finish, the importance of starting with adequate glycogen stores cannot be ignored.

Over the last decades, different regimes for carbohydrate-loading have been researched and most triathletes now use a modification of an original depletion-loading regime. The depletion phase of hard and prolonged training sessions in each of the disciplines to deplete muscle glycogen was initially thought to be essential as depleted muscles store more glycogen. However, it is probably not necessary. After such sessions a couple of days were spent on a fat/protein diet, followed by tapering training and increasing carbohydrate intake to about 70–85 per cent of total energy for the three days leading up to the race.

The above regime does not represent a balanced eating plan, and should *only* be followed a couple of times a year when preparing for a long race, if at all.

A modified version of carbohydrate-loading can be undertaken before all races. On days 7, 6, 5 and 4 before competition, train moderately hard (1–2 hours) and consume a low-carbohydrate diet (350g per day). The muscle becomes carbohydrate-deprived and ready to supercompensate, but there are none of the side-effects that occur when all carbohydrate is eliminated.

In the three days prior to competition, taper training to 30–60 minutes per day of low to moderate intensity, and consume a high-carbohydrate diet (500–600g per day).

Glycogen binds with water, so it is important to take in more fluid. The body will thus hold more fluid after loading and effective loading can be checked by weight gain. You may put on 2–2.5kg during this time, and feel sluggish, but the extra fluids may help offset dehydration and the feeling will disappear as the fuel is used.

Individuals vary as to the most appropriate timing for carbohydrate-loading and the amount of carbohydrate needed to load. As water is stored with glycogen, unloading is accompanied by a high rate of urine production; if this occurs before a race, loading has begun too early. If too much carbohydrate is ingested, diarrhoea occurs, caused by unabsorbed sugars interfering with water uptake in the gut.

Keep fat intake to a minimum. Do not use butter or margarine on bread, avoid use of fats in cooking, avoid high-fat foods such as cream, sour cream, cream cheese, hard cheeses, butter, margarine, oil, peanut butter, nuts and seeds, chocolate, cakes, biscuits, pastries, pies, salad dressing (except low-fat), mayonnaise, fatty take-away foods, crisps and processed meats.

The Pre-Race Meal

The pre-race meals for short-, middle- and long-distance triathlons are all based on similar principles. The objectives are as follows: to provide for a relatively empty stomach, yet avoid hunger; to have no adverse effects on the body's energy stores and possibly contribute to the available amount of energy; to avoid any gastrointestinal problems that may affect performance; to provide adequate hydration.

Food intake will depend on the time of day of the competition and its length. The last big meal should be taken 14–16 hours before the race, usually the night before competition. A light carbohydrate snack prior to bedtime may be useful. After the overnight fast, a pre-exercise carbohydrate meal is recommended, to replenish liver glycogen and to promote the use of carbohydrate as a fuel. Sugar ingestion is generally not recommended. If time permits, a relatively large carbohydrate meal 3–4 hours before the race can improve performance. The meal should be low in fat, protein, fibre and bulk and needs to be well tolerated.

After eating, try to relax; rushing around will slow down the digestion. Avoid eating any last-minute snacks. Remember, anxiety will tend to slow the rate at which food moves out of the stomach; 2–3 hours digestion time may be enough for minor events, but the stress of a major competition may retard emptying even more.

Guidelines for the pre-race meal are:

- avoid fatty foods;
- avoid excessive intake of protein foods;
- avoid gas-forming foods such as legumes and onions;
- avoid high-fibre foods, as they digest slowly;
- avoid excessive intake of high-sugar foods, especially less than one hour before the race; a high intake of sugar at this time may

lead to a reactive low blood sugar level, which can impair performance;

• avoid spicy foods, which may cause indigestion;

• above all, avoid unfamiliar foods; the combination of unfamiliar or unsuitable together with pre-race nerves could have unpleasant consequences.

A suitable breakfast might consist of a bowl of cereal (cornflakes or Rice Krispies) with skimmed milk and fruit *or* white or brown bread toast, without butter, with jam, honey or banana and a drink of fruit juice. If you find a solid meal too difficult to take at this stage or cannot obtain the right food, a liquid replacement such as Maxim or High Five can be a suitable alternative.

In the hours leading up to the race, drink either water or very diluted fruit juice at regular intervals. If possible, drink some water approximately 30 minutes before the race start.

During Exercise

The aim during a race is to avoid glycogen depletion and dehydration. Fatigue due to glycogen depletion only occurs after 1½ to 3 hours of exercise at 60–80 per cent of maximum capacity, so water is probably all you need to take in a short-course triathlon. Some triathletes do use diluted fruit juice, Coca-Cola or energy replacement drinks. Glycogen depletion is an additional factor for all middle-distance and Ironman events, and for some competitors in Olympic-distance races.

Carbohydrate feedings during exercise will delay depletion and fatigue. Energy replacement drinks are ideal, as they provide fluid as well. For a 70kg person it is recommended that 50–60g of high-glycaemic index carbohydrate be ingested each hour (200–249 calories), beginning early in exercise.

There are two different types of drink: those containing simple sugars (glucose, sucrose, dextrose and fructose) and those with glucose polymers (units of glucose linked together). A glucose polymer drink can be taken in high concentrations, whereas simple sugar solutions cannot contain enough glucose to meet the body's need for carbohydrates in intense, endurance exercise. High concentrations of simple glucose can cause adverse gastro-intestinal reactions as well as decreasing the stomach's emptying rate. The relative concentration of the drink you choose will depend on the relative needs for carbohydrate and fluid replacement (*see* 'Fluids', page 146).

In practice, many triathletes like to eat something solid, especially in Ironman races. Choice will be limited, as the food must provide carbohydrate, be easy to prepare and to carry, agree with you and taste good. Popular choices are bananas, oranges, figs and dates, or low-fat energy bars.

Remember, it is essential to experiment in training with any food or drink before taking it in competition.

Other recommendations:

• Start drinking after the swim.
• Take fluids in volumes of 150–250ml every 15–20 minutes (or up to 1 litre per hour).
• If possible, use cold fluids as these are more palatable and add to the cooling effect.
• Use a fluid that tastes good, as you are likely to drink more of it.

Suitable concentrations are 2–5 per cent for simple sugars such as glucose or fruit juice (fruit juices contain approximately 10 per cent sugar, so need to be diluted). Glucose polymers can be 5–10 per cent or 50–100g per litre of fluid. Remember, if you are adding flavours, drinks taste stronger when you are racing.

Recovery

If you want to train and race again shortly, restore your pre-race energy, fluid and electrolyte balances as quickly as possible. Take in plenty of fluids and a high-carbohydrate meal or snack. Try to take at least 1g per kg of body weight of carbohydrate in the first 30 minutes after exercise (*see* 'Carbohydrates', page 138).

CHAPTER 19

Weight-Training and Resistance Training

'Be strong.'

USING WEIGHT-TRAINING FOR TRIATHLON

Triathletes have to become excellent time managers, always looking for ways and methods to short-cut gains and to save time. Careful use of weight and resistance training can help in this respect, although any form of such training should only be geared specifically towards the necessities of triathlon.

Weight-training is one of the most effective methods of developing muscular strength and local endurance and many triathletes use it to supplement their programme. It is important to realize, however, that some consequences of weight-training may not be beneficial to triathlon. Triathlon is, above all, an endurance sport. Extra body weight particularly on the final discipline, the run, is unlikely to be an advantage. You will be gaining general endurance while swimming, cycling and running, so loads of repetitions at a very low weight will also be a waste of time. To make the most use of weight training, look at three main areas:

1. remedial work (if you are weak in one or more areas);
2. strength – if you are weak, you will not get the best out of yourself;
3. specific strength endurance. If a single muscle or muscle group is letting you down, you can do something about it.

Specific skills in swimming, running and cycling can be significantly improved through the proper use of weight-training, but athletes who embark upon a rigorous, non-specific programme will fail to make any gains, and may indeed go backwards.

Weights and resistance work must be designed for the individual triathlete. The basics for the design and development of a basic schedule are given here. Most of the exercises set out can be employed using either free or resistance-type weight-training. Most gymnasiums and fitness centres have a range of resistance machines as well as free weights. Many weight-lifters prefer free weights, but for the non-specialist user of weight-training, the major advantages of resistance machines are that they require less skill and technique, and involve less risk of injury.

Notes:

1. Always seek advice and instruction from a qualified person at a gym or fitness centre.
2. Treat the deadlift, clean and the squat, particularly, with caution; use them only under supervision.

Muscle Groups for Triathlon

The major muscle groups of the three main triathlon sports are:

Latissimus dorsi (upper back)
Deltoids and trapezius (shoulder area)
Biceps and triceps (upper arms)
Rectus abdominus and *Obliquus externus* (stomach/abdominals)
Quadriceps, hamstrings and gastrocnemius/soleus (upper and lower legs)
Hip flexors (abdominals, front legs attachments)
Gluteals (backside/rear pelvis)

3. Weight-training is not the only way of gaining specific strength.

BEFORE YOU START

How Often?

Weight-training has to be an extra to triathlon training but, unless it is done often enough, there will be no gains. Twice a week would be the minimum, three times per week preferable. Many athletes in single sports do weight-training through the off season and make great strength gains. As soon as the season begins, they stop weight-training and their new-found strength starts to slip away. If you need to weight-train, you may need to follow at least a maintenance programme of weight-training in the competition season.

How Heavy?

Before starting on a weights programme, find out how much you are capable of lifting on each exercise. Test yourself to see how much you can lift on a single repetition. This is your maximum.

Warm-Up

As in a swimming, cycling and running workout, it is essential to be properly warmed up before weight-training. The usual strictures and recommendations apply (*see* Chapter 20 on Stretching and Flexibility). Whatever you do, just be sure that you are nice and warm.

Types of Schedule

The triathlete's main aim in weight-lifting is strength rather than endurance, but there is no point in building up to one single lift of a maximum weight. The number of repetitions and sets of exercises will be governed by the muscle group and the body area being worked. Smaller muscles and muscle groups will tend to fatigue more quickly than large groups and should therefore be exercised later in the session.

Exercises for the Triathlon Muscle Groups

Free Weights

Deadlift	Quads, gluteals
Upright row	Trapezius, deltoids, biceps
Clean	Quads, gluteals, gastrocnemius (calves), deltoids, biceps, trapezius
Bicep curl	Biceps
Squat	Quads, gluteals
Neck press	Deltoids, trapezius, triceps
Bench press	Pectorals, triceps
Lateral raise	Deltoids
Triceps extension	Triceps
Pull-overs	Latissimus dorsi, pectorals

Resistance Lifts

Leg curl	Hamstrings, gastrocnemius
Leg press	Quads, gluteals
Leg extension	Quads
Triceps push-down	Triceps
Upright row	Trapezius, deltoids, biceps
Seated row	Latissimus dorsi
Shoulder press	Deltoids, triceps and trapezius
Neck pull-downs	Latissimus dorsi, biceps

Strong stomach muscles are also essential for the triathlete. A range of sit-up type exercises can be used for abdominal work, and there are specialized machines too. The feet and legs should be held free; working the stomach muscles properly in this way makes apparently simple exercises much more difficult. Incorporate some eccentric exercises along with the traditional 'shortening' and 'crunching' abdominal work.

Weight-training is usefully done in a back-to-back manner, with two sets of exercises using complementary groups of muscles being done, one following the other.

The weight-training schedule set out on the right works the entire body. For example, for the first sets (bench press and upright row), twenty repetitions of bench press are followed by twenty repetitions of upright row, then twenty bench press, and so on. Large muscle groups are exercised before small groups, and no group of muscles tired from exercise is immediately worked again. Generally, one area is followed by a different area of the body. The number of sets and repetitions are a guide only, but represent a level at which you are likely to gain maximum benefit without risking injury through over-overtiredness.

The rest period between exercises and sets is kept to a minimum, but the athlete should take care not to become so fatigued that good form is sacrificed when performing the exercise, and the likelihood of injury is increased.

EXERCISES

All the weight-training exercises below are relevant to specific or general needs for triathletes. Not all exercises will be appropriate for all athletes. Read the information carefully in order to perform the exercise properly, but seek proper instruction before embarking upon a programme.

Only the specific exercises that are essential are explained fully here. Triathletes should refer to specialist books and magazines if they wish to pursue their interest.

Free Weights

Deadlift

Prime movers: quadriceps, gluteals, erector spinae

Place the toes underneath the bar with the feet about hip distance apart. The feet may be pointing forwards or slightly outwards but they must be equidistant from both ends of the bar.

Example Weight-Training Session

Bench press	$5 \times 20 \times$ half to two-thirds max
Upright row	$5 \times 20 \times$ half to two-thirds max

Work up to this; when achieved, increase weight

Lat pull-down	$4 \times 12 \times$ half to two-thirds max
Neck press	$4 \times 12 \times$ half max

Work up to 4×15 reps, and then increase weight

Quads (leg extensions)	$3 \times 10 \times$ three-quarters max
Hamstring curl	$3 \times 10 \times$ two-thirds max

Work up to 3×15 reps, then increase weight

Bicep curl	$3 \times 24 \times$ half to two-thirds max
Tricep extension	$3 \times 12 \times$ half to two-thirds max

Do not increase reps, increase weight asap

Quads (half squat)	$3 \times 10 \times$ three-quarters max
Calf raise	$3 \times 10 \times$ three-quarters max

Work up to 3×15 reps, then increase weight

Abdominals – push-throughs, to exhaustion. Repeat 3 times.

Knee raise and straight-leg shoot, to exhaustion.

Fall back (eccentric movement), to exhaustion.

Repeat 3 times.

Fig 62. Joanna Hinde, single leg extension working on right quadricep.

Flex at the knees and hips to adopt the 'Get Set' position, with the arms positioned outside the knees and straight. Grasp the bar with an overhand grip. Ensure that the knees are correctly aligned with the feet and that the back is flat. The backside should be higher than the knees, with the head looking forwards and slightly down.

Position the shoulders slightly in advance of the bar to allow for a vertical line of travel of the bar upwards. Stand up, leading with the shoulders and keeping the bar close to the body throughout the movement.

Ensure that the body moves to a full upright position without any hyperextension at the knee joint.

To return the bar, flex at the knees and hips and keep the back straight.

Upright Row

Prime movers: trapezius, anterior deltoid, biceps and brachialis

Deadlift the bar. Widen the stance to approximately one and a half times hip width apart. Tilt the pelvis and take the lock off the knees.

Narrow the grip to two thumb lengths apart. Replace the thumbs and grip the bar firmly.

Keeping the bar close to the body and leading the movement with the elbows, raise the bar under control to just below the level of the chin.

Lower the bar under control to the starting position, avoiding any temptation to round the back or hyperextend at the elbows.

To return the bar to the floor, widen the grip and narrow the stance and then lower the body by bending at the knees and hips, head facing forwards to help to maintain a straight back.

The Clean

Prime movers: quadriceps, gluteals, gastrocnemius, deltoids, trapezius, erector spinae, soleus, biceps

There are many different ways of teaching this extremely complex lift. The following is a general breakdown of the elements of the clean:

The Set: flex at hips and knees with the back straight. Look forward and slightly down. Keep knees over toes. Maintain feet at hip width apart, with shoulders in front of toes.

Upright Row on to Toes Phase: ensure that weight is distributed over feet to maintain toe, ankle and knee alignment. Ensure that elbows are high at the end of the high pull phase.

The Receive Phase: come down on to heels and flex at the knees, and simultaneously bring elbows forward in advance of the bar so the bar rests securely on the shoulders. Then stand up.

The Return: again keeping bar still, bring elbows high and above the bar. Lower under control to the thighs, keeping bar close to the body. To return, reverse the deadlift.

Biceps Curl

Prime movers: biceps, brachialis

Deadlift the bar with an underhand grip. Widen the stance to approximately one and a half times hip width apart. Narrow the grip to shoulder width. Tilt the pelvis, take the lock off the knees and keep the body upright.

Fix the upper arms into the sides of the body. Curl the bar upwards towards the chest, avoid any excess movement and keep the elbows fixed as the pivot for the movement.

Lower the bar under control until the arms are straight and avoid any hyper-extension at the elbow.

Narrow the stance to about hip width apart. Widen the grip and return the bar to the floor by flexing at the knees and hips, keeping the back flat.

Half Squat

Prime movers: quadriceps, gluteals

Clean the bar to the receive position. Bend the knees slightly and then extend them as the bar is pressed over the head to rest evenly on the top of the shoulders. Widen the grip to a comfortable distance but check that the hands are equidistant from both ends of the bar.

The feet should be placed about hip width apart, either facing forward or slightly outward. In this starting position, the trunk should be upright and the knees slightly bent.

Squat down by bending at the knees and hips and ensure that the back is flat. The bar is lowered in a vertical line. Keep the head facing forward throughout this movement and ensure that the knees travel in line with the feet.

Squat to a position where the thighs are roughly parallel to the ground – do *not* go beyond this level. Extend at the knees and hips to regain the upright position ensuring that no hyperextension occurs at the knee.

To return the bar, narrow the grip, bend at the knees slightly and then press the bar back over the head to the receive position. Return the bar to the floor as for the clean.

Behind-Neck Press

Prime movers: deltoids, trapezius, triceps

Clean the bar to the receive position. Bend the knees slightly and then extend them as the bar is pressed over the head to rest evenly on the top of the shoulders (not on the neck).

Widen the stance to place the feet approximately one and a half times hip width apart. Tilt the pelvis, take the lock off the knees and keep the body upright.

Adjust the grip to place the hands approximately one and a half times shoulder width apart, ensuring that they are placed equidistant from both ends of the bar.

Press the bar directly upwards and under full control until the arms are straight (but without hyperextending at the elbows). The back should be kept straight throughout the movement and the wrists should be locked firm.

Lower the bar to the starting position but avoid resting the bar on the shoulders between repetitions. Breathe out as the bar is raised and make the action smooth and continuous.

To return the bar, narrow both the grip and the stance, bend the knees and then press the bar back over the head to the receive position. Return the bar to the floor as for the clean.

Bench Press

Prime movers: pectorals, triceps, anterior deltoid

Lie face up on the bench with the feet comfortably spaced on either side of the bench.

The back should not be unduly hyperextended – only the natural lumbar curve should be evident (if the hyperextension is excessive, position supports under the feet – avoid raising the legs on to the bench).

A spotter is required for this movement to avoid injury. The spotter stands behind the bench and deadlifts the bar. It is then passed to the athlete who grips the bar with a wide, overhand grip with the hands positioned approximately one and a half to two times shoulder width apart whilst the bar is away from the body. The spotter guides and supports the bar until the athlete's arms are straight with the bar suspended directly above the chest. Only when the athlete is ready does the spotter release his own grip on the bar.

Keeping the wrists firm, the bar should then be lowered under control to the mid-region of the chest leading the movement with the elbows. The forearms should be kept vertical as the bar is lowered. The arms are then extended until they are straight but not hyper-extended.

Lying Triceps Extension

Prime movers: triceps
Lie flat on the bench, face up, take a narrow overhand grip on the bar (hands shoulder width apart or slightly narrower). The arms should be straight with the bar positioned directly above the shoulders. Lock the wrists and keep the upper arms fixed vertically.

Lower the bar under control, leading the movement with the knuckles. The bar should be brought towards the forehead or the bridge of the nose.

Extend the arms until they are straight (but not hyperextended) to return the bar to the starting position.

Dumb-Bell Lunge

Prime movers: quadriceps, gluteals
Proceed with extra caution with this exercise.

Deadlift the dumb-bells from the floor.

Stand with feet hip width apart and toes facing directly forward. Step directly forward with right leg far enough to enable both knees to bend to a right-angle as the body is lowered.

Keep the body upright with toes forward. Keep feet hip width apart for stability. Look forward and slightly down. Ensure that trailing knee does not contact the floor. Relax the shoulders and arms. Avoid excessive tension when gripping dumb-bells.

Drive back with right leg to start position. Repeat, alternating leading legs.

Reverse the deadlift to lower dumb-bells to the floor.

Fixed Resistance Machines

Leg Curl

Prime movers: hamstrings and gastrocnemius

Lie face down on the leg-curl machine with the knees just over the edge of the bench and the ankles underneath the bottom pad. Hold on to the handles or the side of the bench. Curl the weight up by flexing the knees and keep the feet dorsi-flexed. Try to avoid any excess hip flexion (a certain amount is a natural function of the exercise).

On no account hold the hips down on to the bench.

Curl the bar through the full range under control, bringing the pad as close to the backside as possible. Lower slowly back to the starting position. Avoid letting the weight touch the weight stack. Repeat for the desired number of repetitions, breathing out as the weight is curled upwards. Make the action smooth and continuous.

Leg Press

Prime movers: quadriceps, gluteals

Sit on the seat and place the feet evenly on the foot plate, ensuring that the whole of the foot is in contact with the plate. Ensure also that the back is flat against the seat pad. Check that the knee angle is not less than 90 degrees. Grip the handles firmly at the side of the chair. Extend the legs under control until they are straight but without allowing the knees to hyperextend. Return to the starting position working through the full range but without allowing the weight to touch the weight stack. Ensure that the knees travel over the line of the feet throughout the movement.

Leg Extension

Prime movers: quadriceps

Sit on the leg-extension machine and place the feet in a dorsi-flexed position beneath the lower pads. Sit well back on the bench so that the back of the knee joint touches the edge of the bench. Sit with the torso upright or leaning slightly backwards. Hold on (not too tightly) to the handles or the edge of the bench for support. Extend the legs under control until they are fully straight. Tilt the pelvis and take the lock off the knees.

Seated Shoulder Press

Prime movers: deltoids, triceps and trapezius

Sit comfortably on the seat facing the machine so that the bar is positioned slightly in advance of the shoulders. Ensure that the back is upright. Grasp the bar with an overhand grip with the hands positioned about one and a half shoulder width apart.

Keep the wrists straight, knuckles up and the elbows pointing down.

Extend the arms, breathing out, until they are fully straight (but not hyperextended). Take care not to arch the back as this movement takes place. Return the bar under control to the starting position without allowing the weight to touch the weight stack.

Behind-Neck Pull-Down

Prime movers: latissimus dorsi, biceps and brachialis

Take an overhand grip on the bar with the hands positioned about one and a half to two times shoulder width apart.

Go down first on to one knee and then the other until the body is positioned directly below the bar. The arms should be straight but not hyperextended, knees should be placed wide enough to ensure a good base of support (hip width or slightly more).

Ensure that the cable is vertical.

Pull the bar down behind the head to touch the shoulders and lead the movement with the elbows. Maintain a straight back throughout the whole exercise. Return to full extension under control. Control the descent of the weight on to the weights stack.

OTHER WAYS OF GAINING SPECIFIC STRENGTH

Swimming

Using hand paddles (with caution), wearing a T-shirt or baggy swimming costume, or occasionally using tethered swimming will all add strength. Many swimmers make use of rubber bands and slide ropes for stroke work on land to add specific strength.

Cycling

Working on hills, using big gears (with caution), riding into the wind, extra resistance on the turbo trainer; and a combination of all these factors will give great strength benefits. Cyclo-cross and mountain biking in adverse, muddy conditions will also help.

Running

Hill running, running in sand, water running, running with a partner holding you back on stretch cords (with caution), or running with an object tied behind you (for example, a large car tyre, but only with caution) will all add to specific strength.

CHAPTER 20
Stretching and Flexibility

'Every great journey starts with one small step.'

Stretching develops flexibility and suppleness, and improves the efficiency of the muscles to lengthen and to handle eccentric contraction (lengthening under resistance).

Stretching achieves the following:

- relaxes the muscles;
- increases flexibility;
- enhances athletic performance; and
- reduces injury risk.

Flexibility may be defined as the range of movement in joints, and stretching increases this. *Suppleness* may be defined as the lengthening ability of the muscles, which will con-

Fig 63. Stretching for relaxation, flexibility, enhancement of performance and reduction of injury.

tribute towards increased flexibility in the joints. The triathlete needs to develop suppleness and flexibility, in order to enhance performance and reduce the likelihood of injury.

Ironically, muscles that cause movement can also restrict movement because of negative tension. Negative muscle tension wastes energy. Skeletal muscle is affected and pain and aching is felt in fatigued muscles. The will and ability to move diminish. Stretching exercises are included in a fitness programme to relieve that tension in the muscles. Relaxed muscles, or muscles that can lengthen efficiently, allow a better range of movement at the joints.

Muscles may tighten up with nervous tension. Driving in heavy traffic, being late for work or appointments, a difficult situation at home, traumas, crises, and decision-making can all contribute to nervous tension.

BENEFITS OF STRETCHING

Muscles have elastic properties, being able to alter their length and return. They are not like rubber elastic bands, for example, which stretch out and then relax back to their original shortened state. Muscles are contractile; they are relaxed at length and work by contracting. For most of the time, the muscles are in a state of contraction and need to be opened out and stretched regularly. They may often be required to work repeatedly within their inner range and thus become shortened (losing their ability to lengthen fully). This will have an adverse effect on eccentric contraction.

Stretching muscles allows them to relax to their full length so that they do not remain in a semi-contracted, tight, mid-range state. The physical benefits will be obvious: moving better, feeling physically more relaxed, and being better able to cope with physical tasks. Getting the muscles to relax can have psychological benefits too, easing state of mind, and increasing confidence and the ability to cope with mental tasks.

In stretching, the muscle is opened out to its full length and then taken a bit further. This creates a tension in the muscle for a few moments, but this is different from the tension experienced when it contracts.

Stretching should always be carried out before any form of physical activity, from the simplest training session to a competitive event. Stretching should form a vital part of the warm-up, but only *after* the muscles are well warmed up.

With a forceful, explosive movement, the antagonist muscle, which is lengthening to control the movement, may not be able to cope with the speed and force of contraction. In this situation, muscle fibres may be torn. Regular stretching of muscles enables them to cope more efficiently with the quick and powerful lengthening that can occur in training and competition.

TYPES OF STRETCHING

Basically, there are two types of stretching.

Ballistic Stretching

1. Mobilizing exercises, which consist of gentle joint movements to stimulate the secretion of synovial fluid and to warm the muscles affecting that joint.
2. Ballistic bounces, where a muscle is opened to its full length and is then stretched by bouncing movements. (This method of stretching is not recommended as it can cause damage to the connective tissue in the muscle, may invoke a stretch reflex, and may cause damage to muscle fibres.)

Static Stretching

During static stretching the muscle is opened to its full length and gently stretched a little further, with the position being held for a length of time.

Static stretching can be sub-divided into *active* and *passive* stretching:

1. active stretching is when the performer carries out the stretch and holds the position;
2. passive stretching is when the limb is moved and the stretch position is held by another person. (Some authorities consider that passive stretching also includes exercises where gravity or any outside force causes a muscle to be stretched rather than the concentric contraction of an opposing muscle).

Passive stretching can involve PNF (*proprioceptive neuromuscular facilitation*) stretching, sometimes referred to as *contract-relax stretching*. Having held a muscle in a stretch position for a length of time, the muscle is then contracted forcefully and isometrically against a strong resistance for a few seconds and then relaxed and lengthened further. This phenomenon occurs because of an *inverse stretch*

Fig 64. Chris Bailey demonstrates passive stretch.

reflex (a neurological response) in the muscle, which causes the muscle fibres to relax in response to high tension.

Although it can be performed actively, PNF stretching is perhaps better carried out passively with the assistance of another person. Either way, the muscle to be stretched is moved slowly into its maximum (yet comfortable) lengthened position and is held there for a number of seconds. Then the muscle is contracted isometrically for about 5 seconds against resistance provided by the partner. The tension developed is sensed by the *golgi tendon organ* (GTO, a proprioceptor in the musculo-tendon junction), which excites the inverse stretch reflex and gets the muscle fibres to relax. When the isometric contraction (and therefore the tension) is stopped, the muscle will lengthen further because of the relaxing effect of the inverse stretch reflex.

There are two methods of PNF stretching: *contract-relax* (CR) and *contract-relax-agonist-contract* (CRAC). With the CR PNF method, the partner initially assists with the stretch, then provides the resistance, and then assists with the second stretch which should go much further if a good response has been achieved from the GTO and inverse stretch reflex.

With the CRAC method, the same procedure is carried out but after the isometric contraction the performer uses the opposing muscle as a prime mover (agonist) to pull the muscle to be stretched into a further stretch. This part of the stretch is performed actively.

STRETCHING FOR DEVELOPMENT OR MAINTENANCE

Muscles can be stretched either to develop flexibility or to maintain existing flexibility.

Stretching muscles aims to maintain or increase the lengthening ability of the muscle. The bulk of the muscle consists of bundles of muscle fibres bound together by an inelastic connective tissue made of collagen. In order to increase the muscle's ability to lengthen, it is necessary to stretch the connective tissue within the muscle and increase the elongation potential of the muscle fibres.

Ballistic stretching does not increase the length of the connective collagen tissue, although it does have an effect on the muscle fibres. Bouncing a muscle can actually cause damage to the collagen fibres, resulting in muscle pain and not necessarily any increase in the relaxation potential of the belly of the muscle.

Although the collagen fibre is comparatively inelastic, when warm it can become more pliable and can be permanently elongated. When cold, it is brittle and can be damaged. Stretching exercises should always be carried out in warm conditions and when the muscle is well warmed up. Stretches that are part of a preparatory warm-up before training or sport should be done after the mobilizing and pulse-raising components of the warm-up.

Maintenance stretches might be carried out as part of the warm-up before activity, or as part of the cool-down at the end of the activity. This type of stretching involves slowly opening the

---

Stretch Reflex

Muscles contain proprioceptors in the form of muscle spindles, which resemble a coiled wire around muscle fibres. When a muscle is stretched (even slightly), the stretch is sensed by the spindle and a message is sent via a sensory nerve to the central nervous system. A message returns via a motor nerve to the muscle fibre, telling it to contract. Stretch reflex is therefore the basis of muscle tone.

Inverse Stretch Reflex

If a muscle is subjected to excessive tension, for example, when suddenly subjected to a very heavy resistance, the tension is sensed by proprioceptors in the muscle-tendon junction. These sensory organs are known as golgi tendon organs (GTO). When the GTO senses excessive stretch a message is sent to the central nervous system and a message returns telling the muscle fibres to relax. In this way, it acts as a safety device, protecting the muscle fibres from potentially damaging forces.

muscle to its full length, stretching it gently a bit further so that an amount of comfortable tension is developed and holding the stretch position for between 7 to 10 seconds.

The Progressive Stretch Method

Stretches for the development of flexibility should be held for 20 to 30 seconds. They can be done in three progressive stages:

1. Very slowly and gently, ease the muscle into a comfortable lengthened position. This allows the muscle to become desensitized (cancelling out the stretch reflex) and become accustomed to the lengthened state. Hold this stretch for about 7 seconds.
2. Maintain the position but slightly increase the stretch tension very slowly and gently and hold for another 7 seconds. This allows the warm collagen connective tissue fibres to stretch (known as 'creeping').
3. Maintain the stretch position but increase the stretch tension slightly more and hold for a further 7 seconds. This allows the muscle

fibres to elongate along with the connective tissue.

Following this procedure, you will have held the stretch position for just over 20 seconds.

Muscles Prone to Shortening

Not all muscles require developmental stretching. However, the following major muscles are prone to shortening, and may restrict full range of movement in the joints they affect unless they are treated to developmental stretching:

- hamstrings (back of the thigh);
- gluteals;
- calf muscles (back of the lower leg); and
- adductors (inner thigh).

Triathlon involves a high percentage of leg power and will require the athlete to develop suppleness in quadriceps (front of the thigh), hamstrings (back of the thigh), calf muscles – gastrocnemius and soleus (back of the lower leg) – anterior tibial muscles (front of the

Fig 65. Jon David just pre-competition, stretches arms and upper back.

lower leg), gluteals (buttocks), adductors (inner thigh), and hip flexors (ilio-psoas – deep muscles attached to the lumbar spine and to the inside of the femur, which lift up the thigh; the stretch tension will be felt in the groin/top thigh region).

A fairly long stretching session involving all of the above muscles should be incorporated in the warm-up (after gentle, low-intensity activity to warm the muscles), and at the end of a training session or competition as a vital part of the cool-down. This stretching is an important part of the training programme.

THE STRETCHES

It is important to have a comprehensive programme of stretching. Muscles rarely work in isolation and if a muscle is incapable of stretching properly, other groups will be brought into play to compensate for this. Before long, referred pain and injury will be experienced. By all means, work on your weaknesses, but don't avoid an all-round workout.

Below are two groups of stretches. One is generally for the lower body, primarily applying to cycling and running, but also including lower-back stretching; the other is for upper body and shoulder mobility, which will apply primarily to swimming.

There are several excellent books on the subject of stretching.

Lower Body

Lower Back Rotation (Fig 66)

Lie on back, knees bent, feet flat on floor. Drop knees over to left side and then bring back to centre. Repeat to right side. Work up to 3 × 30 seconds on each side.

Step Standing

Place right foot on chair so that hip and knee are at right-angles. Clasp hands around ankle and bend forwards and inwards bringing right shoulder towards right knee and head towards right ankle. Straighten and repeat to left side. Work up to 3 × 30 seconds on each side.

> **Golden Rules for Stretching Correctly**
>
> 1. Stretch *warm* muscles.
> 2. *Do not bounce.*
> 3. Ease the muscle slowly into a comfortable stretch position and hold for a few seconds.
> 4. Then slightly increase the stretch tension and hold for a few seconds more.
> 5. Do not overstretch: keep within the limits of pain.

Hip Hitching

Lie on back with legs stretched out. Alternate stretching and shortening of legs while maintaining knees straight. Repeat up to ten times each side or up to three minutes.

Short Hip Flexors (Fig 67)

Lie on back with right knee pulled up towards the chest. Stretch left leg down while pulling foot up and flattening knee, simultaneously pull right knee upwards and inwards. Straighten and repeat with left knee. Work up to 3 × 30 seconds on each side.

Fig 66. Lower back rotation.

Fig 67. Hip flexor stretch.

Squat Stretch

Stand with feet pointing forward and with heels in contact with floor, feet approximately shoulder width apart. Keeping knees directly above feet, squat down as far as you can and place hands flat on the floor. Hold this position and then, keeping weight on hands, gently attempt to straighten knees. Hold and return to original position. Work up to 3 × 30 seconds on each position in sequence.

Adductors (Inside Upper Leg)

1. Stand with feet wide astride with toes pointing to the front. Push hips across to left, and then slowly bend sideways to right. Feel stretch on inner side of right thigh. Return to upright and repeat to left. Work up to 3 × 30 seconds on each side (Fig 68).
2. Sit with knees dropping outward to sides. Bring soles of feet together. Hold ankles and gradually press knees downwards and outwards with elbows. Relax and repeat. Work up to 3 × 30 seconds (Fig 69).

Quadriceps (Fig 71)

1. Lie flat on stomach. Bend right knee up and reach back to grasp foot behind body. Pull foot towards backside until a stretch is felt in the thigh. Relax and repeat with left knee. Work up to 3 × 30 seconds. (This stretch also effects a plantar flex of the ankle with beneficial results for the foot and leg action in swimming.)
2. Kneel, and then sit back on heels. Gradually lean back and lower body weight down, supporting yourself with your hands until you feel stretch in quadriceps.

Fig 68. Stretching the adductor muscles.

Fig 69. Stretching the adductor muscles.

Fig 70. Becky Mann stretches the sartorius.

(Below right) Fig 71. Quadriceps.

(Below) Fig 72. Stretching the gluteals.

3. Kneel with weight supported on left knee and right foot. Maintain balance by holding fixed object at side. Grasp left foot with left hand and lift towards backside, leaning forward slightly. Relax, change balance and repeat with right foot.

Gluteals (Fig 72)

Lie flat on back with legs bent and feet flat on floor. Lift right leg and place outside of right ankle on to left knee. Relax right leg, allowing knee to fall sideways. Place hands behind left thigh and clasp fingers. Gradually pull left

Fig 73. Progressive calves and achilles tendon stretch: 1.

Fig 74. Progressive calves and achilles tendon stretch: 2.

leg off the floor and towards chest. Relax and repeat with other leg. Work up to 3×30 seconds.

Calves and Achilles Tendon (Figs 73–75)

1. Stand upright facing a wall, approximately at arms' length. Keep heels flat on floor and lean body in towards wall by bending arms until stretch is felt in calves and achilles tendons. Take care to ensure that body remains straight as you lean inwards; letting backside push outwards will negate effect of stretch. Relax and repeat. Work up to 3×30 seconds.
2. Proceed as above. When position is reached, move left foot forward 15cm (6in) and bend left knee slowly until stretch effect is felt. Relax and repeat with right leg. Work up to 3×30 seconds.
3. (Proceed with caution.) Place toes of right foot against wall 8cm (3in) above floor with heel of foot in contact with floor. Slowly bend right knee forward until stretch effect is felt. Relax and repeat with left leg. Work up to 3×30 seconds.

Achilles tendonitis and paratendonitis are a constant risk to runners and triathletes under-

Fig 75. Progressive calves and achilles tendon stretch: 3.

taking a lot of mileage. Stretching of the achilles will help to combat this. However, achilles pain may still be experienced when stiffness and lack of mobility in other lower joints lead to the achilles tendons having to stretch further in order to compensate. This

Fig 76. Shoulder and upper back stretch.

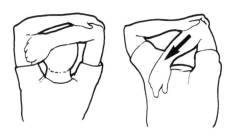

Fig 77. Tricep and shoulder stretch.

referred pain is best combatted by undertaking an *overall* stretching and mobility programme, treating the cause rather than the symptom.

Upper Body

The best stretching programme for triathlon will aim to achieve all-round body mobility. Stretching for swimmers has always included work on shoulders, lower back, ankles and hips. Good shoulder mobility is particularly advantageous for triathletes, as efficiency in the swimming discipline will enable the athlete to go into the following two disciplines less tired and more competitive. Better extension and abduction of the arms will give a longer stroke, less lateral movement (particularly on recovery) and a flatter body position.

Supposed lower-back and hip immobility may actually be referred aspects of poor swimming stroke technique.

1. Hold arms extended upwards slightly behind head, with fingers pointing upwards and palms of hands held against each other. Exert pressure and press palms together (Fig 76).
2. From a starting position, with hands placed behind head, straighten arms and extend to position described above.
3. Place bent left elbow behind head with palm of hand placed against neck or between shoulders. Hold left elbow firmly with right hand and push it down, back and across. Release and repeat with right elbow (Fig 77).

4. Place both hands on back of head with elbows bent and pushed backwards. Partner raises and pulls elbows back and towards each other.
5. Partner holds both arms underneath elbows behind subject's back. Subject presses down.
6. Partner-controlled exercise: subject's arms are extended sideways and held under the elbows by partner. Partner then lifts arms sideways and upwards in their straight position until backs of hands touch above head.
7. Hold left arm in front of chin with right hand. Push left elbow towards right shoulder. Relax and repeat with right arm.
8. Stand at right-angles to the corner of a wall with right arm extended sideways, and with inside of wrist pressing against wall. Try to turn away from arm, so that arm is extended backwards. Relax and repeat with left arm.
9. Stand or sit with back near to a wall, arms extended backwards and fingertips touching wall. Move closer to wall and move the fingertips upwards, extending arms upwards.
10. Kneel on floor with hands linked behind head. Partner stands behind with bent knees, places hands through subject's linked arms, and then clasps own hands together. Partner straightens legs and lifts and stretches subject's upper body.
11. Individually rotate shoulders forwards and backwards.
12. Lock hands together behind back with arms extended. Bend body forward and bring arms forward and upward.

CHAPTER 21

Injuries and Activity-Related Conditions

*'Physicians of the utmost fame
Were called at once, but when they came,
They answered, as they took their fees,
There is no cure for this disease.'*

This chapter deals only with those simpler – yet serious enough to the triathlete – and more common traumatic and over-use injuries which, with an understanding, can be given correct first aid and self-treatment. The identification and treatment of most of the injuries mentioned should be within the scope of an educated and knowledgeable sports therapist (sport scientist, coach, trainer), or the participant/athlete.

The more serious conditions, such as fractures, dislocations, head, neck and back injuries, are not covered. Immediate medical attention should be sought in the case of any of these.

A knowledgeable first-aider should be able to splint and immobilize a broken bone before the casualty is removed to hospital.

With a dislocated joint, the limb can be supported to take the weight (particularly the shoulder). The injured athlete must be removed to hospital as quickly as possible before muscle spasm sets in. No attempt should be made to reduce ('put back') the dislocated joint other than by a medically qualified person.

With head injuries, medical attention should be sought. If any accompanying neck injury is suspected the patient should not be moved. For any neck or spinal injury the patient should not be moved at all except by qualified medical or paramedical personnel.

This chapter does not seek to be a substitute for the expert advice that can be offered by a fully qualified physiotherapist specializing in sports injuries. In some cases, physiotherapist examination and advice from a GP are recommended. Comparatively simple injuries can be prone to complications if full treatment and rehabilitation are not properly carried out.

Many triathletes are reluctant to visit a physiotherapist because of the cost. However, qualified and expert advice is usually worth paying for in the long run, and a good physiotherapist should not impose a long and costly course of treatment if the patient does not need it. Often, advice on correct self-help and rehabilitation may be given to the patient during the initial consultation.

WHAT IS A SPORTS INJURY?

A sports injury is the type of injury that is most likely to occur through participation in sport or regular activity. Sprains, strains, contusions, fractures, and so on, do occur outside sport, but they are more likely to occur in sporting situations where greater stresses are more regularly imposed on the body.

A sports injury may not be any different from an injury that occurs outside sport, but the treatment and desired results may be slightly different for a sportsperson. The sportsperson is often anxious to return to participation and previous fitness as soon as possible, but problems can occur when a return is attempted before full healing has taken place and without proper rehabilitation.

Problems can also occur when a lack of understanding of the injury or condition results in improper treatment and rehabilitation. Healing will be incomplete and complications may develop. Lack of understanding can also cause anxiety, which can be detrimental to the healing process.

The majority of the more common sports injuries occur to the lower part of the body, which has to support and propel the bulk of the body's weight through the numerous muscles and joints. Feet, ankles, legs, knees, thighs, hips and the lower back are particularly vulnerable.

CATEGORIZING SPORTS INJURIES

Sports injuries fall basically into two categories: *traumatic* and *over-use*. Injuries may also be *acute* or *chronic*.

Traumatic Injuries

Traumatic injuries occur suddenly and the injury will be instantly obvious, although the full extent of the injury may not be obvious until investigation and examination has taken place by a qualified person.

Aims of Treatment and Rehabilitation

Short Term
- Prevent further damage
- Limit bleeding
- Reduce pain
- Reduce swelling
- Reduce inflammation
- Prevent stiffness
- Maintain muscle strength

Long Term
- Prevent complications
- Encourage full healing
- Re-educate movement
- Increase mobility
- Increase muscle strength
- Restore function for activity
- Restore confidence in the injured part
- Prevention of return of swelling
- Prevention of re-occurrence

Such injuries usually occur as a result of a sudden twisting, over-stretching or collision and will include joint sprains, dislocations, muscle strains, tendon strains, contusions (bruises) and bone fractures. Although common symptoms usually exist, a qualified examination may be necessary to obtain an accurate diagnosis. For example, a broken bone (fracture) will usually be identified because of severe pain, tenderness over the site of fracture, discoloration, swelling, deformity and immobility; however, not all of these symptoms may be present or obvious and only an X-ray will show the truth.

A twisted joint will usually be painful, will swell fairly rapidly, and may feel insecure. An accompanying fracture may be less obvious and may only be revealed by a qualified examination and an X-ray. Such a condition may occur in a severe sprain of the ankle where strong ligaments may pull away a piece of bone from the fibula in the lower leg (known as an avulsion fracture).

Over-Use Injuries

Over-use injuries occur gradually over a period of time. If ignored, they may become severe and eventually result in immobilization. They are often caused by repetitive actions where incorrect bio-mechanics exist, by a too-rapid progression in training, or excessive competition, incomplete recovery, overtraining, and incomplete muscle glycogen repletion.

Over-use injuries include gradually developing muscle and tendon strains, inflammatory conditions of tendons and tendon sheaths, and inflammation of joints.

Tendonitis is inflammation of a tendon; tenosynovitis is inflammation of a tendon sheath; peritendonitis is inflammation of the soft tissues around the tendon (very similar to tendonitis and tenosynovitis); bursitis is inflammation of a bursa (a small fluid-filled sack, often found near joints, or where tendons pass over a joint, to prevent friction).

The suffix *itis* means inflammation and the beginning of the word usually refers to the tissue that is inflamed. 'Arthritis' literally translated should mean 'inflammation of a joint', but the word is used to describe a joint condition where the articular cartilage has worn. (Inflammatory flare-up can occur in such a joint.)

Acute Injuries

The injury is at the acute stage when it has recently happened, within the first 24 to 48 hours. This is when first aid should be carried out, aimed at reducing internal bleeding, swelling and inflammation.

Chronic Injuries

Chronic injuries are those that have developed complications because of incorrect treatment, lack of treatment, poor rehabilitation, or a return to activity before full fitness of the injured part.

SPRAINS AND STRAINS

The two most common sports injuries are *sprains* and *strains*. The two similar-sounding words are often confused and mis-used.

Sprains are injuries to *joints*. They usually involve damage to the joint capsule, synovial membrane and ligaments (for example, a sprained ankle or a twisted knee).

Strains are injuries to *muscles* and/or *tendons* and usually involve a tearing of fibres (for example, a strained calf muscle, a strained achilles tendon or a pulled hamstring). A 'pulled' muscle is the same as a strained or 'torn' muscle, although the words often refer to the degree of strain or damage.

A muscle or tendon strain may be sudden (traumatic) or gradual (over-use). There can also be 'degrees' of severity of strains, from a minor strain with tearing of a few fibres causing slight pain or discomfort during activity, to a major strain involving tearing of a greater number of fibres. A *rupture* of a muscle or tendon is a complete tear and will require surgery.

As tendons pass over joints, any abnormal wrenching of a joint may also involve damage to those tendons as well as the joint structure, so a joint sprain may also involve accompanying tendon strain.

Grades or Degrees of Sprains and Strains

Joint Sprains

Grade I: minimal damage; some loss of function

Grade II: more ligament fibres damaged; partial detachment; degree of instability; swelling

Grade III: complete rupture; completely unstable; swelling

Muscle Strains

Grade I: small number of muscle fibres torn; fascia (the very thin connective tissue that binds and encapsulates muscle, muscle fibres and myofibrils) intact; minimal bleeding

Grade II: larger number of muscle fibres torn; fascia intact; considerable bleeding which can be felt as mass. (If bleeding heals as a lump, it becomes an intra-muscular haematoma.)

Grade III: large number of muscle fibres torn; fascia torn; bleeding diffuses and fills tissue spaces; inter-muscular haematoma

Grade IV: complete rupture of muscle; gap can be felt between two ends

Intra-muscular haematoma: muscle sheath intact; blood contained within the muscle; haematoma forms within two hours

Inter-muscular haematoma: muscle sheath torn; blood seeps between muscles; blood tracks with gravity

---

SOFT-TISSUE INJURIES

All sports injuries, whether traumatic or over-use, involve damage to soft tissue. Soft tissue includes muscle, tendon, ligament, synovial membrane, tendon sheath, skin, blood vessels, and so on.

Soft-tissue injuries will result from contact (bruising), twisting and stressing joints (sprains), over-stretching muscles or tendons (strains), chaffing and rubbing (local inflammation), fatigue and excessive action (over-use strains).

They can involve conditions such as torn fibres in muscles and tendons, completely torn muscles and tendons, torn ligaments, inflamed ligaments, inflamed tendons, inflamed tendon sheaths, inflammation of other connective tissue around tendon sheaths, inflamed joints, damaged joint capsule, and shrunken joint capsule (frozen shoulder).

Inflammation

Inflammation is the body's reaction to injury or irritation. It involves local heat, pain, redness, and swelling. Some or all of these symptoms may be present.

Inflammation can occur at a muscle's tendonous attachment to the bone. The tendon actually attaches to the periostium, which is the membrane surrounding the bone. This inflammatory condition is known as tenoperiostitis. Groin strain (inflammation of the attachment of the adductor muscles to the pubic bone), and plantar fasciitis (inflammation of the attachment of the plantar fascia of the foot to the calcaneus, or heel bone) are individually named conditions under the general heading of tenoperiostitis.

Anti-inflammatory creams or gels, available from the chemist, can be effective in reducing inflammation. They do require discipline from the patient, who must apply them regularly as directed. Patience is needed, too, as inflammation can often be difficult to get rid of. Depending on the severity, a local inflammation may take one to three weeks, or more, to be cured, even with anti-inflammatory cream applied three times a day. Very severe cases can take months to cure and will involve complete rest of the injured part from the causative action.

Treatment of Soft-Tissue Injuries

All traumatic soft-tissue injuries will involve some degree of pain, inflammation, internal bleeding and swelling. Acute over-use soft-tissue conditions will involve pain, inflammation, possibly some internal bleeding, and swelling.

Immediate first aid treatment is concerned with controlling inflammation, internal bleeding and swelling, and therefore alleviating pain to some degree and promoting faster healing, reducing the likelihood of complications, and perhaps making physiotherapy treatment more effective.

Immediate first aid treatment of a soft-tissue injury involves RICE: rest, ice, compression, elevation.

Rest

Rest may be immediately inevitable, as sudden pain, pain on attempted movement, fear of further damage, and swelling will probably prevent movement. A longer period of rest is essential to allow damaged tissue to start healing. This period of rest will vary according to the severity of the injury and may be a few days or more than a week. Rest may mean complete immobilization, or abstention from attempted use and weight-bearing. After a period of initial healing time, when functional movement may not yet be possible, 'active' rest allows gentle movements that may be beneficial.

Ice

Ice should be applied to the injured part as soon as possible. The ice should be in a polythene bag (to stop leakage) and then applied to the body with a towel or other material against the skin, to prevent ice burn. A bag of frozen peas or beans will mould to the shape of an injured joint or other body part (mark the packet and be sure not to use it for food once it has been used for first aid). Ice should be applied for about 10 minutes, but should not be applied again within an hour. Ice should be applied regularly, at least for the first few days, and may be beneficial if used regularly over a longer period of time.

Physiological effects of ice treatment:

1. reduces pain: by reducing conductivity of nerve fibres;
2. reduces spacticity (stiffness): spasm is a natural reaction to pain; by reducing pain, ice reduces spasm;

3. reduces swelling: the initial response of the tissue is vasoconstriction, which limits the flow of blood (use ice for approximately 10 minutes for inflammatory conditions and the acute stage of injury to reduce bleeding and swelling);
4. promotes repair: after initial vasoconstriction, vasodilation follows, increasing blood flow to help repair and healing. (Use ice for about 20 minutes after the acute stage of injury to promote healing.)

Depth of cooling using ice treatment for 30 minutes:

- skin temperature approximately 14.5°C;
- subcutaneous tissue approximately 24°C;
- muscle at 3cm depth approximately 26°C;
- muscle at 5cm depth approximately 32.3°C.

(Normal body temperature is 37°C.)

Do not apply heat during the acute stage of a soft-tissue injury. Heat will encourage internal bleeding and will aggravate the condition and increase inflammation.

Compression

An elasticated bandage will help control swelling. Swelling is initially not a bad thing. It is the body's natural 'splinting' or safety mechanism, which prevents further damage to an injured part by immobilizing it. However, the body tends to over-compensate and swelling may be excessive, causing pressure, pain and discomfort. Swelling will also be increased by internal bleeding. Excess swelling can hinder the healing process and lead to complications, or may interfere with an early diagnosis by a qualified person.

The swelling is caused by an effusion of fluid into the intercellular spaces or between muscles, or between skin and bone, and is known as oedema. Oedema differs from normal tissue fluid in that it contains plasma proteins and fibrinogen, a substance that causes blood to clot. This viscous fluid can become more viscous (sticky), causing adhesions, which involves tissues that normally slide smoothly over each other becoming stuck together.

Acute Oedema

Swelling during the acute stage of an injury will consist of acute oedema, which needs to be controlled and reduced by RICE treatment. Acute oedema will be soft, puffy, painful and will pit readily on pressure.

Chronic Oedema

Chronic oedema will form if acute oedema is not controlled and reduced. It is then difficult to disperse and will require much massaging and friction to break down adhesions. Chronic oedema is tense; hard; the skin may be shiny; and there is little pitting on pressure.

Ice and compression are intended to reduce swelling and control it to a minimum. Controlling the swelling by ice, compression and elevation, and later by gentle movement, can help prevent the formation of adhesions.

Elevation

Elevation also helps control the swelling because fluids naturally flow downwards with gravity. Raising (elevating) the injured part will help drain the oedema, thus reducing pressure and discomfort.

REHABILITATION (JOINTS)

As soon as possible after injury, and after a short period of healing has taken place, joints thrive on movement. This may be passive (where another person, preferably qualified and experienced, moves the joint through its range), then assisted active, and gentle active (where the patient creates the movement).

Movement for an injured joint during the rehabilitation stage acts as a form of natural massage and helps to disperse oedema, reducing swelling. It lubricates the joint by stimulating the secretion of synovial fluid and helps keep the muscles affecting the joint relaxed and toned.

All remedial movements of an injured joint should be carried out within the limits of pain (the exception might be with a true 'frozen shoulder', where the joint capsule has shrunk and requires stretching to prevent further shortening and a chronic or permanent condition; this will require a qualified diagnosis).

Muscles and Tendons

Injury to a muscle or tendon such as a strain will heal better if the muscle is gently stretched as soon as possible, after an initial period of healing.

During the healing process, scar tissue forms and is laid down. Gentle stretching fairly soon after the injury will help the scar tissue to form long, not tightly, and neatly in the direction of the muscle or tendon fibres. Without movement the scar tissue can be laid down in an irregular fashion and can develop short, resulting in possible future tension in the muscle. Movement also helps to relax, tone and strengthen the muscle.

Soft-Tissue Injuries

Scar tissue is also formed when soft tissue is damaged. It will contract by about the third week after injury and can continue to contract for up to seven months. It is therefore vital to gently stretch the new scar tissue while it is being laid down as soon as possible after the acute injury stage has passed (approximately 48 hours), and it is vital to stretch the scar tissue regularly for at least seven months. (A serious triathlete will be including such stretching as a regular routine anyway.)

Heat should *not* be used during the acute stage of a soft-tissue injury (within the first 48 hours), as it will increase bleeding and encourage swelling.

However, after the acute stage (after 48 hours, and depending on the severity of the injury), when internal bleeding has stopped, heat can be very beneficial in aiding the healing process, relieving pain and relaxing muscles.

Heat can be applied in a variety of ways. A hot-water bottle over the site of injury, or hot, damp towels will be effective (although they may be cumbersome and may drip).

The easiest and most effective application of heat is via an infra-red lamp. Position it approximately 45–50cm (18–20in) away from the skin surface over the site of injury, with the rays at right-angles to the tissue.

Heat in injury treatment has the following physiological effects:

1. vasodilation (promotes blood flow to the affected area);
2. reduces pain by affecting the sensory nerve endings; and
3. relaxes muscles.

Heat can have beneficial effects when the whole body is exposed to it (for example, in a sauna or a hot bath):

1. increases tissue metabolism.
2. relaxes muscles;
3. reduces blood pressure;
4. increases activity of sweat glands; and
5. leads to general relaxation of mind and body.

Inflammatory Conditions

Inflammatory conditions such as tendonitis, tenosynovitis, bursitis, and epicondylitis do *not* require movement. Such conditions often take a comparatively long time to recover and require complete rest from the causative activity. Movement is contra-indicated and qualified advice is recommended in severe cases.

A doctor may prescribe anti-inflammatory drugs and/or cream or gel, but the patient must be disciplined enough to rest the inflamed part until complete recovery is achieved. Another self-help treatment is the application of ice, which, when used regularly (every day for 10 minutes, not repeated within an hour), can be very effective.

CHAPTER 22
Mental Attitude

'The single, most important muscle is the mind.'

This is a crucial chapter for the active triathlete and coach, although it can only scratch the surface of the huge subject of mental attitude, conditioning and toughness and their effect upon physical performance and maximizing potential.

It is fashionable to show an interest in the importance of mental attitude and, in a wider context, sports psychology. However, many athletes and coaches merely pay 'lip service' to the ideas. Some glibly use terms and phrases such as VO_2max, lactate acid tolerance, vertical and horizontal body displacement, psychological re-education and formulation of positive mental strategies – but do they know what they are talking about? A little knowledge can be a dangerous thing.

Others use sports psychology more successfully. Fifty-five-year-old triathlete Harry Barrow is a master of the use of positive mental attitude. Just before setting out on the unique Gozo to Malta triathlon race, which includes a three-mile swim in very cold water after an eight-mile run, he said, 'I don't believe in psychology, I just get out there and do my absolute best and don't let anybody or anything put me off.'

Noureddine Morcelli's mind is full of doubts when he is racing: 'Who will come in second, who will come in third?'

The most important muscle for the triathlete is perhaps the least efficiently used by the majority – the mind.

POSITIVE THOUGHT

Countless races are thrown away every season, from local level right up to Olympic and World finals, by athletes who are always the best in training. What is it that sets champions apart? (For 'champion', read 'anybody who gets the absolute maximum out of themselves'.) It can't be the training; at all levels, training schedules differ only a little and there are fewer and fewer secrets.

The fact is that positive thoughts lead to positive actions. Someone once said about 1500m running that 'of twelve athletes on the starting line, six hope they're going to win, four think they're going to win, and two

Fig 78. Simon Lessing shows focus and concentration.

know they're going to win; the winner will be one of those two'. The theory applies equally to triathlon. To win, you have to have self-belief that you are the best, that you deserve to win, that you will win.

With the phenomenal growth of triathlon, competitive fields have risen to 800-plus entrants in some cases, standards have become higher and higher and the chances of winning tougher and tougher. The training and physical preparation for racing is harder, more intense and more scientific than ever. Winners and losers will often have prepared for competition in exactly the same way, but some will always be winners and some will always be losers.

This happens because of that frequently undertrained body part, the mind. The mental attitude to competition, and to training, is at least as important as the blood, sweat and tears of hard physical work. The triathlete who is properly mentally prepared is the winning triathlete.

PERSONALITIES AND QUALITIES

Successful triathletes need a host of mental qualities if they are to reach their full potential. If those qualities are not present, they have to be learned. In other words, the athlete has to be mentally trained.

An essential list of these qualities would include the following:

- self-discipline;
- self-reliance;
- self-motivation;
- self-belief;
- determination;
- organization; and
- concentration.

Drs Ogilvie and Tutko have isolated eleven personality traits that they consider to be the most important for successful athletes. Dr Ogilvie describes these as representing 'Championship Character'. The eleven traits are present to some degree in everybody, but it is their overall strength and depth in a particular athlete, relative to their strength in other athletes, that is the key factor in winning.

Self-motivation and drive
- A desire to win and to be successful.
- A willingness and aspiration to accomplish and overcome difficulties.
- Setting and maintaining high competition goals and aims.
- A positive attitude to competition.
- A deep, inner desire and need to achieve excellence.

Aggressiveness
- A belief that it is okay to be aggressive, that it is something that is essential to succeed.
- Easily becomes aggressive.
- Enjoys aspects of confrontation and argument.
- Can sometimes use force and intimidation to ensure that personal points of view are accepted.
- A refusal to be intimidated.
- Will not allow others to dominate.
- May try to 'get even' with those whom are perceived as having caused harm.

Determination
- Willing to train hard for a long time.
- Willing to work on skill aspects until exhausted.
- Willing to train alone, often.
- Willing to go on and on, even when results are not immediately forthcoming.
- Patient and relentless in pursuit of triathlon excellence.
- Unwilling to give up quickly on any aspect or problem connected with training or competition.

Proneness to guilt
- Accepts responsibility for actions.
- Accepts blame and criticism, even when they are not deserved.
- Dwells on mistakes and punishes him or herself.
- Willing to endure large amounts of physical and mental pain and discomfort.
- Trains and competes even when injured.

Leadership
- Has an enjoyment of leading and may spontaneously assume the role of leader without consulting others in the group.

- A belief that other athletes see and accept him or her as a leader.
- Will attempt to control and manipulate the environment and training conditions, and will attempt to influence and control other athletes.
- Will express opinions strongly and forcefully.

Self-confidence
- Is completely self-confident personally and also in ability to deal with things.
- Confident in strengths and abilities.
- Is able to cope with unexpected situations.
- Has confidence that when decisions are made, they are correct.
- Confident enough to articulate beliefs to coaches and other athletes.

Emotional control
- A tendency to be emotionally stable and realistic about triathlon.
- Not easily upset or put off.
- Will rarely allow emotions to show, and will not easily allow competition performance to be affected by those emotions.
- Will rarely allow him or herself to become depressed or frustrated by incidents outside control, such as marshal and referee calls, misdirection on race course, or wrongly placed buoys.

Mental toughness
- Will accept strong criticism without feeling hurt or taking the criticism personally.
- Will not become upset or angry when losing or racing poorly.
- An ability to bounce back from adversity.
- Will accept 'rough' or 'strong' coaching.
- Does not need excessive encouragement from coaches.

Coachability
- Respects coaches and the coaching process.
- Receptive to coaches' advice.
- Considers coaching important to becoming a top athlete.
- Accepts and respects leadership of team captain.
- Co-operates with authorities, race organizers, governing bodies.

Conscientiousness
- Likes to follow advice, coaching and training schedules as correctly as possible.
- A tendency to be exacting in character.
- A tendency to be dominated by a sense of duty to triathlon, and the training needed.
- Will not try to make excuses or to try to 'con' the coach or other athletes.

All top-class triathletes will race to their best ability when they are mentally – as well as physically – prepared. Some will want to be relaxed before competition while others will need to be tense, or 'hyped up' for a race. Each athlete will develop strategies and pre-race rituals to ensure that they arrive on the starting line with the best possible attitude for themselves. (For some mental preparations and checklists, *see* page 181.)

Mental strength does not just happen; like physical strength, it needs training to make it fitter, stronger and more controlled.

THE SUCCESS CYCLE

Preparation and training, both physical and mental, are essential for the triathlete to make use to the fullest of their innate potential. There is only one secret to success, but it comes in three parts.

Part I

First, the aspiring triathlete has to decide exactly what standard he or she wants to achieve in triathlon. This really does have to be specific. It is no good thinking, 'I wouldn't mind finishing an Ironman,' or, 'I'd like to go around 2 hours 30 minutes for an Olympic distance.' Accepting only the limits of physical ability, anything is achievable.

Part II

What is required in order to achieve that specific aim? Again, it is essential to be exact. Not, 'Oh, I think I'll have to train pretty hard,' but to lay out the exact requirements for the long-term goal, until every single piece of the intricate jigsaw is in place.

Part III

What will be the cost in terms of time, effort, money, loss of other activities, friends, socializing, job, family – in other words, what others usually call a 'normal life'. One athlete put it this way: 'I don't get much spare time at the moment. Most weekends there's something on, but I wouldn't want to change it. How many other people have travelled like I did last year? When you compare that with going down the pub or just sitting in doing nothing … it's my choice to do this. If it ever stops being enjoyable ….'

Many triathletes have a dream, and think that they are prepared to work for it, but when the crunch comes, it is often that third factor – what they have to give up – that beats all but the best.

The way you feel about yourself is closely related to the way you are likely to perform in a race and in training. Many triathletes fail to examine this relationship and its impact upon performance. The success cycle (Fig 79) is based upon the East European approach to sports psychology, which believes that having a positive self-image means that you are likely to have a positive attitude to triathlon and, indeed, to life in general.

This leads to the following important points of attitude:

- having high expectations of yourself;
- expecting yourself to do well, which itself leads to better training and lifestyle habits;
- eating and drinking properly;
- sleeping regularly;
- not taking part in activities that will have an adverse effect on training; and
- preparing your equipment immaculately for your race or training session.

Everything falls into place very neatly. Improved mental attitude and the physical results will almost inevitably bring better race results and training performances. Everything you have done leads to this and you expect to race well, so you do. Success will make you feel even better about yourself, ensuring that the cycle revolves onwards and upwards.

THE CYCLE OF FAILURE

The success cycle is the positive cycle. Its mirror image is the cycle of failure, which starts with a negative self-image, not liking yourself very much. Just as with the success cycle, each spot on the cycle leads to the next one. The differ-

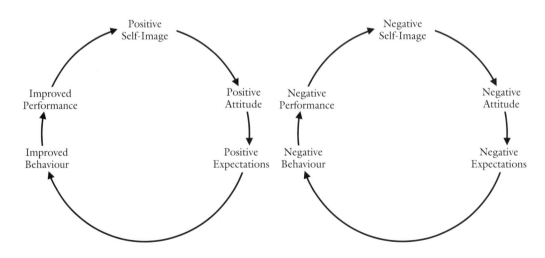

Fig 79. The success cycle.   Fig 80. The cycle of failure.

ence here, of course, is that each spots leads and drags you downwards rather than upwards. Having a negative self-image means that you are likely to think things like, 'I'm scared to try to do that,' or, 'I can't attempt this', and to have a negative attitude to life in general.

This leads to the following points of attitude:

- having low expectations of yourself;
- expecting yourself to do poorly, which it-self leads to poor training and incorrect lifestyle habits;
- eating and drinking badly – and too much;
- not sleeping enough;
- going out on the town and taking part in activities that will have an adverse effect on training; and
- not bothering to prepare your equipment for your race or training session.

Everything jars, and nothing slots into the unfit and ill-prepared niche. The negative mental attitudes and their physical results will almost inevitably bring worse race results and training performances. You expect to race badly, so you do; or you don't even bother! The negative cycle becomes a self-fulfilling prophecy ensuring – unlike the success cycle – that the cycle revolves poorly onwards, but downwards.

FOUR LAWS

One of the crucial things that governs your mental attitude is the way you view the world. Do you make things happen? Or do you allow them to happen to you? Do you always take the initiative, or do you feel that you have no control over what happens to you? The four laws below may give you food for thought, and make you focus on how you see the world.

Law 1: The Law of Control

- You feel good about yourself.
- You are in control of your life and of your training.
- You don't feel right about yourself when you feel that you can't control your own life or your training.

This begins with controlling your own thoughts.

Law 2: The Law of Accident

- You can't control your own life or your train-ing, everything just happens by accident.
- Most people live their life by the law of accident, often without realizing it.
- In triathlon, these people are the athletes who have no goals beyond the short term, they do not have plans and they just hope that somehow things will turn out okay and they will just improve.

Law 3: The Law of Cause and Effect

(The opposite of the Law of Accident.)

- For every effect in your life there is a spe-cific cause.
- For every improvement in competition, there is a specific reason from training.
- You control how you train, what you do in training, and therefore how you improve in competition.

Your thoughts control what you do, what you achieve. If you want to do better in the future, you have to change your thoughts now.

Law 4: The Law of Belief

- Self-belief. 'I can, I will, I must.'
- Whatever you believe can happen, will happen.
- Even if you are a long way from where you would like to be, you plan and you believe you will eventually get there.

MENTAL CONTROL

The winning athlete is the athlete who is in mental control. It is a sport in which there is frequently little or no difference between the physical preparation and training of all the competing athletes. However, a few are able to pull out everything in a race, to win when others may be more fancied. Tom McNab summed it up when he said, 'Training is phys-ical, racing is emotional.'

What sets the winners apart? Some of the points below may give a clue to that winning edge; and how you can go about getting it.

Goal-Setting and Motivation

- Think about the best race you ever had. Try to remember everything connected with the race – before the race, during the race and after it.
- Your brain controls your muscle movements.
- When you swim, cycle or run you do not have to think about it. Years and years, repetition after repetition, grooving into the particular pattern has established it. This is when the going is good.
- When you are tired or you hit a bad patch, you have to go through a conscious set of thought processes to stay in control; this is when the going gets tough.

Ideas Release a Bodily Reaction

How do you go about releasing a mental reaction? If you repeat, 'I want to wake up at 6am' enough times, a sub-conscious reaction will work while you're asleep. Try, 'I will train at 6pm tomorrow;' repeat it enough times and if you don't go out you'll feel guilty.

Thoughts and Reactions

Thoughts influence reactions. If you concentrate enough on a thought, you can actually feel that thought. (Try thinking, 'My arms feel heavy,' and your arms will feel heavy. Think, 'I feel relaxed' and you will feel relaxed.)

In general:

- positive thoughts lead to positive reactions;
- negative thoughts lead to negative reactions;
- systematic, conscious, positive thinking will make your reactions positive.

If you work at it, you can change negative behaviour to positive behaviour. An obvious parallel is the placebo effect, when a patient thinks that something will get them better, and does get better.

As a contrast to your positive thoughts about a good race, think about a particularly bad race. What happened before that bad race? Did you eat too much before starting? Think about it, and you may begin to feel the effects of having eaten too much, and take that reaction into the race.

In triathlon, which has certain complexities, the difference between positive and negative thinking can *dramatically* affect and effect changes in performance.

All athletes talk to themselves. Imagine one of 'those' race days – rough sea, windy conditions, a hill to run up. If you have negative thoughts, you might be saying to yourself, 'I'll never make it, it's stupid, the race should be stopped, they can't expect me to do that.' If you have positive thoughts, you will be saying, 'This'll be fine, I've done worse in training, it will affect all the others more than me, I'll dig in deep and go for it.'

The way you approach such a race will demonstrate your image of yourself. If you have negative thoughts, maybe you feel stupid, scared, or worried that people will laugh at you. A positive thinker will prefer to stay cool, ask what's happening, and trust in his or her strengths.

Triathlon tends to be a self-fulfilling prophecy – in other words, you often do what you think you are going to do.

Just as building up training takes time, so does mental training and learning to think positively. You learn from repetition, but repetition takes time. Use the PASS process:

1. *P*ositive thoughts and words.
2. *A*void negatives: no, never, not.
3. *S*imple thoughts and words.
4. *S*chedule mental training; get used to the habit of positive mental thoughts

Thoughts + Feelings + Energy = Performance

Try these positive thoughts:

- I feel calm.
- My mind is clear and ready to go.
- I can concentrate intensely on the race.
- I will attack/go out fast/respond.
- I dare to attack/go out fast/respond.

- I feel ready and happy.
- I'm really looking forward to this race, and I feel in a good mood.

PRE-RACE THOUGHTS AND ACTIONS

The state of your mental attitude in the hours and minutes before an important race will be especially significant, and will have maximum impact on how well or badly you do. To prepare yourself fully, it is as well to have a list of actions and positive thoughts (almost a mantra).

The physical warm-up can be the key with which to turn on the mental preparation. The easy stretch and jog/swim/cycle, the technique run-through, and the transition awareness should lead to the establishment of a physical and mental comfort zone within the competition area. Using positive imagery, creating 'space', talking to yourself about your own strengths and skills, and reminding yourself of your immediate goals will establish a proper focus and the correct mental attitude.

From these general thoughts, go on to specific psychological preparation: pre-planned thoughts, a short mental review of the race, establishing the correct level of activation (or 'hype') that is appropriate for you, establishing total readiness and a 100 per cent focus on the race.

1. Relax (as well as you can).
2. Try to imagine yourself doing well in the actual race.
3. Think through the positive thoughts above.

A checklist for positive thoughts in the last few minutes should include the following:

1. I have *prepared* extremely well, physically and psychologically.
2. I am *capable* of accepting any weather or course condition. Wind, cold, waves and surf, a greasy surface, hills and descents, the other athletes, will make no difference. *I am under my own control.*

3. My goal is realistic and *I can achieve it.* Nothing will distract or stop me from gaining that achievement.
4. I have a huge background of preparation and training, both physical and mental. *I can extend myself* and *stretch my limits* further than I have ever done before.
5. I will follow my race plan. I will be fast and in control throughout every discipline.
6. I am *ready*. I am at my *very best*. I will do it!

In the final few seconds, think about the following:

1. I will race my race.
2. I will think about what I am doing, not about what anyone else is doing.
3. I will start fast, stay there, concentrate.
4. I will be with the leaders, I will stay with them, and then I will kick away from them.
5. Concentrate, concentrate, concentrate.

WINNERS AND LOSERS

Open your mind to the possibilities that are available with a strong, positive, mental attitude. Consider these last few questions – no answers, just questions …

'Man was designed for accomplishment, engineered for success and endowed with the seeds of greatness.' (Napoleon Hill, *Think and Grow Rich*)

So why do so few athletes fulfil their potential?

'Most men lead lives of quiet desperation.' (Henry Thoreau)

Why do so few athletes really go for it? Are they waiting for another life to do it? Why do some athletes live under the law of accident, refusing to take control of their own athletic career?

Are some athletes waiting for that lucky break (which never comes), rather than creating their own luck? Are they so tied up in complaining about not having that good luck that they do not recognize it when it does come along?

Adrian Trier vs Joe Plodder

Adrian Trier	*Joe Plodder*
Wants to race	Passive and nervous, not sure …
Strongly motivated	Tired, feels sluggish
Can concentrate totally	Indecisive
Happy with himself	Insecure, not happy with himself
Feels 'flowing' in swim/cycle/run	Feels heavy and slow
Happy, good mood	Feels low and down
No inner conflicts	I've got this problem …
Self-confident	Worried … doesn't dare try
No anxieties about performance/race	Scared about own performance/race
Aims high/dares to win/goes for it	Anxious/defensive/evasive
So what? If I don't …	I'm scared to try, in case …
Thinks/talks positive to self	Thinks/talks negative to self
There is no number 13 in positive thoughts	I'm achieving nothing, everything's wrong

Positive Mental Attitude (PMA) checklist

- Set your dream goal.
- Set specific goals.
- Plan specifically how you will achieve those goals.
- Imagine success. If you can't imagine, you can't do it.
- Always act as if you will achieve success.
- Prepare and train mentally.
- Train to race well, don't train to train.
- Focus on your strengths.
- Work on your weaknesses.
- Assess your progress. And then re-assess. And then re-assess again.
- Learn from every race, every training session.
- Don't be afraid to refine and change your aims, objectives and goals.
- Be persistent. Try, try, try … and then try again.
- Liking yourself is the single most important starting point.
- Enjoy your good luck at being a triathlete.
- Always remember that there is life outside triathlon.

Isn't 'luck' really the result of 'preparation meeting opportunity'?

Many truly great sportspeople have overcome an appalling start in life; triathletes who aspire to reach the highest level can have no excuses. Indeed, they should not *want* to have any excuses. It's not the cards that life deals you, it's how you play those cards.

Why do some athletes always attract 'bad' luck? Why do some athletes always attract 'good' luck?

Is winning in sport (and in life) a habit? Is losing in sport (and in life) a habit?

Winning and losing are the results of choices. You can choose to go for your goals, or you can choose to be controlled by other people's goals. The awesome responsibility is that winning and losing are both a question of attitude. And you choose your own attitude.

CHAPTER 23

Stress and the Triathlete

'It's not the cards that life deals you, it's how you play those cards.'

Does the following sound familiar?

5am. Not already! I'm still shattered from yesterday's run; just couldn't sleep last night. I don't know how I'll get through this morning's swim session.

8am. I'm knackered! Still, running to work's better than sitting in the car ... it's just that my legs feel so heavy.

9am. Oh God, I'm behind on yesterday's account and I haven't even started today. Hope the boss doesn't single me out.

12.00 Thank goodness that's the morning over. I'll grab a cup of tea and then get out for a few intervals on the road. Got to shake out of this lethargy.

1.30pm. Damn! I forgot all about the figures the office wanted. Better get my head down and get them done.

3.30pm. I am so, so tired. Roll on 5.30.

6pm. What a day; I'm finished, just absolutely finished. I'll have to take the bus home instead of running.

8.30pm. Is that the time? Must have dozed off .... I'll have to dash for the pool.

Midnight. Why can't I sleep? I work hard enough. You'd think I'd be out before my head touched the pillow, but everything just keeps spinning round. I'll have to catch up tomorrow.

5am. Not already!

Do you recognize anyone ... or yourself?

WHAT IS STRESS?

Stress is a much-used, much-maligned, much-misunderstood word. In the 1980s and 90s it came to be used to describe the business-person in a high-pressure work environment, who lacks the time to do everything and is constantly juggling work schedules, meetings, and family life. This kind of stress is *distress*, the opposite of the 'good' type, *eustress*.

Stress could be better defined as 'coping with change'.

Stress is an everyday part of life, and a life without stress is a life without anything. Everyone has to deal with stress in some form or to some degree, depending on their lifestyle. Some stress is always there; other stress is self-imposed by work or by social and leisure choices (such as triathlon training).

When the brain anticipates a potentially stressful situation, it alerts the body, which reacts by releasing a surge of adrenalin. This, in turn, leads to good performance. Along with the adrenalin, the following physical changes also occur:

1. an increased level of blood sugar is released into the bloodstream;
2. there is an increase in heart rate;
3. there is a rise in blood pressure;
4. breathing becomes more rapid;
5. the muscles tense, preparing the body for action; and
6. the body starts to perspire.

That surge of adrenalin as an athlete turns the last corner and hears the crowd applauding is essential. Getting rid of stress and its effects in this situation would not be beneficial. The secret is to recognize stress and to get rid of the *harmful* effects of too much of it.

Different levels of stress, or lack of stress, are placed upon 'fun' triathletes, non-competitive, competitive and professional triathletes. Competition is largely irrelevant to the fun triathlete, who will often swim, cycle and run purely as a relaxation from everyday work. Rather than increasing stress, this kind of activity will often alleviate it.

As competition becomes more important, up to a point at which a triathlete's living depends upon success, stress can increase enormously. The lifestyle of a pro triathlete may sound great, but the reality of having to compete, succeed and win for sponsors, and earn enough money just to exist can be rather different. A small number of stars do nothing but train all day, and reap well-justified rewards, but the other 90 per cent train just as long and hard without winning the races, and without earning the money.

It may be tough at the top, but it is even tougher a couple of rungs down.

THE FOUR SUPPORTS

One way at looking at stress is to imagine your life balanced upon four pillars, which all take an equal load:

1. Support 1 is your family and your home life.
2. Support 2 is your work.
3. Support 3 is your friends.
4. Support 4 is your hobbies and relaxation.

Fig 81. The four supports.

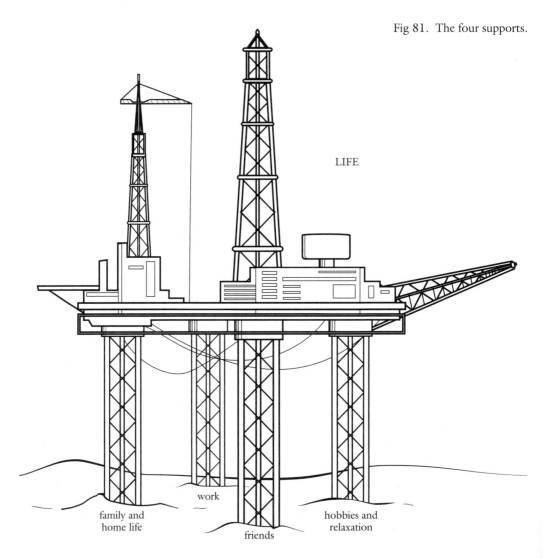

For triathletes, Support 4 – almost by definition – has to be triathlon.

Most people jog along quite happily balancing the four aspects of their life on these four supporting pillars, until one day something happens to upset the status quo. Say the awful spectre of redundancy comes along. At a single stroke, one support pillar is demolished, but with the support of the three remaining pillars, most people can cope (at least temporarily). Life is less stable, but it's liveable.

However, when a second pillar crumbles, things really get tough. Suppose that most of the redundancy casualty's friends were connected with work; they may start to slip away. Life will be precariously balanced on two pillars. The lucky ones will survive with the support of family and their sport, but if another support goes …

The successful full-time triathlete is sponsored, wins races, earns money, gets the glory. In a single incident, a serious injury can remove that athlete's work, relaxation, sport and, probably, many friends. Is it possible to continue balancing on just one pillar?

What about Joe Average triathlete? Most live from day to day competently combatting everyday stress. When the stress builds up, there is no single easy solution.

Imagine there is a magic substance in Joe called 'anti-stress syndrome' (ASS), which allows him to combat stress. Assume that Joe has twelve ASS tablets to use up each day. His job uses up four (say), travelling to and from work another two, looking after the house one, training moderately hard another three. That leaves two in reserve to take care of any extra stresses that come along.

Then Joe decides that he wants to win his age group in the nationals. He ups his training and uses his last two ASS tablets. He is balanced on a fine edge, which is okay unless something else comes along. Then he gets promotion at work – more money, but also more hours, more responsibility, less time for home, less time for training. Joe needs more ASS tablets than he possesses. He has to structure his life so that the stress becomes less. At this point, he needs to deal with it immediately. And at this point, the self-imposed stress of training hard can lead to the downward spiral of fatigue, working harder, more fatigue, and so on.

Stress is cumulative. It cannot be isolated from other areas of life, and should be considered along with the whole.

DEALING WITH STRESS AND MAKING IT LESS

In the simplest terms, stress is the physical and emotional reaction to change. The important factor is how it is perceived, and how the stressed person reacts to it. Ideally, stress can be made to work for the benefit of the athlete.

Reacting Well

In a work situation, deadlines mean that work has to be done. The body tenses and all the attention is focused on the job, and it gets done, on time. The same is true of a race or training. When you have finished, in the best time that you can, you feel pleased with yourself. Then you can relax. You have handled the situation that caused you stress; your body and mind responded by accepting the challenge and working through it.

Although you may not have been aware of it, changes would have been taking place in your body during this stressful period. Your body would have been gearing itself up for the stress – muscles tensing, jaw clenching, pulse rate going up, blood pressure rising, hands feeling cold, stomach feeling upset.

These body changes will be familiar to the triathlete. They are exactly what happens in a race or in a hard training session. The reactions are entirely normal, being physical reactions to stress.

Reacting Badly

What if you had not accepted the work (or the training, or the race situation) as a challenge to be overcome? What if you had been afraid of not being able to do well? The same body reactions would have occurred, but you would not have used the energy created positively to focus your attention on the task.

Example 1: you get passed early on the bike discipline and the rider starts to disappear into the distance. What do you do? How do you react? Do you say, 'I'll try to pull her back,' or 'That's it for today. What's the point?'

Example 2: in a track session (your strongest discipline), your training partner comes up to your shoulder. Normally, you take great pleasure in grinding him into the dust, but he pulls away from you and then does it for the next three reps. What's your reaction? What does that situation do to you and to your thinking?

If you see potential stress situations as something to be *avoided* or *feared*, the stress will be carried over after the job/training/race is finished. It will become a source of worry and you may still feel tense when you are trying to sleep, which means that you are likely still to be tense the following day. It is all too easy to get caught up in this vicious circle.

PERCEIVING AND HANDLING STRESS

The first important step is to understand that it is not usually the stress or the stressor that creates a problem. It is the way that stress or challenge is *perceived* or *handled*. The key to coping properly is to react positively. If you perceive stress negatively, you react negatively. If you welcome the stress of a challenge, you react positively. Face jobs, races and training sessions equally positively; and then reward yourself with the enjoyment and satisfaction of having tried as hard as you could.

Even in one of those races where everything goes wrong, there is a positive aspect. You may have overcome the challenges and stresses of cold water, crashing, going off course, cramping, panicking, and finished the race. For world-class triathletes, experiencing such a race, and persevering to overcome the problems and upsets, makes them remarkably strong-minded for the future.

A healthy reaction to stress involves not only the way you perceive stress, but also the way you reverse or counteract its physical effects. The stress reaction gears you up inside. In order to prevent this pent-up energy from accumulating in your body, you have to shift gears. Training and taking part in triathlons is the obvious physical answer to the stress created from working, but it is important also to utilize relaxation and methods of controlling breathing. For the full-time triathlete, a physical effort in a sport outside triathlon might be relaxing. Scott Tinley often plays tennis immediately after competing; it is a different physical release, and therefore a relaxation for him.

Relaxation

In the early 1900s, Edmund Jacobson theorized that when the body experienced stress, the muscles tensed and the extra physical discomfort of the tensed muscles made the stress worse.

The objective is to break that cycle. Progressive relaxation (*see also* Chapter 24) consists of focusing how it feels to relax alternately tensing and relaxing different groups of muscles in a series of eleven progressive steps:

1. Sit in a comfortable chair, or lie on the floor with your feet against the wall, and close your eyes.
2. Make a tight fist with your right hand, hold it for about 5 seconds and experience the tension.
3. Unclench your fist and let the tension flow out, noting how different it feels to relax.
4. Do the same with your left hand and the muscles in your upper arms and shoulders.
5. Tense your neck, hold and then relax, noting the feeling of relaxed tension.
6. Frown as hard as you can and then relax.
7. Smile as hard as you can and then relax.
8. Raise your toes (or push against the wall), feeling the leg tension, and then relax. Again, notice how the tension drains away.
9. Take a deep breath, feeling the tension in your chest. Breathe out and then relax. Breathe in again and hold, then breathe out and concentrate on how calm you are.
10. Conjure up in your mind a peaceful, pleasant setting and enjoy it for a while.
11. Now count slowly to four and open your eyes. You will be fully alert and relaxed.

A daily session using this technique may take about 20 minutes at first, but with practice it can be much shorter.

Deep Breathing

Deep breathing is another simple technique to help combat tension build-up:

1. Sit in your chair or stand comfortably, but erect.
2. Place the palms of your hands against your stomach.
3. Breathe in slowly through your nose, allowing your stomach to expand forwards against your hands.
4. Hold this deep breath for a few seconds.
5. Breathe out slowly through your mouth, pursing your lips slightly, and feel the tension draining away.
6. When you have breathed out as much as you can, repeat the technique.

You should repeat this cycle a couple of times at first and work up to taking four or five breaths in this manner after some practice.

Be careful not to breathe too fast as this may cause hyperventilation or light-headedness.

Positive Imagery

Positive imagery or controlled daydreams represent a less time-consuming but enjoyable method of relaxing the mind. Follow these simple steps:

1. Lean back in your chair and get as comfortable as possible.
2. Breathe in slowly through your nose and out through your mouth ten to twelve times with your eyes closed.
3. As you breathe out say to yourself 'calm' or 'relax'.
4. After about 2 minutes, picture a positive triathlon scene from your own experience and imagine yourself in it. Stay engrossed in the scene until you feel the tension drain away from you.
5. Open your eyes, get out of your chair, stretch, and you will be ready to go.

Focusing

Focusing is a valuable method of recognizing the body's signals that something is wrong, that the body is reacting to stressors with tensed muscles or gritted teeth, and of dealing with it.

Take a 'strain inventory' every day. Check situations that might be stressful and that keep you from feeling good. First, you need to recognize how stress affects your body, perhaps causing tense neck or back muscles, headaches or stomach aches. Write down which stressors affect you and to what degree. (Writing them down gives you a better chance of finding solutions to them.)

Using this focusing or analysing, you can gain a sense of control over stress and find yourself in a better position to adapt to the changes you encounter.

Helpful Relaxing Practices

Monitoring your food and fluid intake can be helpful. Caffeine is a stimulant, and while you may feel alert for a short time after taking it, you will soon feel sluggish, anxious and irritable.

Eliminate various items from your diet and see how you feel. The consumption of meat, cheese, eggs, nuts, vegetables, fruits, fruit juices and water instead of sweets, caffeine and highly processed food may help you to meet challenges in a more relaxed and positive way. Be aware that withdrawal symptoms such as headaches and fatigue can occur when you remove refined sugar and caffeine from your diet.

The feeling of soft-tissue stretching and relaxing experienced in a good massage can also help to counteract the cumulative tensing effects of stress. Massage should only be administered by properly qualified individuals. It may be wise to check with your doctor before starting a course of massage.

THE STRESS-RESISTANT PERSON

If you want to survive and thrive in this stressful life, you will need to work to acquire the attributes and perspective of a stress-resistant person. Two stress experts, Suzanne 0. Kobasa and Salvatore R. Maddi, have found that people who cope successfully with stress have three characteristics that are not found in the less hardy.

Unlike others, who see change as a threat to their security, these individuals perceive change as a natural challenge to be mastered. They regard life as strenuous, yet exciting, and welcome change as an opportunity for improvement. They also have a strong sense of commitment to themselves, their families and their jobs, as well as other important values. In contrast to less hardy people who find tasks boring or meaningless. They throw themselves enthusiastically and with maximum effort and interest into what they consider important missions. Hardy individuals exhibit a sense of optimism or control over their lives.

Less hardy people see themselves as passive victims of forces beyond their control and expect the worse. Hardy individuals believe they can influence events and try to turn a possible negative into an advantage.

In what way will it benefit you to work hard and acquire these hardy characteristics? Drs Kobasa and Maddi have shown in their research that people who view life's stresses and change with challenge, commitment and control are only half as likely to become ill as less

hardy people exposed to the same stress levels. Inner resources prove to be more important and effective as antistress factors than genetic make-up, relaxation methods or exercise.

These hardy characteristics, usually learned during childhood, *can* be developed, with a change of attitude and an acquisition of the appropriate habits.

STRESS MANAGEMENT

Unfinished business on your desk or in your home life can be a major contributor to stress. Worrying subconsciously about unfinished business may prevent you from releasing stress and its effects when necessary. Finish those projects that you set out to do, or make a decision to put them behind you as soon as is possible and practical. Completing your office work can be as mentally exhilarating as finishing a race, depending on how you look at it.

Stress management is essential to your health as well as your job performance and satisfaction. You can do a great deal to prevent uncontrolled stress reactions, which could otherwise make you ill with headaches, backache, insomnia, depression, high blood pressure, ulcers, heart disease, and so on. Take the necessary steps to turn this potential enemy into a friend. If you need to, seek professional guidance.

CHAPTER 24
Relaxation

'Count backwards from one hundred – one hundred, ninety-nine...'

Fig 82. Rick Collard takes the opportunity to relax immediately after the race.

The levels of training expected from triathletes wishing to maximize their potential are extremely high. They often find it very difficult to relax, perhaps because of the constant pressure to perform well in training. All highly trained athletes are familiar with tight muscles and fatigue, and triathletes are no exception.

There is a connection between stress and training, and a difference between 'good' stress, or eustress, and 'bad' stress, or distress. The downward spiral of the stress cycle can quickly become apparent when so little time is given to rest and relaxation. However, there are methods of consciously and actively relaxing the different muscle groups of the body. By gradually progressing through the individual muscle groups and, in time, putting them together in a smaller number of groups as your own awareness becomes more pronounced, relaxing almost at will becomes easier and easier.

When you first attempt practical relaxation, it is important to be comfortable, without tight or restricting clothing. It might be preferable

the first few times to go through this with a group, or in your triathlon club with an experienced coach, instructor or teacher helping you through the different stages.

After a few attempts, you may wish to progress a little further, perhaps with a relaxation or self-induced hypnosis tape.

PROGRESSIVE MUSCLE RELAXATION (PMR)

This procedure uses the overshoot principle to initiate the relaxation response.

Try this experiment: quickly scan your body; notice the way your right arm feels; now tighten your muscles and squeeze; hold this contraction for 5 seconds and then release. Do you notice a difference in the way your right arm feels?

Most people will notice that their tight arm feels a little more relaxed, because the normal level of tension has been overshot. Everyone has

Fig 83. Sam Larkin in stretch and relaxation mode.

a particular level of tension in their body, their own personal adaptation level. Tension is necessary to allow standing, sitting and moving. Tensing the muscles results in a momentary move into a zone of additional tension. With the release of the tensed muscle, the tension level is reduced below normal. This becomes the starting point of the relaxation response.

PMR can be done with 16, 7, 4 or 1 muscle groups. The table opposite lists the major muscle groupings for each of the techniques.

Usually, it is best to start by relaxing the 16 muscle groups. As you become more proficient, combine the divisions until you can relax your whole body at one. Most athletes have a fairly good knowledge of their bodies and may be able to begin with the 7 muscle group programme. Use the programme that is most effective for you, remembering that your objective is to relax your whole body as quickly as possible.

After you have decided which muscle groups to relax, the next step is to learn *how* to relax

them. The tension table opposite is a guide to follow when tensing particular muscle groups. In each instance, completely relax the muscle following each period of tension. Be sure that you understand how to relax each muscle group before attempting your first relaxation session.

POINTS TO REMEMBER

The following guidelines should help you to have a successful relaxation experience. Remember, relaxation is a skill and it will take you some time to develop it to its fullest capacity.

- Find a comfortable, quiet environment.
- Lie (preferably on a carpeted floor) on your back and stretch out; avoid crossing your arms or legs.
- Once you relax a muscle group, try not to move that set of muscles as the procedure continues.
- Tense a muscle group for 5 seconds; then relax for 30 seconds. Repeat this process as needed to relax each muscle group completely.
- When you release a contraction, release it sharply and completely. Gradually releasing the contraction does not provide a sharp enough contrast to learn to distinguish between tension and relaxation.
- Concentrate on the feelings of relaxation.

Your objective in practising PMR is to move from using the 16-muscle group procedure to relaxing at will. To do this take the following steps:

1. learn to distinguish tension from relaxation;
2. become aware of your breathing. Breathe in deeply through the nose and exhale slowly through the mouth;
3. repeat the word 'relax' to yourself each time you exhale; focus on the sensation of relaxation;
4. develop a cue or image of what relaxation sensation feels like for you; as you progress, you will be able to use the cue or image or the word relax to initiate the relaxation response.

Muscle Groups for PMR Training

16 Muscle Groups	7 Muscle Groups	4 Muscle Groups
Dominant hand/forearm	Dominant arm	
Dominant biceps		Arms and hands
Nondominant hand/forearm	Nondominant arm	
Nondominant biceps		
Upper face and forehead	Face	
Central face		Face and neck
Lower face and jaw		
Neck	Neck	
Chest/shoulders/upper back	Chest/shoulders/back and abdomen	Chest/shoulders/back and abdomen
Abdomen		
Dominant upper leg and thigh	Dominant leg and foot	
Dominant lower leg and calf		
Dominant foot		
Nondominant upper leg and thigh	Nondominant leg and foot	Legs and feet
Nondominant lower leg and calf		
Nondominant foot		

PMR Tension Instructions

Muscle Group	Tension Activity
Hand and forearm	Make a tight fist
Biceps	Push elbow down against a surface and in towards side
Upper face	Lift eyebrows as high as possible
Central face	Squint and wriggle the nose
Lower face	Clench teeth and pull corners of mouth back
Neck	Pull chin down to touch your chest; at the same time, resist the action
Chest/shoulders/upper back	Take a deep breath, hold it, pull shoulders back and together
Abdomen	Pull stomach in as far as possible and hold it (as if someone has punched you in the stomach)
Upper leg and thigh	Extend and lift the leg slightly and hold
Lower leg and calf	Pull toes towards head and hold
Foot	Point toes, turn foot inwards, and then curl the toes

CHAPTER 25
Travel

'Treat every long journey as if it were a hard training session.'

Travelling places the athlete under a number of stresses. Travel stress may arise from the planning prior to departure, and the procedures of getting through security, passport and customs, and boarding the aircraft; travel fatigue comes from spending hours in cramped conditions. Many people also suffer the collection of symptoms known as jet lag, caused by the disruption of the body clock.

FLYING

Travelling on long flights, even within the same time zone (for example, from the UK to South Africa) may cause all sorts of difficulties, which can be made worse by delays. Travel can be more of a drain on mental resources than on the body, so a positive psychological attitude towards it is important.

Dehydration, both while waiting to board and on the plane, can be a problem. Taking plenty of fluid will help to prevent this and also prevent headaches, which can be a result of the combination of low air pressure and loss of body water in the cabin. Coffee and tea should be limited as these are diuretics; have fruit juice, squash or still mineral water as an alternative. You may prefer to take your own sports drink.

Avoid stiffness caused by staying a long time in a cramped position by periodically walking up and down the aisle of the plane. Do simple stretching exercises at the back of the plane, or do isometric exercises in your seat.

After-effects attributable to the flight itself wear off quickly after arrival. A shower, a change of clothing and perhaps a light exercise session provide a good antidote to 'travel fatigue'.

JET LAG

Travellers flying west or east may suffer a number of after-effects, due to disturbances of the body clock. Jet lag is the name given to the group of symptoms, which affect travellers in different ways and to different extents. The symptoms include fatigue, inability to sleep at an appropriate time, loss of appetite, constipation, loss of concentration and drive, and headache. The general malaise may prevent travelling athletes from performing at their best. Physical exertion will be more difficult, and fine skills are likely to be accomplished less well.

Jet lag affects individuals differently, but in general:

- it is more pronounced (that is, it is more severe and lasts longer) after a flight to the east than one to the west through the same number of time zones;
- it is more pronounced as more time zones are crossed;
- younger and fitter people tend to suffer less than older members of the population.

On average it will take about one day for every time zone crossed to recover completely from the effects of jet lag. After travelling to the USA from the UK, for example, it may take 5–6 days for the majority of athletes to be completely clear of jet lag symptoms, although a few may recover by the third day. If travelling to New Zealand or Australia, UK athletes may need ten days.

The effects are periodic and can be more intense at particular times of the day. It is possible to be totally unaware of any adverse effects, until you have to do something quickly, take decisions or train or race.

Causes of Jet Lag

Jet lag is due to the disruption of the body's so-called 'circadian rhythm'. This rhythm is a function of the body clock that controls a whole host of physiological functions. It determines the cyclical rise in body temperature during the day to an evening peak and a subsequent drop to a trough in the middle of the night's sleep. It also determines the sleep-wakefulness cycle. Research also suggests that the body clock affects physiological measures that themselves influence sports performance.

Normally, the body clock is in harmony with the 24-hour changes between daylight and darkness. Since the earth spins on its axis, the sun is at its maximum height above the horizon at any point on the earth's surface once in every 24-hour period. This time is called 'local noon'. The world's 24 time zones are related to Greenwich Mean Time (GMT), based upon the Greenwich Meridian in London. Countries to the east of the Greenwich Meridian, where the sun rises earlier, are ahead of GMT, while those to the west are behind. For example, when it is 4pm in London, it is 8pm in Abu Dhabi and midnight (at the end of the day) in Singapore, 11am in Florida and 8am on the west coast of the USA. Adjusting to a new local time when flying to a different time zone can cause difficulties for the body's internal clock.

Adjusting to a Different Time Zone

The body clock is slow to adjust to the change in schedule that is required when travelling to a country with a different local time. Before adjustment, the athlete might be training or competing at a time when the body would prefer to be asleep, and attempting to sleep when the body clock wants to be awake. It is during this period that jet lag is experienced. Once the body clock has adjusted, jet lag does not return until crossing time zones again (usually on the return journey home).

Full adjustment of the body clock takes several days. The aim must be to speed up the process of adjustment as much and as safely as possible. Performance can only be at its peak when the body is fully adjusted to the new time zone. This applies to training as well as to competition. Until that time, an individual will struggle to give 100 per cent.

The body clock is a poor time-keeper. Under normal circumstances, it is adjusted by external signals. Making use of such signals can help with adjustment to time zone transitions. The main signals that adjust the body clock are the following:

- pattern of sleep and activity (including exercise);
- timing and type of meals;
- exposure to social influences and the alternation of natural daylight and darkness in the environment; and
- the body's exposure to ultraviolet light, generally by receiving direct sunlight out of doors.

Adjustment can be started during the flight, but most takes place during the first few days in the new time zone. The measures taken depend on the direction in which you travel.

Travelling west (UK to USA, for example) requires a delay in the body clock – comparatively easier than advancing it. In the days immediately before departure, try going to bed one or two hours later than normal and getting up one or two hours later. Trying to adjust fully to time-zone transitions before the journey will interrupt your training schedule and lifestyle too much and will not adjust your body clock very much. Where you have a choice of flight times and airports, select a schedule that makes planning to adjust easier. Aim, for example, to get to the USA in the evening.

Set your watch to the new time zone immediately after take-off. It is a good tactic to find somebody to talk to, read a book, listen to the in-flight music or watch the in-flight film.

On arrival, your new local time will be behind (later than) your body's time, so you will tend to wake early and feel tired in the afternoon or evening. Recommendations are:

1. try to sleep in surroundings that are quiet, dark and comfortable;
2. if you wake early (often because you need to use the toilet), return quietly to bed until the correct rising time;

3. if you feel tired during the day, resist the temptation to take a nap. If you are genuinely exhausted from lack of sleep, take a short nap of no more than 1 hour; it is far better, however, to fight through the feelings of drowsiness until bedtime.

For the first day or so after the flight you might find it helps to go to bed one or two hours earlier than normal, but no earlier than that. You may not feel like a full training session at first, but light training outside at your usual training time (local time) will help you to adjust and make you feel ready for sleep at bedtime. Prearranged social activities are a very good way of adjusting to the new time zone, particularly if they enable you to spend time out of doors in natural daylight.

Try to take meals of the 'correct' type (breakfast, lunch, and so on) at the appropriate time; do not eat a large supper, which may make sleep difficult. There is some evidence that high-protein foods such as fish and meat, and caffeine-containing drinks (such as coffee and tea) are best taken in the morning and that a light snack rich in carbohydrates (fruit juice and dessert) is best for supper. Alcohol sends you to sleep, but will also act as a diuretic and cause you to wake up to go to the toilet.

Drugs and Treatments

A number of pills and other treatments are supposed to reduce the effects of jet lag, and some travellers also make considerable use of sleeping pills (particularly some short-acting benzodiazepines). Apart from any rules that might govern their use by athletes, these drugs have not been tested extensively for any side-effects they might have upon maximum performance in top-class athletes. Although there might be a role for drugs known as 'hypnotic' in promoting sleep during the nights immediately after a flight, their use is more appropriate for non-athletes. They should only be used in *exceptional* cases and under prescription of the medical advisor to the squad. It is better not to use them less than four days prior to competition.

The effects of sleep loss are not as pronounced as many athletes fear, and in any case the nature of the problem makes it self-limiting.

Travelling Eastwards

Returning to the UK from training camps or competition in the USA will present some problems to the athlete for some days after arrival, as 'body time' lags behind local time. Advancing the body clock is more difficult than delaying it, which is why it takes longer to adapt, even when the athlete is returning to a home environment.

The advice is the same in principle as for travelling westwards, with regard to physical and social activities, meals and drinks, with the following specific recommendations:

1. if you cannot get to sleep at night, stay in bed and rest;
2. if you feel tired when it is time to get up, do not stay in bed. A lie-in of 1–2 hours – but no more – might be allowed for the first day or so.

Acknowledgement
Much of this material appears as advice to athletes competing abroad in *Coaching Focus*, published by the National Coaching Foundation, and in the BOA advice to athletes.

CHAPTER 26
Examples of Individual Training Programmes

'The life of the nothing men hurts harder and deeper than anything you do in training or in a race.'

This chapter includes a number of examples of individuals' training sessions. You will note many particular training schemes, individual training sessions and patterns that have been discussed in other chapters. These training programmes are included for interest and appraisal. They give a practical view of how different triathletes – often of the same or similar standard – may follow very diverse schedules.

From the coaching point of view, the most important thing in planning a programme is to *know the athlete well*. Breaking point for one may well be ticking over for another, with all the various stages in between.

Each athlete will be able to work on similar sessions where heart rates are the guidelines and main monitor, but will work to their own individual heart rates. Each set of training schedules is aimed at specific athletes, and some of the terminology used will be appropriate to that athlete and their maturity and experience.

Where reference is made to a session that is not included in full, these sessions are included in the relevant chapter on the relevant discipline.

EXAMPLE 1

JOH is a female junior international triathlete and duathlete who has a swimming background. The schedule below was used for her running training before a recent world championships when she was returning from a 'minor' injury. After Week 10, she began a two-week HIT taper going into the championships.

Week 1
Session 1: easy run for 15 mins
Session 2: long run for 30 mins
Session 3: run for 20 mins with 5 strides (not flat out) of 30 secs, 60 secs easy running in between.

Weeks 2 and 3
Session 1: easy run for 20 mins
Session 2: long run for 35 mins
Session 3: hills 10 × 30 secs, with jog down recovery
Session 4: hard run for 20 mins, pulse at 85 per cent plus of max HR
Session 5: fartlek to include 12 × 30 secs effort with 30 secs recovery
Session 6: intervals – 4 × 3 mins with 3 mins jog recovery, pulse at 90 per cent of max HR.
Session 7: run fairly hard for 45 secs, jog for 90 secs
Run fairly hard for 45 secs, jog for 75 secs
Run fairly hard for 45 secs, jog for 60 secs
Run fairly hard for 45 secs, jog for 45 secs
Run fairly hard for 45 secs, jog for 30 secs
Run fairly hard for 45 secs, jog for 15 secs

Weeks 4 and 5
Session 1: easy run for 25 mins
Session 2: long run for 40 mins
Session 3: hills – 10 × 40 secs, with jog down recovery
Session 4: hard run for 20 mins, pulse at 85 per cent plus of max HR
Session 5: fartlek to include 5 × 3 mins stride out effort with 90 secs recovery
Session 6: intervals – 3 × 4 mins with 3 mins jog recovery, pulse at 90 per cent of max HR
Session 7: run fairly hard for 45 secs, jog for 90 secs
Run fairly hard for 45 secs, jog for 75 secs
Run fairly hard for 45 secs, jog for 60 secs

Run fairly hard for 45 secs, jog for 45 secs
Run fairly hard for 45 secs, jog for 30 secs
Run fairly hard for 45 secs, jog for 15 secs

Weeks 6 and 7
Session 1: easy run for 30 mins
Session 2: long run for 40 mins
Session 3: hills – 8 × 60 secs, with jog down recovery
Session 4: hard run for 25 mins, pulse at 85 per cent plus of max HR
Session 5: fartlek to include 4 × 4 mins effort with 2 mins recovery
Session 6: rest
Session 7: rest

Weeks 8 and 9
Session 1: easy run for 20 mins
Session 2: rest
Session 3: hills – 12 × 60 secs, with jog down recovery
Session 4: hard run for 25 mins, pulse at 85 per cent plus of max HR
Session 5: fartlek to include 18 × 30 secs effort with 30 secs recovery
Session 6: intervals – 3 × 1 mile with 400m jog recovery, pulse at 85/90 per cent of max HR (concentrating on running technique, not pushing too hard)
Session 7: run fairly hard for 45 secs, jog for 90 secs
Run fairly hard for 45 secs, jog for 75 secs
Run fairly hard for 45 secs, jog for 60 secs
Run fairly hard for 45 secs, jog for 45 secs
Run fairly hard for 45 secs, jog for 30 secs
Run fairly hard for 45 secs, jog for 15 secs
And repeat

Week 10
Session 1: easy run for 20 mins or rest
Session 2: long run for 60 mins
Session 3: hard run for 30 mins, pulse at 85 per cent plus of max HR

EXAMPLE 2

HAI is an extremely well-motivated 20-year-old male, 6ft tall, 11 stone, a four-time team medallist at world and European level in the junior age group. His background is as a county-level track runner at 800 and 1500m. He is now very successful at cross-country running at county and area level as well as being a GB international triathlete. The training programme is for the four weeks covering a triathlon world championships. At the time he worked part-time and lived at home.

Week 1 (week commencing 26 July)
Monday
Swim: easy session; 800 warm-up, to include 4 × 100 full, pull, catch up, drill; repeat twice; then 5 × 100, concentrating on long stroke on all; 1st, 3rd and 5th full; 2nd and 4th broken at 100; no times, 1 min between each cycle; easy spin if he feels like it
Tuesday
Run: easy 5 miles, pick up pace on 2nd half if feeling good
Cycle: warm up, then ride for 1 hour with each succeeding 10 mins slightly harder than the 10 before
Wednesday
Swim: directed session
Cycle: long warm-up, time trial 10 miles
Thursday
Swim: directed session
Run: warm up 2 miles, then 6-miler with each mile 10 secs faster than previous one. Start at 5.40 pace, last one in 4.50 or faster. Do not start too fast
Friday
Cycle: 1½ to 2 hours steady to fast
Run: hard and hilly 8 miles
Saturday
Swim: 1500m swim made up as 400 crawl, 100 back, 300 crawl, 100 back, 200 crawl, 100 back, 100 crawl, 100 back, 100 crawl. Then 10 × 50 with 5 secs rest only; 5 × 100 rest 15 secs, 10 × 50 with 10 secs rest. All at 90 per cent. Rest 2 mins between sets
Cycle: 20 × 1 min flat out in 53 × 12/13. 1 min between
Run: warm up then 15 mins flat out (note distance)
Sunday
Cycle: 4 × 5 miles at time-trial pace plus 2 miles recovery between

Week 2 (week commencing 2 August)
Monday
Swim: 400 warm-up, 2 × 200 pull, 4 × 100 catch up, 8 × 50 drill, 4 × 100 pull with extended stretch, 2 × 200 (with 4 × 50 different drills), 1 × 400 full stroke with extended stretch; 90 secs between sets; 30 secs between 200s, 20 on 100s, 10 on 50s
Run: 8 miles, 4 miles out steady to fast, return flat out
Tuesday
Cycle: 8 × 2 miles hard with 4 mins recovery between
Wednesday
Swim: directed session
Run: long easy 80 mins plus
Thursday
Swim: directed session
Cycle: time trial, preferably 25 miles
Friday
Run: 3 × 2 miles at 10 secs per mile faster than 10km pace, jog easy 2 mins between
Cycle: hilly 2-hour ride
Saturday
Rest
Sunday
Cycle: 35–40 miles, out and back. Out at 80 per cent, turn round and flat out return at 110 per cent
Run: 4 × 1 mile at race pace less 15 secs, recover 2 mins 30 secs between

Week 3 (week commencing 9 August)
Monday
Swim: 2000 straight swim, made up of 400 full, 100 pull, 300 full, 200 pull, 200 full, 300 pull, 100 full, 400 pull (with a pull-buoy if wanted); then 1 × 400 at 8 mins, 2 × 200 at 4 mins, 4 × 100 at 3 mins, all at 95 per cent
Cycle: 20 × 1 min flat out
Tuesday
Run: race pace 10k, but try to hold on up to 8 miles
Wednesday
Swim: directed session
Cycle: 2 hours, steady to hardish
Run: reducing rest 200m at around 32–33 secs, rest 90 secs, then, 75, 60, 45, 30, 15 secs and repeat twice.
Thursday
Swim: directed session

Run: easy jog or rest
Cycle: 10-mile time trial, jog immediately after if not done in morning
Friday
5-mile running road race
Saturday
National relays
Sunday
Rest

Week 4 (week commencing 16 August)
Monday
Swim: warm up, then 10 × 50 or 15 × 33 at 90/60 secs, 5 × 100 at 3 mins, 1 × 500 at 99 per cent; warm down
Run: easy 30 mins
Tuesday
Cycle: 1½ hours, easy but attacking hills
Wednesday
Swim: warm up, then 2 × 400 at 95 per cent on 8 mins, 1 × 200 at 95 per cent; warm down
Run: 3 or 4 miles with 3 × 1 min stride out
Thursday
Swim: 1500m (preferably in open water)
Cycle: 25 miles/1+ hours – on course if possible
Friday
Easy swim, easy run (a couple of strides maybe)
Saturday
Easy swim and cycle and stretch
Sunday
World triathlon championships

EXAMPLE 3

SMT is a 26-year-old male in his third year of triathlon. He is 5ft 10in tall and weighs 11 stone 2lb (he weighed 13 stone 7lb before starting triathlon). He comes from a general sports background and has always worked out intensively with weight-training. He is in the fortunate position of not having to work, and has set his sights on completing an Ironman distance race in 9 hours. He has completed one full Ironman where he had a good swim, an excellent bike ride and a very good first ten miles of the run; then he suffered.

SMT thrives on hard work and is able to handle an extremely heavy training load (*see* opposite). He was extremely immobile before taking up triathlon, particularly in the upper body. He now stretches daily for at least 30 minutes and works religiously on flexibility and mobility. Perhaps because of this, he does not suffer from injuries, despite his arduous training programme. When he started training for triathlon, his swimming discipline was particularly poor. His first season's times for 1500m open-water swimming averaged 46 minutes. His swimming splits in the season discussed averaged 20 minutes and 30 secs.

The training programme opposite was a hard-work phase approaching a major Ironman-distance race, not including the taper phase.

All swimming sessions – apart from one session per week when he swam in open water – were in a swimming club environment. The average distance covered in each 1½-hour session was approximately 4500m. One-third of this distance in all sessions concentrated on drills. 3000m per week (the major part of one session) were swum with hand paddles.

After this, SMT started on a severe two-week taper with a drastically reduced workload going into the Ironman race. He finished in a personal best time of 9 hours and 18 minutes.

EXAMPLE 4

ROX is a 30-year-old female athlete. Previously an ultra-distance runner (with world records at 24-hour and 6-day running), she is also an experienced triathlete and duathlete. She is very strong on the bike and is a competent swimmer, although with a poor technique. She is married with three children and during the following training programme she was holding down a part-time job. (Much of her run training was done by running between worksites.)

The schedule and the comments apply to a four-week period before a European Ironman championship.

Her priorities have to be as follows:

Swimming: working on long stroke, drills, some speed work (but not flat-out 50s and 100s) and drafting; aiming to cover 1500m

per half an hour, 3000m per hour on intervals and more on a straight swim.

Cycling: all the base work is done, so priorities are long distance, hill work, speed work and technique. There is no time to do the really long rides; the options are to ride out to time trials, race hard and then ride home; to do the medium-distance rides – 50s, 60s and so on – pretty hard and combine them with as much hilly work as possible. Speed work should be pretty much taken care of with time trials and triathlons at Olympic distance and half-distance. Technique should be worked on at all times, practising eating and drinking while riding. She should also work on single-leg spinning on the turbo.

Running: 50 per cent of the run sessions should be used as some form of quality even if they are long(ish) efforts. It might be necessary to cut down on some distance to make room for the cycle sessions and to avoid the fatigue of running faster than usual. Back-to-back and brick sessions with cycling will also be added (*see* box, page 201).

EXAMPLE 5

JEN is a 21-year-old triathlete of national top-ten ranking. She is also a county-level cross-country runner and a nationally ranked cyclist. Her weakness is swimming although she is far better outdoors wearing a wetsuit than in the pool. The following programme is a comprehensive shorthand of one eighteen-week period over the conditioning and early pre-season phase of her training.

Base Work: Winter

From 1 November: Phase 1 – mainly aerobic work on run and cycle; technique on swimming
Week 1
Swimming: 4 sessions per week. Untimed, work on skills and drills; minimum 4 hours.
Cycling: 3 sessions per week: long, easy ride up to 3 hours (no pulsemeter to be used); medium ride between 1½ and 2 hours (generally faster than long ride but no real pace);

EXAMPLE 3

Week 1 (week commencing 14 June)

	SWIM	CYCLE	RUN
Monday	Swim	Easy 2 hours	Very easy 15 miles
Tuesday	Swim	Hilly 60 miles	1 hour fartlek, 10 mins easy then 60 secs on 60 off
Wednesday	Open 45 mins minimum	Rest	80 miles
Thursday	Rest	Time trial or turbo 20 × 90 secs/60 rec	Hard 10k
Friday	Swim	Hill reps 1½ hours	6 miles, 1 easy, 2 + 3 hard and repeat
Saturday	Rest	Rest	Rest
Sunday	Swim/open?	Rest	20 miles steady

Week 2 (week commencing 21 June)

	SWIM	CYCLE	RUN
Monday	Swim	Hilly 60–70 miles	Jog 3 miles
Tuesday	Swim	Rest	4 × 2000m at 175 HRM, 2 mins jog recovery
Wednesday	Open	100 miles	Rest
Thursday	Rest	Time trial or turbo at anaerobic thresh. 75 mins	15 miles steady
Friday	Swim	2 hours hard hills or hill reps	Rest
Saturday	Rest	Easy ride/rest	Rest
Sunday	Swim	Rest	22 miles

Week 3 (week commencing 28 June)

	SWIM	CYCLE	RUN
Monday	Swim	3-hour honest ride, not silly hard	Jog 3 or 4 miles
Tuesday	Swim	Hilly 60 miles	10 × 800m at 175 HRM, recovery 1 min
Wednesday	Open 1 hour	80 miles plus	Straight into 7-mile run
Thursday	Rest	Time trial or rest	Rest
Friday	Swim	Rest	18 miles
Saturday	Rest	Easy ride or mountain bike ride	Rest
Sunday	Swim	Rest	22 miles

Week 4 (week commencing 5 July)

	SWIM	CYCLE	RUN
Monday	Swim	80 miles	Jog 3 miles
Tuesday	Swim	Hilly 70 miles	10km tempo at 165 HRM
Wednesday	Open concentrating on stroke, 75 mins	110 miles steady	Rest
Thursday	Rest	Time trial	3 × 2 miles, jog ½ mile recovery (175 HRM)
Friday	Swim	Rest	1 hour of 30 secs on/off

(continued overleaf)

EXAMPLE 3   *(continued from previous page)*

Week 4 (continued)

	SWIM	CYCLE	RUN
Saturday	Rest	Hard 50 miles or time trial 50 miles	Rest
Sunday	Swim	Rest	Easy pace 18 miles

Week 5 (week commencing 12 July)

	SWIM	CYCLE	RUN
Monday	Swim	Hilly 80 miles	Hard 8 miles
Tuesday	Swim	Rest	20–22 miles
Wednesday	Open	Easy 80 miles	Easy pace fartlek 45–75 mins
Thursday	Rest	25-mile time trial	Rest
Friday	Rest	Rest	Rest
Saturday	Race half-Ironman distance		
Sunday	Rest	Rest	Rest

Week 6 (week commencing 19 July)

	SWIM	CYCLE	RUN
Monday	Swim	Hilly 80 miles	Jog 5 miles
Tuesday	Swim	120 miles	REST
Wednesday	Rest	Rest	Rest
Thursday	Rest	Time trial 50 miles?	Easy 6–8 miles
Friday	Swim	Hard 2 hours	Rest
Saturday	Rest	Rest	Rest
Sunday	Rest	4-hour brick session: 30 mins bike then 30 mins (5 miles) run, repeated four times	

Week 7 (week commencing 26 July)

	SWIM	CYCLE	RUN
Monday	Swim	Very easy spin	Rest
Tuesday	Swim	60 miles easy pace	Jog 5 miles
Wednesday	Open	6 hours plus	3-mile jog
Thursday	Rest	Time trial	Jog 5 miles
Friday	Swim	Rest	22 miles or 3 hours
Saturday	Rest	Easy 2 hours	Rest
Sunday	Swim	Rest	Rest

Week 8 (week commencing 2 August)

	SWIM	CYCLE	RUN
Monday	Swim	4-hour brick session: 30 mins bike then 30 mins (5 miles) run, repeated four times	
Tuesday	Swim	2 hours easy	Rest
Wednesday	Open	100 miles	40 mins of 30 secs on/30 secs off, striding fast
Thursday	Rest	Time trial	Hard 10 miles
Friday	Swim	2 hours hard hilly	12 × 400m at just sub max; 200m slow jog recovery

EXAMPLE 3

Week 8 (continued)

	SWIM	CYCLE	RUN
Saturday	Rest	Rest	Rest
Sunday	Rest	Rest	20 miles am then 12 miles pm; eat lightly between

Week 9 (week commencing 9 August)

	SWIM	CYCLE	RUN
Monday	Swim	2 hours fairly easy	Rest
Tuesday	Swim	60 miles easy pace	Jog 5 miles
Wednesday	Open 6 hours	6 or 8 miles easy fartlek	
Thursday	Rest	Time trial, then hard 5-mile run	
Friday	Swim	Single leg on turbo, spinning easy 1 hour	Warm up and strides only
Saturday	Rest	Rest	15 miles with 10×30 secs pick-ups
Sunday	Swim	130 miles, followed by honest 10km run	

EXAMPLE 4

Week 1

	SWIM	CYCLE	RUN
Monday	2000m straight	Rest	3-part 8, 5, 4 miler; maybe try and fartlek the 5 miles
Tuesday	Rest	As long and as hilly as possible; work all hills	Rest
Wednesday	Warm up, then Hungarian rep 8×50m on 1 min, 4×100m on 2 mins, 2×200m on 4 mins, 1×400m on 8 mins, and come back down	Brick session: 30 mins bike then 5-mile run, repeated twice	
Thursday	Rest	Fast 2 hours	4×1 mile, 2-min jog recovery
Friday	Swim	All hills in low gear and spin	90-min steady run
Saturday	Rest	Rest	Rest
Sunday	Rest	25-mile time trial, ride in and out	

Week 2

	SWIM	CYCLE	RUN
Monday	2000m straight	Rest	3-part 8, 5, 4 miler; try and fartlek the 8 and the 5 miles
Tuesday	Rest	Long, hilly and hard	Rest

(continued overleaf)

EXAMPLE 4   *(continued from previous page)*

Week 2 (continued)

	SWIM	CYCLE	RUN
Wednesday	Drills warm up, then 6 × 100m, 3 × 200m, 6 × 100m, 3 × 200m	Brick session: 45-min cycle, 7-mile run then 30-min cycle, 5-mile run, then 30-min cycle, 5-mile run, repeated twice	
Thursday	Rest	2-hour quality ride attacking all hills in biggish gear	Warm up, then 10 mins hard, 3-min jog, 10 × 30/30 secs, 3 mins jog, 1 min hard, 2 mins hard, 3 mins hard. 1 min between × 3!
Friday	Swim	3 hours (if possible) thinking spinning and staying on aerobars	1–1½ hours easy with 10 strides of 20 secs somewhere in the middle
Saturday	Rest	Rest	Rest
Sunday	Long course (2k/110k/18k) or long hard ride or time trial		

Week 3

	SWIM	CYCLE	RUN
Monday	Rest	Rest	16 miles
Tuesday	Rest	Hard, quality ride	Rest
Wednesday	Rest	Ride 15 miles to race; race 10-mile time trial; ride 15 miles home	1 hour
Thursday	Swim?	Brick: turbo 30/run 5 × 2 miles	
Friday	Rest	Long ride	Rest
Saturday	Rest	Rest	Rest
Sunday	Rest	Rest	Cross-country marathon race

tempo ride either on road or turbo for 1 hour (working quite hard but at less than race pace).

Running: 4 sessions per week: road or cross-country race; fartlek for 50–60 mins; steady run for 1 hour; long run, starting at 1 hour 20 mins, very easy pace.

Mobility: at least 2 sessions per week of 30 mins plus short stretch especially after each run.

Weeks 2/3/4/5/6

As for Week 1, but increase the medium cycle ride and long cycle ride by 15 mins each week up to a maximum of 2½ and 4 hours respectively.

Increase length of efforts and reduce recovery on fartlek sessions, increase 1-hour run to 1 hour 20 mins (10 mins extra every 2 weeks); increase long run up to 1 hour 45 mins.

Continue to emphasize mobility exercises, using any spare time available, particularly hip, glute and hamstring work.

From 12 December: Phase 2 – still mainly aerobic work. Add small amounts of pace and tempo. Maintain technique on swimming. Add some slow pace work and intervals

Weeks 7/8/9/10/11/12

Swimming: maintain 4 sessions per week; mostly untimed; minimum 4 hours.

Cycling: 4 sessions per week: long, easy ride up to 4 hours (no pulsemeter to be used); cycle/run brick session, 30 mins/20 mins × 2, cycle turbo 30 mins, run 20 mins (approx. 3 plus miles), repeat cycle, repeat run; tempo ride either on road or turbo for 1 hour, working quite hard but at less than race pace; tempo ride either on road or turbo for 1½ or 2 hours, working quite hard by alternating 10 mins at 85 per cent of max heart rate and 70 per cent.

Running: 4 sessions per week:

1. road or cross-country race;
2. fartlek for 1 hour;
3. different sessions for each week of this phase: warm up, then 20 × 30 secs stride effort/30 secs easy jog recovery; warm up, then 6 × 2 mins 85 per cent effort/60 secs easy jog recovery; warm up, then 14 × 1 min 90 per cent effort/60 secs easy jog recovery; warm up, then 6 × 3 mins 85 per cent effort/60 secs easy jog recovery; warm up, then 4 × 6 mins at just faster than 10km race pace effort, 2 mins easy jog recovery; warm up, then 10 × 3 mins at just faster than 10km race pace effort, 3 mins recovery, but not dropping to a jog;
4. long run, start at 1 hour 45 mins, very easy pace.

Mobility: at least 2 sessions per week of 30 mins plus short stretch especially after each run.

From 31 January: Phase 3 – first transition phase, beginning to put emphasis on pace and tempo
Weeks 13/14/15/16/17/18
Swimming: maintain 4 plus sessions per week. Work at race pace and faster than race pace. To get an indication of race pace, do a timed swim of 15 mins and work out 100, 200, 400m times from this. Aim to do repetition times as follows: race pace 3 secs faster per 100, 5 secs faster per 200, 9 secs faster per 400m, recovery 10–15 secs between reps at race pace. Faster than race pace 5–6 secs faster per 100, 8–11 secs faster per 200, 15–20 secs faster per 400m, recovery 30–45 secs between reps at faster than race pace.

Aim for a main set each time of 1500–2500m, shorter end of spectrum for faster than race pace, longer set for race pace. Occasionally go up to 3000m for main set race pace. Also once a month do a 30- or 45- or 60-min swim for distance, emphasizing good stroke. Minimum 4 hours.

Cycling: 4 sessions per week: long, easy ride 3–6 hours (no pulsemeter to be used; distance to be covered depends on racing distance); group ride, 2 hours plus, good/hard pace;

time trial every week of 10/25/30 miles (make the first one a 10-miler if possible); interval sessions, either on turbo or road. Progress each week as follows:

- 7 × 2 mins on 52 × 14 or whatever gear you can turn over at 100rpm. Important: recover 1 min between efforts;
- 3 × 6 mins on 52 × 15 for 3 mins, 14 for 2 mins, 13 for 1 min. Recover 1 min between efforts;
- 2 × 12 mins, made up as follows: 52 × 18 for 2 mins, 52 × 17 for 2 mins, 52 × 16 for 2 mins, 52 × 15 for 2 mins, 52 × 14 for 2 mins, 52 × 13 for 2 mins (these gears are guidelines only – remember it is the 100rpm that is important). Recover for 2 mins between the 12-min efforts;
- 5 × 4 mins made up as follows: 52 × 17 for 4 mins, 52 × 16 for 4 mins, 52 × 15 for 4 mins, 52 × 14 for 4 mins, 52 × 13 for 4 mins; remember importance of 100rpm. Recover for 1 min between the 4-min efforts;
- 4 × 8 mins made up as follows: 52 × 16 for 8 mins, 52 × 15 for 8 mins, 52 × 14 for 8 mins, 52 × 13 for 8 mins; remember 100rpm. Recover for 2 mins between the 8-min efforts.

Running: 6 sessions every 2 weeks. *Warning*: if tired, reduce run sessions before any other.

1. Road or cross-country race or hard sustained pace run of 35–40 mins.
2. Hills or hilly fartlek for 1 hour. Aim to cover 3 miles of going up the hills.
3. Long run. Up to 1½ hours but increased steady pace.
4. 3 × 7½ mins at race pace plus. Start with 2½-min recovery, aim to reduce by 30 secs each time down to 1 min. Then raise to 4 reps.
5. Reducing recovery. 45-sec efforts at 95 per cent with a reducing recovery of 90 secs, then 75 secs, 60, 45, 30 and finally 15 secs before repeating immediately. Continue until you are so tired that you cannot maintain speed. You should work up to 3 repeats eventually.

The first session should be done twice in each two-week period, all the others once.

EXAMPLE 6

CHR is a 35-year-old male age-grouper triathlete who is hoping to improve his Olympic-distance time from 2 hours 12 mins to 2 hours 5 min. The following schedule covers the period of six weeks before the first important race of the season. The swimming sessions were similar to those in phase one of the examples given in the third swimming chapter concerned with periodization and appropriate sessions.

Week 1 – Cycling
Session 1: lactate tolerance. Warm up steadily to 80–85 per cent of MHR. Hold this percentage for 40 mins with 90–110rpm. You will almost certainly need to change gears to maintain this heart rate.
Session 2: 3 reps of 52 × 18 for 3 mins, aim for 100rpm, straight into: 52 × 16 for 2 mins, aim for 100rpm, straight into: 52 × 15 for 1 min, aim for 100rpm. Recovery: 42 × 20 for 1 min at 60rpm after each 6-min effort.
Session 3: 2 hours hard road ride.

Week 2 – Cycling
Session 4: HR turbo session No.2. Anaerobic threshold.
Session 5: 12 reps of 52 × 16 for 1 min, aim for 100rpm. Recovery: 52 × 22 for 1 min at 60rpm.
Session 6: 3–3½ hours steady road ride.

Week 3 – Cycling
Session 7: HR turbo session No.3. Progressive resistance/increasing demand.
Session 8: 3 reps of 52 × 20 for 4 mins, aim for 100rpm, straight into: 52 × 18 for 3 mins, aim for 100rpm, straight into: 52 × 16 for 2 mins, aim for 100rpm. Recovery: 42 × 20 for 1 min at 60rpm after each 9-min effort.
Session 9: 2½–3 hours hilly ride.

Week 4 – Cycling
Session 10: HR turbo session No.4. Speed endurance/increasing demand.
Session 11: 10 reps of 52 × 18 for 2 mins, aim for 100rpm. Recovery: 42 × 18 for 1 min at 60rpm.
Session 12: 2½ hours hard road ride.

Week 5 – Cycling
Session 13: HR turbo session No.5. Hills: warm up; into 52 × 13 pedal flat out for 1 min, out of the saddle; recover for 1 min in easy gear; as before in 52 × 13 but hold for 2 mins, recover for 1 min; repeat for 3, 4, 5 mins.
Session 14: 2 reps of 52 × 22 for 2 mins, aim for 100rpm; straight into 52 × 20 for 2 mins, aim for 100rpm; straight into 52 × 18 for 2 mins, aim for 100rpm; straight into 52 × 16 for 2 mins, aim for 100rpm; straight into 52 × 15 for 2 mins, aim for 100rpm; straight into 52 × 14 for 2 mins, aim for 100rpm; straight into recovery, 42 × 22 for 2 mins at 60rpm after first set of 12 mins effort.
Session 15: 3½–4 hours steady road ride.

Week 6 – Cycling
Session 16: lactate tolerance. Warm up steadily to 80–85 per cent of MHR. Hold this percentage for 50 mins with 90–110rpm. You will almost certainly need to change gears to maintain this heart rate.
Session 17: 3 reps of 52 × 20 for 3 mins, aim for 100rpm; straight into 52 × 18 for 3 mins, aim for 100rpm; straight into 52 × 16 for 3 mins, aim for 100rpm; straight into recovery, 42 × 22 for 2 mins at 60rpm after each set of 9 mins effort.
Session 18: 2½–3 hours hilly ride.

Week 1 – Running
Session 1: 12 miles steady pace.
Session 2: 10km pace. 3 × 2 miles with 200m jog (90 secs to 2 mins recovery) in 11.30 mins (5.45-min mile pace). Increase to four repetitions when you hit the target pace.
Session 3: warm up 10 mins, then 30 × 15 secs fast stride/15 secs cruise, warm down 10–15 mins.

Week 2 – Running
Session 4: 8 miles fast pace.
Session 5: 5km pace. 3 × 1 mile in 5.25 mins with 200m jog (90 secs to 2 mins recovery). Increase to four repetitions when you hit the target pace.
Session 6: Warm up 10 mins, then 5 × 3 mins/90 secs recovery at 170bpm.

Week 3 – Running
Session 7: 10 miles easy pace.

Session 8: 3km pace. 5 × 800m in 2.35 mins with 200m jog (90 secs to 2 mins recovery). Increase to six repetitions when you hit the target pace.
Session 9: warm up 10 mins, then 20 × 30 secs stride/30 secs jog – not silly slow, warm down 10 mins.

Week 4 – Running
Session 10: 12 miles steady run.
Session 11: 1500m pace. 6 × 500m, going through the 400m in 70 secs with 250m jog recovery (2.00–2.30 mins recovery).
Session 12: warm up 10 mins, then 5 × 4 mins at 165/170 HR, jog recovery of 1.30–2.00 mins.

Week 5 – Running
Session 13: 8 miles fast run.
Session 14: 800m pace. 16 × 200m in 33–35 secs with 200m jog recovery of 1.30–2.00 mins.
Session 15: warm up 10 mins, straight into 15 × 60 secs/30–45 secs recovery at HR starting at 165 and building to 175/180 by end; warm down 10 mins.

Week 6 – Running
Session 16: 10 miles slow run.
Session 17: 400m pace. 8 × 100m at sprint pace with 200m jog/walk recovery of 1.30–2.00 mins. (If this feels too easy you aren't working hard enough; do another set!)
Session 18: warm up 10 mins, 4 × 6 mins at 170/175 HR (working up to this) with 2 mins jog recovery (or 3 mins if you must).

EXAMPLE 7

PAU is a 34-year-old male triathlete whose ambition was to finish an Ironman distance race in a time of under 11 hours. The following programme covers a transitional phase in his training, from general fitness to gradually building endurance. PAU works full-time and travels a lot for his work, and has a number of other responsibilities. Shortly after this phase of training, he finished a long-distance triathlon (2200m swim, 78km cycle and 20km run) in 4 hours 20 minutes. His previous best

had been 5 hours and 55 minutes. He attempted nine sessions of training each week.

Swimming during this phase moved on from aerobic endurance into the pacing phase:
Session 1: warm up; 3 × 3 × 100, 1st kick, 2nd stroke drill, 3rd swim, and repeat. 10 secs between 100s, then 30 × 50 on 60 secs. 1st kick, 2nd stroke drill, 3rd swim, and repeat. 10 secs between 50s. 60 secs after ten. 4 × 4 × 150 plus 15 secs, as 50 stroke – 100 swim – 50 kick – 100 swim – 100 swim – 50 kick – 100 swim – 50 stroke: Total 4800

Session 2 (*key session*): 4 × 200 full stroke on 3.15; 1 × 800 timed; 2 × 400 hitting half of 800 time; 4 × 200 hitting half of 400 time; 16 × 100 hitting half of 200 time. (+10 secs, 30 after 8 reps); 10 × 50 build speed and hold stroke 1 to 5 and repeat. 20 secs recovery: Total 5300

Session 3: warm up 6 × 200 as 100 drill, 50 kick, 50 swim (+15), then 6 × 50 kick, 100 swim, 150 drill, 200 pull, recovery 15 secs after each rep. 60 secs after each set: Total 4200

Session 4 (*key session*): warm up 400 easy, 5000 timed, 400 easy: Total 5800

Session 5 (*relaxing session*): 2 × 300 drill (+10); 2 × 300 pull (+10), aiming for 4.40 mins; 2 × 300 full (+10), aiming for 4.40 mins; 5 × 100 kick (+10); 5 × 100 pull (+10) with paddles; 5 × 100 full stroke (+10), all concentrating on long stroke: Total 3300

Session 6: 6 × 400 as 100 full, 100 drill, 200 full, aim for 6.15 with +15 secs only; 4 × 100 kick, relaxed long downbeat (+10); 20 × 50 as 25 drill, 25 full stroke, aim for 45–48 secs with 10 rest, 30 secs after 10 reps; 1 × 400 hard full stroke for time: Total 4200

Session 7: 2 × 1500, 1 min recovery, aiming for 21.30 mins on each, optional pull on 2nd rep; 500 kick easy; 12 × 100 alternate full and pull with paddles, stay constant on time; 15 secs recovery: Total 4700

Session 8 (*key session*): 6 × 100 full stroke (+10), aim for 90 secs; 1 × 400, aim for 6 mins;

16 × 50, aim for 44 secs (+10); 2 × 200, aim for 3 mins (+15); 16 × 50, aim for 44 secs pull (+15); 1500 time trial: Total 4500

Session 9: 1 × 500 full in 7 mins, 1 × 100 kick; 1 × 500 full in 6.45, 1 × 100 kick; 1 × 500 full in 6.30, 1 × 100 kick; 1 × 500 full in 6.15, 1 × 100 kick; 1 × 500 full in 6.00: Total 2900

Session 10: 1 × 2000 concentrating on stroke; 4 × 100 kick easy (+15); 5 × 200, aim is hitting best 200 of 2000 swim (+15 secs only); 1 × 1000 alternate drill 100/swim full stroke 100: Total 4400

Session 11: 6 × 400 alternate long stroke and hard swim (+30), take times; 2 × 100 kick easy (+10); 8 × 50 hard swims (+30), all at sub-38 secs; 1 × 800 timed swim: Total 3800

Session 12: 7 × 100, first 4 pull, then 3 on full stroke (+15); 4 × 500 concentrating on stroke throughout, hold pace (7.20 mins?), 45 secs between swims; 4 × 200 as above, hold sub 3 mins (+30): Total 3500

Session 13: 6 × 50 drill; 6 × 50 pull; 6 × 50 kick; 6 × 50 full, all on +10, 30 secs between sets; 2 × 800, 1st full stroke, 2nd pull with paddles, aim 11.30 mins on both; 1 min between swims: Total 2800

Session 14: 3 × 200 drill (+10); 3 × 200 pull (+15); 3 × 200 full (+20); 3 × 400, 1st on drill, 2nd pull with paddles, 3rd full stroke (+30); 15 × 100, 1st 3 kick (+10), next 4 drill (+15), next 5 pull with paddles (+10), last 3 full stroke, hard (+30): Total 4500

Session 15: 16 × 50 reduce on 1–4 etc., 46, 43, 40, 37 (+15); 4 × 400 alternate drill and full (+30); no times taken: Total 2400

Session 16: 4000 swim, take time; then 400 drill, 300 pull, 200 kick, 100 full (+30): Total 5000

Session 17: 6 × 200 alternate pull with paddles/full stroke (+15); 3 sets of: 1 × 200 easy, 1 × 200 hard, 4 × 50 hard, 1 × 100 easy, 1 × 100 hard (+15 on each), 1 min after each set;

6 × 6 × 50 alternate sets on drill/pull/full (+10), 1 min between sets: Total 5400

Session 18: 2 × 300/400/500 with 30 secs rest, 2 mins between sets, 2nd set pulling with paddles, hold times from 1st set; 16 × 50 drill/pull alternate (+10); 16 × 50 full, 3 secs faster than above, 15 secs recovery: Total 4000

Week 1 – Cycling
Session 1: 4 reps of 52 × 20 for 2 mins, aim for 100rpm. 52 × 18 for 2 mins, aim for 100rpm. Recovery 42 × 20 for 1 min at 60rpm after each 4-min effort.
Session 2: repeat HR turbo session from Phase 1 but increase time by 10 per cent.
Session 3: 3-hour long ride (*see* page 212 for turbo suggestions and examples).

Week 2 – Cycling
Session 1: 3 reps of 52 × 20 for 2 mins, aim for 100rpm; 52 × 18 for 2 mins, aim for 100rpm; 52 × 16 for 1 min, aim for 100rpm. Recovery 42 × 20 for 1 min at 60rpm after each 5-min effort.
Session 2: repeat HR turbo session from Phase 1 but increase time by 15 per cent.
Session 3: 2-hour hard ride, try to hold above 80 per cent HR for two-thirds of time (*see* page 212 for turbo suggestions and examples).

Week 3 – Cycling
Session 1: 3 reps of 52 × 18 for 3 mins, aim for 100rpm; 52 × 16 for 2 mins, aim for 100rpm; 52 × 15 for 1 min, aim for 100rpm. Recovery 42 × 20 for 1 min at 60rpm after each 6-min effort.
Session 2: repeat HR turbo session from Phase 1 but increase time by 20 per cent.
Session 3: 3½-hour long ride.

Week 4 – Cycling
Session 1: 3 reps of 52 × 20 for 4 mins, aim for 100rpm; 52 × 18 for 3 mins, aim for 100rpm; 52 × 16 for 2 mins, aim for 100rpm. Recovery 42 × 20 for 1 min at 60rpm after each 9-min effort.
Session 2: repeat HR turbo session from Phase 1 but increase time by 25 per cent.
Session 3: 2 hours 20 mins hard ride (*see* page

212 for turbo suggestions and examples), followed by 30-min run.

Week 5 – Cycling
Session 1: 10 reps of 52 × 18 for 2 mins, aim for 100rpm. Recovery 42 × 18 for 1 min at 60rpm.
Session 2: repeat HR turbo session from Phase 1 but increase time by 30 per cent.
Session 3: 4-hour long ride (*see* page 212 for turbo suggestions and examples).

Week 6 – Cycling
Session 1: 2 reps of 52 × 22 for 2 mins, aim for 100rpm; 52 × 20 for 2 mins, aim for 100rpm; 52 × 18 for 2 mins, aim for 100rpm; 52 × 16 for 2 mins, aim for 100rpm; 52 × 15 for 2 mins, aim for 100rpm; 52 × 14 for 2 mins, aim for 100rpm. Recovery 42 × 22 for 2 mins at 60rpm after first set of 12-min effort.
Session 2: turbo hills. Warm up for at least 15 mins, then hills in hardest gear for 2, 3, 4, 5, 6 mins with 1 min between. Warm down for at least 15 mins.
Session 3: 3-hour long ride (*see* page 212 for turbo suggestions and examples), followed by 40-min run.

Week 1 – Running
1. 1-hour run, steady at around 80 per cent HR.
2. Warm up 10 mins, then 5 × 5 mins at 10km race pace (slightly faster than 6-min miling, so 1500 yards, 1350m) with 2 mins jog recovery, 10 mins warm down.
3. 90 mins run at easy HR, around 70 per cent. If comfortable, add 15 mins to this and each of the long runs for the next 6 weeks.

Week 2 – Running
1. 60 mins structured fartlek pace run, as 10 mins easy, 10 mins hard at 5km pace, 3 mins jog, 10 × 30 secs/30 secs recovery at 1500m pace, 3 mins jog, 1/2/3 mins with 1 min recovery at 3km pace, 10 mins jog at end.
2. 5 × 6 mins at 10km pace, 90 secs jog between.
3. 105 mins easy run (+15 as above if okay).

Week 3 – Running
1. Up and down ladder run: after warm-up 1/2/3/4/5/4/3/2/1 min holding at

5km pace. 60 secs recovery between, 3 mins jog after the 5-min effort. Warm down.
2. Pace-change run: warm up, then 20 × 15 secs hard stride with 15 secs float (but not jog) between. 5 mins jog, then 20 × 30/30secs the same, 5 mins jog, and repeat the 15/15 secs effort.
3. 105-min easy run (+15 as above if okay).

Week 4 – Running
1. 1 hour steady.
2. 1 hour as hilly as you can find.
3. 2 hour run (+15 as above if okay).

Week 5 – Running
1. 40 mins hard at 85 per cent plus effort.
2. 3 × 10 mins at slightly faster than 10km pace, 2 mins jog between.
3. 2 hour run (+15 as above if okay).

Week 6 – Running
1. 1 hour hilly, work all uphills and try to stride downhills.
2. Warm up, then 6 × 2 mins/1 min jog recovery, 3 mins easy, 1 × 6 mins, 3 mins easy, 3 × 3 mins/1 min jog recovery. All at 5km pace.
3. 2 hour 15 mins run (+ 15 as above if okay).

Leading directly into Phase 3:

Week 1 – Running
1. 75- to 90-min run, steady at around 80 per cent HR.
2. Warm up 10 mins, then 6 × 6 mins at 10km-race pace (aiming to cover just over a mile with each rep) with 90 secs jog recovery, 10 mins warm down.
3. 2-hour run at easy HR, around 70 per cent. If comfortable, add 15 mins to this and each of the long runs for this phase.

Week 2 – Running
1. 75 mins structured fartlek pace run, as 12 mins easy, 12 mins hard at 5km to 10km pace, 3 mins jog, 12 × 45/30 secs recovery at 1500m pace, 3 mins jog, 2/3/4 mins with 1 min recovery at 3km pace, 12 mins jog at end.
2. 4 × 9 mins at 10km pace, 90 secs jog between.
3. 2 hours 15 mins easy run (+ 15 as above if okay).

Week 3 – Running
1. Up and down ladder run: after warm up, 2/ 3/4/5/6/5/4/3/2 mins holding at 5km to 8km pace. 60 secs recovery between, 3 mins jog after the 6 mins effort. Warm down.
2. Pace-change run: warm up, then 24 × 25 secs hard stride with 20 secs float (but not jog) between. 5 mins jog, then 24 × 40/20 secs the same, 5 mins jog, and repeat the 25/20 secs effort.
3. Back-to-back session: 1-hour easy run, 2-hour cycle (75 mins if on turbo), 1-hour run trying to hold form. Drink loads throughout the cycle so that you have to go to the loo before the 2nd run.

Week 4 – Running
1. 1½-hour steady.
2. 1½-hour working all the hills at a bound while holding form (head up, chest out, knees high).
3. 2½- to 3-hour run.

Week 5 – Running
1. Time trial: 10km or 40 mins, hard and fast. With warm up and down. Try to spin on turbo after for 30 mins.
2. 3 × 2 miles (or 12 mins) at slightly faster than 10km pace, 3 to 5 mins jog between and try to hold quality.
3. 3-hour run (+15 as above if okay).

Week 6 – Running
1. 75 to 90 mins hilly, work all uphills and try to stride downhills.
2. Warm up, then 8 × 2 mins/1 min jog recovery, 3 mins easy, 1 × 8 mins, 3 mins easy, 4 × 4 mins/1 min jog recovery. All at 75/80 per cent max HR.
3. Back-to-back session: 1-hour easy run, 2½-hour cycle (90 mins if on turbo), 1½-hour run trying to hold form. Again, drink loads throughout the cycle so that you have to go to the loo before the 2nd run, and you have to stop on the run.

EXAMPLE 8

ONA is an experienced senior female International triathlete who was running poorly after the bike stage in major (ITU) races. The following running programme (combined with four cycle and five swim sessions) was designed to put some speed and speed endurance back into her performance. The time aimed at was 37 mins 30 secs for 10km, which should indicate times of around 17 mins 50 secs for 5km, 10 mins 15 secs for 3km, 4 mins 45 secs for 1500m, and 2 mins 26 secs for 800m. The programme covers a six-week period in mid-season with no major races in between. ONA has recently gained Olympic selection.

Phase 1
Session 1: 12 miles steady pace, HR at max minus 50 beats.
Session 2: 10km pace, 3 × 2 miles in 12 mins with 200m jog (1.30–2 mins recovery). Do four repetitions if the target pace is okay.
Session 3: 8 miles fast pace, about 25–30 beats below max HR.
Session 4: 5km pace, 4 × 1 mile in 5.45 mins with 200m jog (1.30–2 mins recovery).
Session 5: 25 to 30 mins hard run at anaerobic threshold; around 12–15 beats below max HR.
Session 6: 3km pace, 6 × 800m in 2.45 mins with 200m jog (1.30–2 mins recovery).
Session 7: 12 miles steady run, HR 50 below max.
Session 8: 1500m pace, 6 × 500m in 1.35 mins with 250m jog recovery (2–2.30 mins recovery).
Session 9: 8-mile fast run, 30 beats below max HR.
Session 10: 800m pace, 16 × 200m in 36 secs with 200m jog recovery (1.30–2 mins recovery).
Session 11: tough back-to-back session: 5 sets of 5km turbo (or road cycle) at race pace (40kph or 20–25 beats below max HR), straight into 1km run, each 1km getting faster, as 4.00, 3.50, 3.40, 3.30, and 3.20 mins.
Session 12: 400m pace, 8 × 100m at just under sprint pace (95 per cent effort) with 200m jog/walk recovery (1.30–2 mins).

Phase 2
Session 1: 6 × 6 mins at max HR minus 25 with 1 min recovery only.

Session 2: 10km pace, 5 × 2000m in 7.15 mins with 75–90 secs jog recovery.

Session 3: 8 miles easy, maybe 1 hour.

Session 4: 5km pace, 6 × 1000m in 3.30 mins with 60–75 secs recovery.

Session 5: 60–75 mins hilly run with at least 6 × 90 sec hard intervals uphill.

Session 6: 3km pace, 7 × 600m in 2 mins with 200m jog (1.30–2 mins recovery).

Session 7: back-to-back session: 5 sets of 5km turbo (or road cycle) at race pace (40kph or 20–25 beats below max HR), straight into 1km run, each 1km getting faster, as 3.50, 3.40, 3.30, 3.20, and 3.10 mins; take up to 2 mins between reps if needed.

Session 8: 1500m pace, 8 × 400m in 75–77 secs with 1.30–2 mins recovery.

Session 9: 8-mile hard run, 30 beats below max HR.

Session 10: back-to-back session: 3 sets of 5km turbo (or road cycle) at race pace, straight into 1km run, each 1km getting faster, as 3.20, 3.10, and 3.10 mins. Take 4 mins between reps.

Session 11: 1-hour relaxed recovery run, 50 beats below max HR.

Session 12: 400m pace, 8 × 100m at just under sprint pace (95 per cent effort), with 200m jog/walk recovery (1.30–2 mins).

EXAMPLE 9

WIL is a late thirties age-grouper making a comeback into triathlon after suffering several knee injury problems, and having exploratory operations on both knees. WIL is a hard worker who fits his training around a forty-five-hour working week, plus major travelling commitments.

Swimming
From Monday 2 February
All swim sessions were taken from a programme appropriate for the time of year (*see* Chapter 11, on swim periodization).

Cycling
Week 1, Monday 2 February
Session 1: warm up 10 mins; 30/40/50/60 secs/1.10/1.20/1.30/1.40/1.50/2 mins and then come back down at 5 HR beats below anaerobic threshold, all at 100–110rpm; take 20 secs spin in between. Warm down 10 mins.

Session 2: 10 reps of 52 × 20 for 1 min, aim for 100rpm; recovery 42 × 20 for 1 min at 60rpm.

Session 3: 2- or 3-hour steady ride.

Session 4: warm up steadily to 80–85 per cent of max HR. Hold this percentage for 40 mins with 90–110rpm. You will almost certainly need to change gears to maintain this heart rate.

Week 2, Monday 9 February
Session 1: Warm up 10 mins. Single legs: right at 30 secs, then left at 30 secs, then right and left at 60 secs, 1.30, 2 mins all with 1 min in between; then come back down. Warm down 10mins.

Session 2: 5 reps of 52 × 20 for 2 mins, aiming for 100rpm; recovery 42 × 20 for 1 min at 60rpm.

Session 3: 2- or 3-hour steady ride.

Session 4: HR turbo session No.2. Anaerobic threshold.

Week 3, Monday 16 February
Session 1: 5 reps of 52 × 18 for 2 mins, aiming for 100rpm; recovery 42 × 18 for 1 min at 60rpm.

Session 2: warm up 10 mins. Alternate 1 min only at whatever gear you can hold 130rpm, with your biggest gear (52 × 13?), smoothly and sitting down. Take 1 min recovery between reps and repeat 6 times on each gear. Warm down 10 mins.

Session 3: 2- or 3-hour steady ride. Include efforts on hills.

Session 4: HR turbo session No.3. Progressive resistance, increasing demand.

Week 4, Monday 23 February
Session 1: 10 reps of 52 × 18 for 1 min, aiming for 100rpm; recovery 42 × 18 for 1 min at 60rpm.

Session 2: start in your smallest gear (42 × 21/23?) and work for 8 mins at 110rpm, then go straight into next gear up (42 × 19?) and work for 7 mins, then into 42 × 18 and 6 mins right up to 42 × 13. Try to maintain at least

100rpm right the way through. If you feel like it, come back down again.

Session 3: 2- or 3-hour steady ride. Include efforts on hills.

Session 4: HR turbo session No.4. Speed endurance/increasing demand.

Week 5, Monday 2 March
Session 1: 7 reps of 52 × 18 for 2 mins, aiming for 100rpm; recovery 42 × 18 for 1 min at 60rpm.

Session 2: start in your smallest gear (42 × 21/23?) and work for 2 mins only at 110rpm, then go straight into next gear up (42 × 19?) and work for 2 mins again, then into 42 × 18 and 2 mins right up to 42 × 13. Try to maintain at least 100rpm right the way through. Then go into the big chainring and start again at 52 × 23. Warm down 10 mins

Session 3: 3-hour steady ride. Efforts on hills now a must.

Session 4: warm up; into 52 × 13 pedalling flat out for 1 min, out of the saddle; recover for 1 min in easy gear; as before in 52 × 13 but hold for 2 mins, recover for 1 min; repeat for 3, 4, and 5 mins.

Week 6, Monday 9 March
Session 1: 5 reps of 52 × 20 for 3 mins, aiming for 100rpm; recovery 42 × 20 for 1 min at 60rpm.

Session 2: 4 sets of 6 mins on turbo (1 min recovery) in whatever gear you can hold 95–100rpm.

Session 3: 3-hour easy, steady ride.

Session 4: 1-hour turbo. Alternate 10 mins at 105rpm and 10 mins at 85rpm, using appropriate gears.

Running
Week 1, Monday 2 February
Session 1: 30 mins at 85 per cent effort. Measure HR.

Session 2: 40 mins at 80 per cent effort. Measure HR.

Week 2, Monday 9 February
Session 1: 35 mins at 85 per cent effort. Measure HR.

Session 2: 45 mins at 80 per cent effort. Measure HR.

Week 3, Monday 16 February
Session 1: warm up, then run 15 mins at maximum effort on track or wherever you can measure distance exactly. Note distance covered and HR at finish.

Session 2: 45 mins at 80 per cent effort. Measure HR.

Week 4, Monday 23 February
Session 1: warm up, then run 12 × 30 secs only, with 30 secs jog recovery. Aim to finish each 30 secs at max HR from last week minus 15 beats.

Session 2: 45 mins at 80 per cent effort. Measure HR.

Week 5, Monday 2 March
Session 1: warm up, then run 12 × 45 secs only, with 30 secs jog recovery. Aim to finish each 45 secs at max HR minus 15 beats (as before).

Session 2: 50 mins at 80 per cent effort. Measure HR.

Week 6, Monday 9 March
Session 1: warm up, then run 20 × 30 secs only, with 20 secs jog recovery. Aim to finish each 30 secs at Max HR minus 15 beats (as before).

Session 2: 50 mins at 80 per cent effort. Measure HR.

EXAMPLE 10

BOU is a 31-year-old age-grouper who has made the decision to enter his first Ironman-distance triathlon after ten years of competing at the standard distance. A full-time worker, his training time is restricted. His training includes three structured swim sessions (not included here), three runs and three cycles. The phase (*see* box opposite) shows a move from general conditioning into a more specific pace-type workout.

EXAMPLE 10

Strength Endurance Phase, Moving into Start of Pace Work, from Monday 26 January

Week 1

RUN

40 mins hard pace (10km)

2.15 hours below 155bpm

90 mins below 145bpm, including
10 × 3 mins strides with 60 secs
jog recovery (HR on efforts?)

CYCLE

3-hour ride with HR below 145bpm

Turbo session 1

4-hour ride with HR below 140bpm
(including hills or mountain bike)

Week 2

RUN

45 mins hard pace (10km)

2.15 hours below 155 bpm
(as Week 1)

90 mins below 145 bpm, including
1, 2, 3, 4, 5 mins strides with
60 secs jog recovery, and repeat

CYCLE

3½-hour ride with HR 145bpm

Turbo session 2

4-hour ride with HR below 140bpm (as Week 1)

Week 3

RUN

11 miles at 6.40-min mile pace
or slower. What is comfortable?

13 miles as 15 mins easy, 15 mins
steady, and remainder (1 hour?)
hard run

Warm up, then 3 × 2 miles at 5.55-
min mile pace, 90 secs recovery

CYCLE

60 miles at 32kph (20mph)

30 mins easy twiddle, 30 mins steady, 2–3 hours
steady/hard ride

Warm up, 3 × 20 or 4 × 15 mins at 40kph (25mph), 300
watts or best 25-mile time-trial pace; recovery 60–90 secs

Week 4

RUN

12 miles at 6.40-min mile pace or
last week's pace

4 × 1 mile in 5.40 mins, recovery
90 secs between

Warm up, then 16 × 400m at
77–80 secs pace, 45 secs recovery

CYCLE

60–65 miles at 32kph (20mph)

16 × 2 mins (recovery 60 secs) at just sub max HR?

Warm up, 5 × 10 or 4 × 12 mins at 43kph (27mph), 340
watts or best 10-mile time-trial pace; recovery 60–90 secs

Week 5

RUN

13 miles at 6.40-min mile pace or
last week's pace

2 × 10km at 6.10-min miling pace;
recovery 60secs between; do this
on an out and back course

Warm up, then 24 to 30 × 400m as
straight run with each consecutive
400 alternating between 1 min
25 secs and 1 min 35 secs

CYCLE

65–70 miles at 32kph (20mph)

Similar to run, after warm-up, 2 × 25 miles (out and
back) as 2 hard straight rides; 5 mins between

Warm up, then similar to run (can do on turbo) with
alternating 3 mins at 40kph (25mph) and 34–35kph
(21–22 mph). Go through 15 to 20 times if you can

Week 6

Recovery week – to be negotiated after feedback

EXAMPLE 11

EMM is a 25-year-old female runner-turned-duathlete. She has a history of some running-related injuries going back to university. Although she is a good runner, she is a comparative novice on the bike. The programme (*see* box above) covers her introductory three weeks into duathlon training.

EXAMPLE 12

CER is an 18-year-old female junior in full-time education. She is an international cyclist, duathlete and triathlete who has medalled at both European and world competitions. A number of factors needed to be taken into account when planning her training programme: following a very long domestic and international season, including five major international races, she was tired; and her swimming training was about to undergo a radical reappraisal. The aim was to get her to *lose* a feel for the water initially, so only two swim sessions were included to begin with (*see* box opposite).

Turbo Sessions
Phase 1 – Winter Period
Session 1: warm up 10 mins. 30/40/50/60 secs/1.10/1.20/1.30/1.40/1.50/2 mins, then come back down at 5 HR beats below anaerobic threshold, all at 100–110rpm. Take 20 secs spin in between. Warm down 10 mins.
Session 2: warm up 10 mins. Single legs: right at 30 secs, then left at 30 secs, then right and left at 60 secs/1.30/2 mins all with 1 min in between, then come back down. Warm down 10 mins.
Session 3: warm up 10 mins. Alternate 1 min only at whatever gear you can hold 130rpm, with your biggest gear (52 × 13?), smoothly and sitting down. Take 1 min recovery between reps

EXAMPLE 12

Winter Preparation

Week 1, beginning Monday 1 December

SWIM: 2 sessions only

RUN	CYCLE
Easy 30 mins	Easy ride 1 hour or turbo 40 mins
Easy 40 mins	Easy ride 90 mins or turbo 50 mins

Week 2, beginning Monday 8 December

SWIM: 3 sessions only

RUN	CYCLE
Easy 30 mins	Easy ride 1 hour or turbo 40 mins
Easy 40 mins	Easy ride 90 mins or turbo 50 mins
Rest	Turbo session 1 (*see* page 212)

Week 3, beginning Monday 15 December

SWIM: 3 sessions only

Run	Cycle
Easy 30 mins	Easy ride 1 hour or turbo 40 mins
Easy 40 mins	Easy ride 90 mins or turbo 50 mins
Easy 1-hour or club session	Turbo session 2 (*see* page 212)

Week 4, beginning Monday 22 December

SWIM: 4 sessions if possible

RUN	CYCLE
Easy 30 mins	Easy ride 1 hour or turbo 50 mins
Easy 40 mins	Easy ride 90 mins or turbo 60 mins
Easy 1-hour or club session	Turbo session 3 (*see* page 212)
40 mins with 20 × 30 secs strides with 30 secs jog recovery	Turbo 4 × 3 mins (1 min recovery) in 52 × 16, max HR minus 40 beats

Week 5, beginning Monday 5 January

SWIM: 4 sessions if possible

RUN	CYCLE
Easy 30 mins	Easy ride 1 hour or turbo 50 mins
Easy 40 mins	Easy ride 90 mins or turbo 60 mins
Easy 1-hour or club session	Turbo session 4 (*see* page 215)
40 mins with 20 × 45 secs strides with 30 secs jog recovery	Turbo 4 × 4 mins (1 min recovery) in 52 × 16, max HR minus 40 beats

Week 5, beginning Monday 12 January

SWIM: 4 sessions if possible

Run	Cycle
Easy 40 mins	Easy ride 2 hours or turbo 75 mins
Easy 45–50 mins	Easy ride 90 mins or turbo 60 mins
Easy 1-hour or club session	Turbo session 5 (*see* page 215)
40 mins with 12 × 60 secs strides with 30 secs jog recovery	Turbo 5 × 3 mins (1 min recovery) in 52 × 16, max HR minus 40 beats

| **EXAMPLE 12** | *(continued from previous page)* |

Spring Preparation

Week 1, beginning Monday 19 January

SWIM: as arranged

RUN	CYCLE
Easy 40 mins with hard pace 10 mins in middle	Easy ride 2–3 hours or turbo 90 mins
Easy 45–50 mins	Easy ride 1.30–2 hours or turbo 75 mins
Easy 60–70 mins (or club)	Turbo session 1 HR
40 mins with 10 × 90 secs strides with 30 secs jog recovery	Turbo hills (1 min recovery) 1, 2, 3, 4, 5 mins

Week 2, beginning Monday 26 January

SWIM: as arranged

RUN	CYCLE
Easy 40 mins with hard pace 10 mins in middle	Easy ride 3 hours or turbo 90 mins
Easy 45–50 mins	Easy ride 1.30–2 hours or turbo 75 mins
Easy 60–70 mins (or club)	Turbo session 2 HR
40 mins with 8 × 2 mins strides with 60 secs jog recovery	Turbo 4 × 5 mins (1 min recovery) in 52 × 16 at max HR minus 40 beats

Week 3, beginning Monday 2 February

SWIM: as arranged

RUN	CYCLE
Easy 40 mins with hard pace 12 mins in middle	Easy ride 60 miles
Easy 45–50 mins	Easy ride 2 hours or turbo 75 mins
Easy 60–70 mins (or club)	Turbo session 3 HR
40 mins with hill reps 12 mins in total, 6 × 2 mins, or 12 × 1 min, etc.	Turbo hills (1 min recovery) 2, 3, 4, 5, 6 mins

Week 4, beginning Monday 9 February

SWIM: as arranged, to include a time trial over 1000m

Run	Cycle
Easy 40 mins with hard pace 12 mins in middle	Easy ride 60 miles or turbo 90 mins
Easy 45–50 mins	Easy ride 2 hours or turbo 75 mins
Easy 60–75 mins (or club)	Turbo session 4 HR
40 mins with 30 × 30 secs strides with 15 secs jog recovery	Turbo 7 × 3 mins (1 min recovery) in 52 × 16 at max HR minus 35 beats

Week 5, beginning Monday 16 February

SWIM: as arranged

RUN	CYCLE
Easy 40 mins with hard pace 15 mins in middle	Easy ride 60 miles
Easy 45–50 mins	Easy ride 2 hours or turbo 75 mins
Easy 60–70 mins (or club)	Turbo session 1 HR
40 mins with hill reps 12 mins in total, 6 × 2 mins, or 12 × 1 min, etc.	Turbo hills (1 min recovery) 3, 3, 4, 5, 6 mins

EXAMPLE 12

Spring Preparation *(continued)*

Week 6, beginning Monday 23 February

SWIM: as arranged

RUN	CYCLE
Easy 40 mins with hard pace 15 mins in middle	Easy ride 60 miles or turbo 90 mins
Easy 45–50 mins	Easy ride 2 hours or turbo 75 mins
Easy 60–75 mins (or club)	Turbo session 2 HR
40 mins with 1, 2, 3 mins strides with 1 min jog recovery and repeat 3 times with 3 mins recovery after each set	Turbo 4×6 mins (1 min recovery) in 52×16 at max HR minus 35 beats

and repeat 6 times on each gear. Warm down 10 mins.

Session 4: Start in your smallest gear ($42 \times 21/23$?) and work for 8 mins at 110rpm, then go straight into next gear up (42×19?) and work for 7 mins, then into 42×18 and 6 mins right up to 42×13. Try to maintain at least 100rpm right the way through. If you feel like it, come back down again.

Session 5: Start in your smallest gear ($42 \times 21/23$?) and work for 2 mins only at 110rpm, then go straight into next gear up (42×19?) and work for 2 mins again, then into 42×18 and 2 mins right up to 42×13. Try to maintain at least 100rpm right the way through. Then go into the big chainring and start again at 52×23. Warm down 10 mins.

EXAMPLE 13

SIA is an extremely talented and hard-working female triathlete who has won national championship triathlon titles and has also had winning success at ETU Cup level. An excellent runner with a good middle-distance competitive record, and also a very good swimmer, SIA needed to work on two major aspects: cycling (strength), and running coming off the bike.

A large amount of swimming work – perhaps as much as 35 per cent per session – was also emphasized using paddles. Swimming sessions were largely quality repetitions over distances of 200m, 400m and 1000m. Two main swim sessions were also used to monitor

progress: 20×100m swim and rest 90 seconds only, and 4×400m with 2 minutes rest between swims.

The following programme covers the pre-season and early-season phase. Primary aims for this period were:

1. keep upper body rock steady on bike, especially on turbo;
2. extend the push away as far as possible on each swim stroke;
3. have confidence about being able to run faster than anybody coming off the bike.

SIA has recently won Olympic selection.

Tuesday 20 May
7.30–9.00am swim.
9.00am–12.00pm long cycle, really steady.
1.00pm circuits/massage/sauna.

Wednesday 21 May
5.30–7.00am swim.
2.00–5.00pm run 30 mins/turbo (cycle) 50 mins/run 30 mins. In run, both runs are steady pace, HR below 150bpm. Turbo to include 6 × 6 mins (recovery 90 secs) at 30 beats below max HR. Hold rpm at 100 if possible.

Thursday 22 May
7.30–9.00am swim, long – aim for 6km per session.
9.00–10.30am steady cycle – include 3 sets of 8 mins in biggest gear you can handle, but holding it smooth.
pm: fartlek/intervals 50 mins. 3 × 2 miles or

10 mins, jog 2 mins recovery, this is aimed at 5km pace.

Friday 23 May
Rest day.

Saturday 24 May
3-hour long ride followed by 6–8 mile run, gradually increasing pace.

Sunday 25 May
Back-to-back, 1-hour ride plus 1-hour run. If turbo, do 1st HR session from list, if on road, 1-hour hard ride or time trial. Run to have 4 × 1 mile or 5 mins (2 mins jog recovery), done at 3–5km race pace so HR at almost anaerobic threshold.

Monday 26 May
5.30–7.00am swim.
7.30–10.00am steady cycle.
pm: run/bike/run – both runs extremely easy, 5 miles each. Bike or turbo as hill reps! If on turbo, do 1, 2, 3, 4, 5 mins with 1 min recovery. If on road, at least 20 mins of climbing (3 × 8 mins, or 4 × 6 mins, etc,).

Tuesday 27 May
7.30–9.00am swim.
9.00am–12.00pm long cycle, steady.
1.00pm circuits/massage/sauna.

Wednesday 28 May
5.30–7.00am swim.
2.00–5.00pm run 30 mins/turbo (cycle) 50 mins/run 30 mins. In run, 1st run is steady pace, HR below 160bpm, 2nd run to include 6 × 800m (1st one straight off bike) or 2.30 mins with 2 mins recovery at 1500m–3km pace. Turbo is 2nd HR session from list. Alternate big and small (100rpm) gears.

Thursday 29 May
7.30–9.00am swim, long – aim for 6km per session.
9.00–10.30am steady cycle. Include 6 sets of 4 mins in biggest gear you can handle, but holding it smooth.
pm: long, straight run without slowing to a jog.

Friday 30 May
Rest day.

Saturday 31 May
Turbo 30 mins, include 10 × 30 secs at 99 per cent, recovery 1 min between, or cycle course. Run, 20–30 mins to include 6 × 30 secs accelerating strides.

Sunday 1 June
Race – sprint distance.

Monday 2 June
5.30–7.00am swim.
7.30–10.00am steady cycle.
pm: run 8 miles easy. No cycle turbo.

Tuesday 3 June
7.30–9.00am swim.
9.00am–12.00pm long steady cycle.
1.00pm circuits/massage/sauna.

Wednesday 4 June
5.30–7.00am swim.
2.00–5.00pm run 30 mins/turbo (cycle) 50 mins/run 30 mins. In run, 1st run is steady pace, HR below 160bpm, 2nd run is increasing pace throughout. Turbo is 3rd HR session; again playing with big/small gears alternately.

Thursday 5 June
7.30–9.00am swim, long – aiming for 6km per session.
9.00–10.30am steady cycle. Include 10 sets of 1 mins in biggest gear you can handle, *hard*.
pm: 20× 200m or 30 secs (recovery 200m jog or 90 secs) at 800m pace.

Friday 6 June
Rest day.

Saturday 7 June
Long ride.
Run, 10 miles easy.

Sunday 8 June
Run 3 × 7.30 mins, recovery 1 min only at 5km race pace. *Hurt!*
Cycle 10- or 15-mile time trial or 1-hour hard ride.

Monday 9 June
5.30–7.00am swim.
7.30–10.00am steady cycle.
pm: run 8 miles easy with 2 sets of 20 × 15/15 strides and recovery, 10 mins easy running between sets.
Bike or turbo as hill reps (as 26 May). If on turbo, do 1, 2, 3, 4, 5 mins with 1 min recovery or 4 × 5 mins out of saddle (recovery 2 mins). If on road, at least 15 mins of climbing but shorter 30-sec hills.

Tuesday 10 June
7.30–9.00am swim.
9.00am–12.00pm long cycle.
1.00pm circuits/massage/sauna.

Wednesday 11 June
5.30–7.00am swim.
2.00–5.00pm run 30 mins/turbo (cycle) 50 mins/run 30 mins. In run, 1st run includes 5 × 3 mins (1 min recovery) at 10km pace only. If feeling really good, only up to 5km pace, 2nd run is steady pace. Turbo is 4th HR session.

Thursday 12 June
7.30–9.00am swim, long – aim for 6km per session.
9.00–10.30am steady cycle. Include 3 sets of 8 mins in easy smooth gear with at least 110rpm.
pm: run – warm up, then a set of 250m or 40 secs with reducing recovery of 90, 75, 60, 45, 30, 15 secs between, and then go straight in and repeat. If feeling completely unstressed, repeat 1 final set.

Friday 13 June
Rest day.

Saturday 14 June
Turbo 30 mins, include 10 × 30 secs at 99 per cent, recovery 1 min between, or cycle 1st 6 miles and last 6 miles of course.
Run, easy 3–4 miles with 6 × 30 sec strides, full recovery.

Sunday 15 June
Race. After this event, an HIT taper was used going into the national championships, followed by a consolidation week and then a further taper before the European championships.

EXAMPLE 14

RRR is a full-time professional triathlete. With adaptations for individual quirks, the programme shown overleaf is also the basis of the winter schedule for a number of other triathletes. All swim sessions (five or six per week) are in swimming club sessions with an emphasis towards middle-distance swimming (400m front crawl, 400m IM, 1500m front crawl). The three six-week phases place the emphasis on:

1. endurance;
2. endurance and strength;
3. endurance and preparation for specific phase.

Interval Session 1:
1 rep of 52 × 18 for 8 mins, aim for 100rpm.
  Recovery 52 × 22 for 2 mins at 60rpm.
1 rep of 52 × 17 for 8 mins, aim for 100rpm.
  Recovery 52 × 22 for 2 mins at 60rpm.
1 rep of 52 × 16 for 8 mins, aim for 100rpm.
  Recovery 52 × 22 for 2 mins at 60rpm.
1 rep of 52 × 15 for 8 mins, aim for 100rpm.
  Recovery 52 × 22 for 2 mins at 60rpm.
1 rep of 52 × 14 for 8 mins, aim for 100rpm.
  Recovery 52 × 22 for 2 mins at 60rpm.

Interval Session 2:
3 reps of :
52 × 17 for 6 mins, aim for 100rpm, straight into:
52 × 16 for 6 mins, aim for 100rpm, straight into:
52 × 15 for 6 mins, aim for 100rpm.
  Recovery 52 × 22 for 2 mins at 60rpm after each set of 18 mins.

Interval Session 3:
10 reps of 52 × 13 for 3 mins, aim for 100rpm.
  Recovery 52 × 22 for 1 min at 60rpm.

EXAMPLE 14

First Six-Week Phase

Week 1, Monday 3 November

RUN

Cross-country race or hard 40 mins; note HR

Long run, 90 mins +

Hilly run of 75–90 mins to include 30 mins
of running uphill, or 10 × 3 mins hill reps,
or 6 × 5 etc.,

Long run, 2 hours

Recovery, easy run 35–50 mins

CYCLE

Turbo 50 mins, 10 mins warm up, then 30
mins at 110rpm, 10 mins warm down

Medium steady ride, 2 hours +

Hilly ride of 2 hours (+) or hill reps of 10 ×
3–4 mins

Long ride, 2½–3 hours

Recovery, easy ride; choose time

Week 2, Monday 10 November

RUN

Cross-country race or hard 40 mins

Long run, 60 mins +

Hilly run of 45–60 mins to include 20 mins
of running uphill, or 10 × 2 mins hill reps

Long run, 100 mins +

Recovery, easy run 25–40 mins

CYCLE

Turbo 50 mins, 10 mins warm up, then 30
mins at 110rpm, 10 mins warm down

Medium steady ride, 2 hours +

Hilly ride of 2 hours (+) or hill reps of
10 × 3–4 mins

Long ride, 2½–3 hours

Recovery, easy ride; choose time

Week 3, Monday 17 November

RUN

Cross-country race or hard 40 mins

Long run, 70 mins +

Hilly run of 45–60 mins to include 20 mins
of running uphill, or 10 × 2 mins hill reps

Long run, 100 mins +

Recovery, easy run 25–40 min

CYCLE

Turbo 50 mins, 10 mins warm up, then
30 mins at 110rpm, 10 mins warm down

Medium steady ride, 2 hours +

Hilly ride of 2 hours (+) or hill reps of
10 × 3–4 mins

Long ride, 3–3½ hours

Recovery, easy ride; choose time

Week 4, Monday 24 November

RUN

Cross-country race or hard 40 mins

Long run, 75 mins +

Hilly run of 50–60 mins to include 24 mins
of running uphill, or 12 × 2 mins hill reps

Long run, 1½ hours

Recovery, easy run 25–40 mins

CYCLE

Turbo 60 mins, 10 mins warm up, then
5 × 1 min on right leg with 30 secs
recovery, then 30 mins at 110rpm, then
5 × 1 min on left leg with 30 secs
recovery, then 10 mins warm down. Try
to spin one gear higher

Medium steady ride, 2½ hours

Hilly ride of 2½ hours or hill reps of
12 × 3–4 mins

Long ride, 3½ hours +

Recovery, easy ride; choose time

Week 5, Monday 1 December

Exactly the same as Week 4

EXAMPLE 14

Week 6, Monday 8 December

RUN
Cross-country race or hard 40 mins

CYCLE
Turbo 60 mins, 10 mins warm up, then 5 × 1 min on right leg with 30 secs recovery, then 30 mins at 110rpm, then 5 × 1 min on left leg with 30 secs recovery, then 10 mins warm down. Try to spin one gear higher than Week 5

Long run, 75–90 mins +
Hilly run of 60–75 mins to include 27 mins of running uphill, or 14 × 2, 9 × 3, or 7 × 4 mins hill reps
Long run, 2 hours
Recovery, easy run 25–40 mins

Medium steady ride, 3 hours
Hilly ride of 2½ hours or hill reps of 8 × 5 mins

Long ride, 4 hours
Recovery, easy ride; 1½–2 hours

Second Six-Week Phase

Week 1, Monday 15 December

RUN
Cross-country race or hard 40 mins; note HR

CYCLE
Turbo 50 mins, 10 mins warm up, then 30 mins at anaerobic threshold (max HR minus 30 beats), 10 mins warm down

Long run, 90 mins to include 30 × 30 secs stride with 30 secs jog recovery
Hilly run of 75–90 mins to include 30 mins of running uphill, or 10 × 3 mins hill reps, or 6 × 5 etc.
Long run, 2 hours
Recovery, easy run 35–50 mins

Medium steady ride, 2 hours +

Hilly ride of 3 hours or hill reps to include 36 mins up of 12 × 3 or 8 × 4 mins, etc.

Long ride, 4–5 hours
Recovery, easy ride; choose time

Week 2, Monday 22 and 29 December
(spread over two-week Christmas period)

RUN
Cross-country race or hard 40 mins; note HR

CYCLE
Turbo 50 mins, 10 mins warm up, then 5 × 6 mins at 46kph (30mph) or 360–380 watts with 1 min spin recovery, 10 mins warm down

Long run, 90 mins to include 10 × 2 mins stride with 60 secs jog recovery
Hilly run of 75–90 mins to include 30 mins of running uphill, or 10 × 3 mins hill reps, or 6 × 5 etc.
Long run, 2 hours
Recovery, easy run 35–50 mins

Medium steady ride, 2½ hours

Hilly ride of 3 hours or hill reps to include 36 mins up of 12 × 3 or 8 × 4 mins, etc., or preferably long hill of 3 × 12 mins

Long ride, 4–5 hours
Recovery, easy ride; choose time

(continued overleaf)

EXAMPLE 14   *(continued from previous page)*

Week 3, Monday 5 January

RUN

Cross-country race or hard 40 mins; note HR

Long run, 90 mins to include 16 × 60 secs
stride with 60 secs jog recovery

Hilly run of 75–90 mins to include 35 mins
of running uphill, or 12 × 3 mins hill reps,
or 6 × 6, etc.

Long run, 2 hours

Recovery, easy run 35–50 mins

CYCLE

Turbo 50 mins, 10 mins warm up, then
40 mins at anaerobic threshold (max HR
minus 30 beats), 10 mins warm down

Medium steady ride, 2 hours +

Hilly ride of 3 hours or hill reps to include
40 mins up of 10 × 4, or 4 × 10 mins, etc.

Long ride, 4–5 hours

Recovery, easy ride; choose time

Week 4, Monday 12 January

RUN

Cross-country race or hard 40 mins; note HR

Long run, 90 mins to include 6 × 4 mins
stride with 2 mins jog recovery

Hilly run of 75–90 mins to include 36 mins
of running uphill, or 12 × 3 mins hill reps,
or 6 × 6, etc.

Long run, 2 hours

Recovery, easy run 35–50 mins

CYCLE

Turbo 50 mins, 10 mins warm up, then
6 × 6 mins at 46kph (30mph) or 360–
380 watts with 1 min spin recovery, 10
mins warm down

Medium steady ride, 2½ hours

Hilly ride of 3 hours or hill reps to include
40 mins up of 10 × 4, or 4 × 10 mins,
etc., preferably the longer reps

Long ride, 4–5 hours

Recovery, easy ride; choose time

Week 5, Monday 19 January

RUN

Cross-country race or hard 40 mins; note HR

Long run, 90 mins to include 10 × 3 mins stride
with 60–90 secs jog recovery

Hilly run of 75–90 mins to include 40 mins
of running uphill, or 13 × 3 mins hill reps,
or 5 × 8, etc.

Long run, 2 hours

Recovery, easy run 35–50 mins

CYCLE

Turbo 50 mins, 10 mins warm up, then 40
mins at anaerobic threshold (max HR
minus 30 beats), 10 mins warm down

Medium steady ride, 3 hours +

Hilly ride of 3 hours or hill reps to include
50 mins up of 10 × 5, or 5 × 10 mins,
etc.

Long ride, 4–5 hours

Recovery, easy ride; choose time

Week 6, Monday 26 January

RUN

Cross-country race or hard 40 mins; note HR

Long run, 90 mins to include 6 × 6 mins stride
with 30 secs jog recovery

CYCLE

Turbo 50 mins, 10 mins warm up, then
5 × 8 mins at 46kph (30mph) or 360–
380 watts with 1 min spin recovery, 10
mins warm down

Medium steady ride, 3 hours (+ 30 mins)

EXAMPLE 14

Week 6, Monday 26 January (continued)

RUN

Hilly run of 75–90 mins to include 40 mins of running uphill, or 10 × 4 mins hill reps, or 8 × 5, etc.

Long run, 2 hours

Recovery, easy run 35–50 mins

CYCLE

Hilly ride of 3 hours or hill reps to include 50 mins up of 10 × 5, or 5 × 10 mins etc., preferably the longer reps

Long ride, 4–5 hours

Recovery, easy ride; choose time

Third Six-Week Phase

Week 1, Monday 2 February

RUN

Cross-country race or hard 40 mins; note HR

Warm up, then 1, 2, 3, 4 mins at 5km pace (14.30–14.45 mins?) with 60 secs jog recovery, and repeat × 3; 3 mins after each set

Hills of 75–90 mins total to include 10 sets of running 600m (approx.) as 200m up, 200m flat, 200m up, concentrating on 2nd uphill

Long run, 2 hours; distance should be greater, or time slightly shorter, or HR down

Recovery, easy run 35–50 mins

CYCLE

Turbo 10 mins warm up, then HR session 1, 10 mins warm down

Medium steady ride, 3 hours +

Hilly ride of 3 hours or hill reps to include 40–45 mins of 15 × 3 or 11 × 4 mins

Long ride, 5 hours

Recovery, easy ride; choose time

Week 2, Monday 9 February

RUN

Cross-country race or hard 40 mins; note HR

Warm up, then 10 mins at 5km pace (14.30–14.45 mins?), with 3 mins jog recovery, then 10 × 3 secs at 800m speed (200m), with 30 secs recovery; jog 3 mins; then 1, 2, 3 mins with 60 secs jog recovery at 1500m pace

Hilly run of 75–90 mins to include 4 × 8-min reps

Long run, 2 hours

Recovery, easy run 35–50 mins

CYCLE

Turbo 10 mins warm up, then HR session 2, 10 mins warm down

See Interval Session 1

Hilly ride of 3 hours or hill reps to include 45 mins as 15 × 3, or 12 × 4 mins, etc.

Long ride, 5 hours

Recovery, easy ride; choose time

Week 3, Monday 16 February

RUN

Cross-country race or hard 40 mins; note HR

Warm up, then 4 × 7.30 mins at 5km pace (14.30–14.45 mins?), with 60–90 secs jog recovery, aiming for 2400m

Hilly run of 75–90 mins, 10 × 2 mins, and then flat out on flat surface for 20 secs

CYCLE

Turbo 10 mins warm up, then 8 × 6 mins at 49kph (31mph) or 380–400 watts, recovery 1 min, 10 mins warm down

Medium ride, 3 hours +

Hilly ride of 3 hours or hill reps to include 45 mins up of 4 × 11 or 3 × 15 mins

(continued overleaf)

EXAMPLE 14   *(continued from previous page)*

Week 3, Monday 16 February (continued)

RUN	CYCLE
Long run, 2 hours	Long ride, 5 hours
Recovery, easy run 35–50 mins	Recovery, easy ride; choose time

Week 4, Monday 23 February

RUN

Cross-country race or hard 40 mins; note HR

Warm up, then 45-sec efforts at 800m/1500m
pace, with 90, 75, 60, 45, 30, 15 secs jog
recovery, and repeat × 4; no extra recovery after
each set

Hills of 75–90 mins total to include 10 sets
of running 600m (approx.) as 200m flat, 400m
up; go into uphill hard but stride/bound

Long run, 2 hours

Recovery, easy run 35–50 mins

CYCLE

Turbo 10 mins warm up, then HR session
3, 10 mins warm down
See Interval Session 2

Hilly ride of 3 hours or hill reps to include
40–45 mins hill reps of short, fast hills

Long ride, 5 hours

Recovery, easy ride; choose time

Week 5, Monday 2 March

RUN

Cross-country race or hard 40 mins; note HR

Warm up, then 10 mins at 5km pace (14.30–
14.45 mins?) with 3 mins jog recovery, then
10 × 30 secs at 800m speed (200m) with 30 secs
recovery, jog 3 mins; then 1, 2, 3 mins with
60 secs jog recovery at 1500m pace; repeat × 3;
3 mins after each set

Hills of 75–90 mins total to include 10 sets of
running 600m (approx.) as 200m up, 200m
flat, 200m up, concentrating on 2nd uphill

Long run, 2 hours

Recovery, easy run, 35–50 mins

CYCLE

Turbo 10 mins warm up, then HR session
4, 10 mins warm down
Medium steady ride, 3 hours +

Hilly ride of 3 hours or hill reps to include
50 mins of 2 × 20–25 mins

Long ride, 5 hours

Recovery, easy ride; choose time

Week 6, Monday 9 March

RUN

Cross-country race or hard 40 mins; note HR

Warm-up, then 1 × 5 mins at 5km pace, 5 × 1 min,
and repeat with recovery of 3 mins after each
set; 30 secs between 1-min efforts (these at 90
per cent max)

Rest

Long run, 2 hours

Recovery, easy run 35–50 mins

CYCLE

Turbo 10 mins warm up, then 7 × 8 mins
at 49kph (31mph) or 380–400 watts
with 1 min spin recovery, 10 mins warm
down

See Interval Session 3

Rest

Long ride, 5 hours

Recovery, easy ride; choose time

Index